PATHWAYS
THIRD EDITION

Listening, Speaking, and Critical Thinking

PAUL MACINTYRE

NATIONAL GEOGRAPHIC
LEARNING

Australia · Brazil · Canada · Mexico · Singapore · United Kingdom · United States

National Geographic Learning,
a Cengage Company

Pathways 4: Listening, Speaking, and Critical Thinking, 3rd Edition
Paul MacIntyre

Publisher: Sherrise Roehr

Executive Editor: Laura Le Dréan

Managing Editor: Jennifer Monaghan

Director of Global Marketing: Ian Martin

Heads of Regional Marketing:

  Charlotte Ellis (Europe, Middle East and Africa)

  Justin Kaley (Asia and Greater China)

  Irina Pereyra (Latin America)

  Joy MacFarland (US and Canada)

Product Marketing Manager: Tracy Bailie

Content Project Manager: Samantha Bertschmann

Media Researcher: Leila Hishmeh

Senior Designer: Heather Marshall

Operations Support: Hayley Chwazik-Gee

Manufacturing Planner: Terry Isabella

Composition: MPS North America LLC

For permission to use material from this text or product, submit all requests online at **cengage.com/permissions**
Further permissions questions can be emailed to
permissionrequest@cengage.com

Student's Book:
ISBN: 978-0-357-97928-0
Student's Book with the Spark platform:
ISBN: 978-0-357-97927-3

National Geographic Learning
5191 Natorp Blvd,
Mason, OH 45040
USA

Locate your local office at **international.cengage.com/region**

Visit National Geographic Learning online at **ELTNGL.com**
Visit our corporate website at **www.cengage.com**

Printed in China
Print Number: 01 Print Year: 2023

Scope and Sequence

	Unit Title & Theme	Listenings & Videos	Listening & Note Taking
	1 **HOSPITALITY AND TOURISM** *page 1* ACADEMIC TRACK: Career Studies / Hospitality	**Lesson A** A Career in Hospitality and Tourism◆ **VIDEO** Sustainable Surfing **Lesson B** Cutting-Edge Resort Technology	• Recognize Three-Word Phrasal Verbs
	2 **SOLVING URBAN CHALLENGES** *page 21* ACADEMIC TRACK: Urban Studies	**Lesson A** The Impact of Tourism in Venice, Italy* **VIDEO** Urban Solution: Farming on Rooftops **Lesson B** The City-State of Singapore	• Infer Meaning from Intonation and Stress • Use Symbols and Abbreviations
	3 **BEAUTY AND APPEARANCE** *page 41* ACADEMIC TRACK: Sociology	**Lesson A** Perceptions of Beauty* **VIDEO** The Future of Fashion **Lesson B** Fashion Influences	• Recognize Arguments *For* and *Against* • Use an Outline
	4 **GOING GLOBAL** *page 61* ACADEMIC TRACK: Global Studies	**Lesson A** Skills for Global Business* **VIDEO** What Is a Global Citizen? **Lesson B** Global Trend: Augmented Reality	• Listen for a Summary
	5 **FACING YOUR FEARS** *page 81* ACADEMIC TRACK: Social Science	**Lesson A** Science vs. Fear* **VIDEO** How Fear and Anxiety Drove Human Evolution **Lesson B** Victory Over Fear	• Recognize Metaphor

* With slideshow
◆ With animation

Speaking & Pronunciation	Grammar & Vocabulary	Critical Thinking	Final Tasks
• Express Approximations • Handle Audience Questions • Linking with *You* or *Your*	• Mixed Conditionals • Adjective Suffixes *-ous, -ful,* and *-less*	• Identify and Solve Problems	**Option 1** Discuss What's Important in a Job **Option 2** Give a Recruitment Presentation for a Job
• Add and Emphasize Information • Present with a Partner • Word Stress with Suffixes	• Passive Voice • Word Families	• Consider Different Perspectives	**Option 1** Discuss How to Make Your City Smarter **Option 2** Give a Presentation About Laws or Rules
• Paraphrase • Prepare Visuals for Display • Consonant Clusters Across Words	• Noun Modifiers • Adjective Suffix *-ive*	• Interpret a Bar Graph	**Option 1** Discuss and Rank Clothing Influences **Option 2** Present Fashion Trends
• Define Terms • Manage Nervousness • Silent Letters	• Adjective Clauses • Collocations	• Interpret Data in Charts and Graphs	**Option 1** Discuss the Role of New Technologies in Globalization **Option 2** Give a Presentation About a Social Media Platform
• Respond to Suggestions • Listen Actively • Recognize Reduced Vowels in Unstressed Syllables	• Separable Two-Word Phrasal Verbs • Noun Suffixes *-ist* and *-ant*	• Recognize Logical Fallacies	**Option 1** Tell a Story About When You've Been Courageous **Option 2** Give a Presentation About a Courageous Person

Scope and Sequence

	Unit Title & Theme	Listenings & Videos	Listening & Note Taking
	6 **TRADITION AND PROGRESS** *page 101* ACADEMIC TRACK: Anthropology / Sociology	**Lesson A** Opening Up Bhutan* VIDEO The Way of Indigenous Boatbuilding **Lesson B** The Return of American Indian Lands	• Recognize Repetition and Addition • Use an Idea Map
	7 **MONEY IN OUR LIVES** *page 121* ACADEMIC TRACK: Economics	**Lesson A** Money and Happiness◆ VIDEO The Money Illusion **Lesson B** Financial Innovations	• Listen for Shifts in Topic
	8 **HEALTH AND TECHNOLOGY** *page 141* ACADEMIC TRACK: Health / Technology	**Lesson A** Big Data in Health Care* VIDEO Biking in the City **Lesson B** Wearable Health Care Technology	• Listen for Pros and Cons • Use a T-Chart
	9 **THE MYSTERIOUS MIND** *page 161* ACADEMIC TRACK: Psychology / Brain Science	**Lesson A** A History of Intelligence* VIDEO Your Memory Under Stress **Lesson B** The Brain and Memory	• Recognize Definitions
	10 **THE FUTURE OF FOOD** *page 181* ACADEMIC TRACK: Environmental Studies	**Lesson A** Genetically Modified Foods* VIDEO Food-Waste Rebel **Lesson B** Rising Food Prices	• Recognize References • Use the Cornell Method

Appendix   *page 201*

* With slideshow
◆ With animation

Speaking & Pronunciation	Grammar & Vocabulary	Critical Thinking	Final Tasks
• Ask Rhetorical Questions • Speak with Confidence • Long and Short Vowels	• Noun Phrase Appositives • Collocations: Verb/ Adjective + Preposition	• Express Original Ideas	**Option 1** Discuss a Tradition **Option 2** Interview and Present About Gross National Happiness
• Refer to Sources • Collaborate Fairly and Responsibly • Aspirated /k/, /p/, and /t/	• Modals in the Past • Words with Multiple Meanings	• Prioritize	**Option 1** Discuss Ways to Budget **Option 2** Give a Presentation on How to Save and Manage Money
• Make and Respond to Suggestions • Engage Your Audience • Recognize Dropped Syllables	• Noun Clauses with *Wh*-Words and *That* • Synonyms	• Synthesize Information	**Option 1** Discuss Your City's Health **Option 2** Present on a Wearable Health Care Device
• Express Causal Relationships • Use Gestures and Facial Expressions • Recognize Reduced Function Words	• Subject-Verb Agreement with Quantifiers • Adjective Suffixes *-al*, *-tial*, and *-ical*	• Identify Premises and Conclusions	**Option 1** Discuss Your Learning Style **Option 2** Give a Presentation on "Study/Learning Hacks"
• Concede and Refute • Follow Debate Rules • Recognize Reduced Auxiliary Phrases	• Noun Clauses as Subject Complements • Concordancers	• Categorize	**Option 1** Discuss Ways of Saving Money on Food **Option 2** Have a Debate About a Food-Related Issue

and Critical Thinking, Third Edition

Compelling photography and infographics in **Explore the Theme** draw students into the unit, develop their visual and information literacy skills, and get them speaking.

A **multimedia approach** featuring videos, slideshows, and animations supports listening comprehension while making content accessible and engaging.

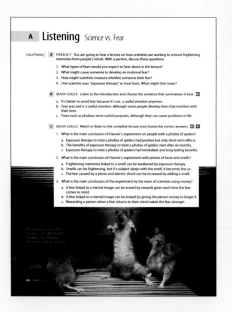

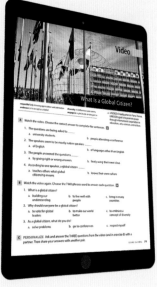

Updated Speaking Activities give more guided instruction and language support, building fluency, accuracy, and learner independence.

Academic competency skills like collaboration, communication, and problem-solving help students develop the skills and behaviors needed to succeed in school and their lives.

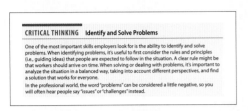

CRITICAL THINKING   Identify and Solve Problems

One of the most important skills employers look for is the ability to identify and solve problems. When identifying problems, it's useful to first consider the rules and principles (i.e., guiding ideas) that people are expected to follow in the situation. A clear rule might be that workers should arrive on time. When solving or dealing with problems, it's important to analyze the situation in a balanced way, taking into account different perspectives, and find a solution that works for everyone.

In the professional world, the word "problems" can be considered a little negative, so you will often hear people say "issues" or "challenges" instead.

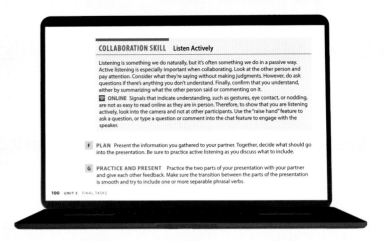

COLLABORATION SKILL   Listen Actively

Listening is something we do naturally, but it's often something we do in a passive way. Active listening is especially important when collaborating. Look at the other person and pay attention. Consider what they're saying without making judgments. However, do ask questions if there's anything you don't understand. Finally, confirm that you understand, either by summarizing what the other person said or commenting on it.

🛜 ONLINE Signals that indicate understanding, such as gestures, eye contact, or nodding, are not as easy to read online as they are in person. Therefore, to show that you are listening actively, look into the camera and not at other participants. Use the "raise hand" feature to ask a question, or type a question or comment into the chat feature to engage with the speaker.

F PLAN Present the information you gathered to your partner. Together, decide what should go into the presentation. Be sure to practice active listening as you discuss what to include.

G PRACTICE AND PRESENT Practice the two parts of your presentation with your partner and give each other feedback. Make sure the transition between the parts of the presentation is smooth and try to include one or more separable phrasal verbs.

100 UNIT 5 FINAL TASKS

Assessment

Pathways Listening, Speaking, and Critical Thinking supports teachers and learners with various forms of assessment, with the goal of helping students achieve real-world success.

A **new Review section** provides additional opportunities for formative assessment and encourages students to take control of their learning journey through guided self-assessment.

The **Final Tasks** section with two options provides flexibility for various learning environments and another opportunity for formative assessment.

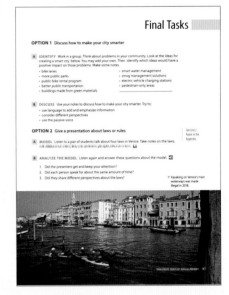

Opportunities for online assessment on the **new Spark platform** include:

- The National Geographic Learning Online Placement Test, which places students into the correct level of *Pathways*

- Interactive Online Practice activities and online tests from the Assessment Suite, for formative and summative assessment

- A Course Gradebook that tracks student and class performance against learning objectives, providing teachers with actionable insights to support student's progress

spark

Bring the world to the classroom and the classroom to life with the Spark platform — where you can prepare, teach and assess your classes all in one place!

Manage your course and teach great classes with integrated digital teaching and learning tools. Spark brings together everything you need on an all-in-one platform with a single log-in.

Track student and class performance on independent online practice and assessment. The Course Gradebook helps you turn information into insights to make the most of valuable classroom time.

Set up classes and roster students quickly and easily on Spark. Seamless integration options and point-of-use support helps you focus on what matters most: student success.

CLASSROOM PRESENTATION TOOL

STUDENT'S eBOOK

TEACHER RESOURCES

ONLINE PRACTICE

ONLINE PLACEMENT

ASSESSMENT SUITE

ADMIN TOOLS

COURSE GRADEBOOK

Photo credit: ©Brian Yen

Visit *ELTNGL.com/spark* to learn more

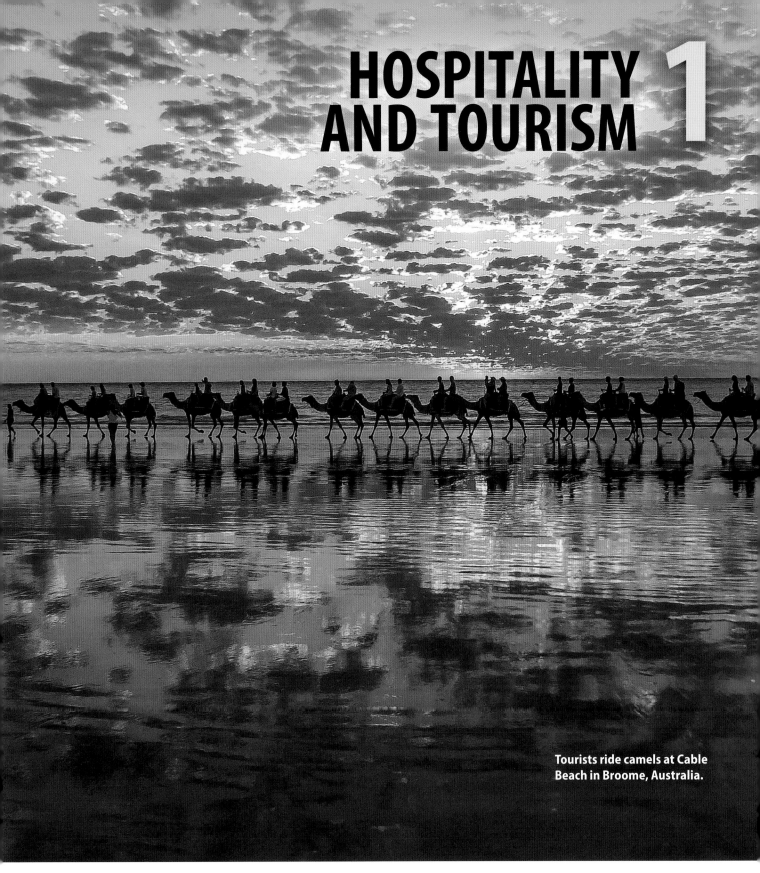

HOSPITALITY AND TOURISM 1

Tourists ride camels at Cable Beach in Broome, Australia.

IN THIS UNIT, YOU WILL:

- Watch or listen to a lecture about a career in hospitality and tourism
- Watch a video about sustainable surfing
- Listen to a conversation about innovations at resorts
- Discuss what's important in a job
  OR Give a recruitment presentation for a job

THINK AND DISCUSS:

1. If you could be a tourist in any location, where would you go and why?
2. If someone wanted to visit your region or country, what would you tell them to see?
3. What does hospitality mean to you? What culture do you think of as especially hospitable?

1

Look at the photo and read the information. Then discuss the questions.

1. Which of these eco-friendly activities looks the most fun to you?

2. Which of these activities are available where you live?

3. What do you consider when you make travel plans?

What is Ecotourism?

Visitors to Pelileo, Ecuador, can swing into the clouds at La Casa del Árbol.

What is ecotourism?

The International Ecotourism Society defines ecotourism as "responsible travel to natural areas that conserves the environment and improves the welfare of local people."

How can I be an ecotourist?

Choose eco-friendly transportation.

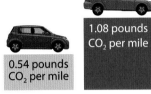

1.08 pounds CO_2 per mile

0.54 pounds CO_2 per mile

HYBRID vs. GAS

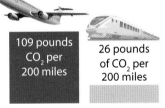

109 pounds CO_2 per 200 miles

26 pounds of CO_2 per 200 miles

AIRPLANE vs. TRAIN

Is it popular?

The World Tourism Organization estimates that ecotourism is 10-15% of total global tourism. It is the fastest-growing tourism sector.

10-15%

Global Tourism

■ Ecotourism

Do activities that focus on nature, wildlife, and culture:

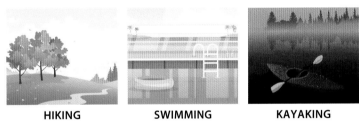

HIKING   **SWIMMING**   **KAYAKING**

Stay in an eco-friendly place with these green features:

is involved in nature &/or conservation efforts

offers locally grown food options

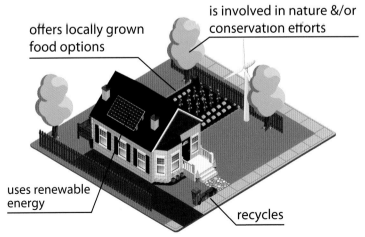

uses renewable energy

recycles

A Vocabulary

A **MEANING FROM CONTEXT** Read and listen to the job advertisement. Pay attention to the words in blue. Then tell a partner whether you would be interested in the job and why. 🔊

> **EXOTIC BREEZE RESORT** *We're hiring!*
>
> At the Exotic Breeze Resort, we put **hospitality** first. That's why our guests consistently **rate** our staff as the friendliest and most helpful in the industry. Services that few hotels offer, such as free in-room yoga lessons and pet day care, are **the norm** at Exotic Breeze. We've also won a **sustainability** award from the **prestigious** *Resort Review* magazine for our low impact on the environment, including our careful water use, our efforts to **cut down on** waste, and our recycling program.
>
> We're looking for an **outgoing** person to encourage guests to participate in the many activities our resort offers, from exercise classes on the beach to small group cruises. You'll promote existing activities, **come up with** ideas for new ones, and **recruit** the staff necessary to make them happen. If you're comfortable in a dynamic work situation and think helping others is **rewarding**, you're welcome to apply to be our Activities Director.

B Use the words in blue from exercise A to complete the sentences.

1. I'm new on the hotel staff, so it's hard for me to _____ answers to guests' questions.

2. At a five-star hotel, excellent, polite service by the staff should be _____.

3. Businesses following _____ guidelines use resources in a responsible way.

4. Being a travel agent is _____ . You make people's dreams come true.

5. The Nobel Peace Prize is possibly the most _____ award that a person can receive. It's a real honor.

6. In the Middle East, _____ is part of the culture. Guests must be warmly welcomed.

7. If you asked me to _____ my experience at this hotel, I'd give it five stars.

8. Many travel and tourism companies _____ employees on university campuses.

9. We change the sheets every other day to _____ the amount of water we use.

10. Flight attendants need a(n) _____ personality to deal with people successfully.

C Match each word with its synonym.

1. _____ hospitality (n)
2. _____ outgoing (adj)
3. _____ prestigious (adj)
4. _____ come up with (v phr)
5. _____ the norm (n)
6. _____ rewarding (adj)
7. _____ cut down on (v phr)
8. _____ rate (v)

a. well-respected
b. judge
c. satisfying
d. friendly and warm reception
e. reduce
f. sociable
g. standard
h. think of

See Word Families in the Appendix.

VOCABULARY SKILL   Adjective Suffixes *–ous*, *–ful*, and *–less*

The suffixes *–ous, –ful,* and *–less* are adjective endings. They are added to some nouns and verbs or word roots to form adjectives.

–ous means *characterized by*
   envi**ous**, fam**ous**, nerv**ous**, cauti**ous**, courage**ous**

–ful means *full of*
   help**ful**, joy**ful**, beauti**ful**, meaning**ful**, forget**ful**

–less means *without*
   breath**less**, care**less**, harm**less**, hope**less**, use**less**

D Complete the sentences with a noun from the box and the correct adjective suffix. Use a dictionary if necessary.

adventure	forget	harm	hazard	home	pain	use	vary

1. My neighbor has a large dog that looks scary but is really quite _____.
2. I prefer the comfort and safety of home, but my _____ sister loves to travel.
3. My grandfather used to have a good memory, but he's becoming _____.
4. The bridge was badly damaged by the storm, so it's too _____ to cross.
5. I want to thank you again for the set of pots and pans. It was a very _____ gift!
6. Our family plays _____ card games and board games together.
7. Many people became _____ after the storm destroyed their houses.
8. The dentist promised that fixing my tooth will be completely _____.

A Listening A Career in Hospitality and Tourism

Critical Thinking | **A** **PREDICT** You are going to watch a video about a career in the hospitality and tourism industry. With a partner, predict the kind of information you expect to hear and who you expect to be in the audience.

B **MAIN IDEAS** Watch or listen to the talk. Number the FOUR main topics in the order you hear them. TWO topics are not discussed. 🔊 ▶

a. _____ Personal qualities suitable for the hospitality and tourism industry

b. _____ The current state of the hospitality and tourism industry

c. _____ The importance of obtaining a degree in hospitality and tourism

d. _____ Future problems for the hospitality and tourism industry

e. _____ Why the hospitality and tourism industry is an excellent career choice

f. _____ The history of the hospitality and tourism industry

C **DETAILS** Listen again. Choose the TWO correct answers that complete each sentence. 🔊

1. A career in hospitality and tourism is a great choice because _____.
   a. there are many positions available
   b. people aren't focused on money
   c. it offers excellent salaries

2. You'll have a better chance of success in hospitality and tourism if you _____.
   a. enjoy dealing with other people
   b. are comfortable in a busy and changing work environment
   c. have worked with famous people before

3. A related degree _____.
   a. focuses on event planning
   b. takes about four years to complete
   c. will help you advance at work

4. The speaker recommends studying abroad because _____.
   a. it's enjoyable
   b. you will get more respect from customers
   c. it can make getting a job easier

5. Current trends in the hospitality and tourism industry include _____.
   a. larger rooms
   b. healthier dishes
   c. cleaner facilities

See Common
Phrasal Verbs in
the Appendix.

LISTENING SKILL   Recognize Three-Word Phrasal Verbs

A three-word phrasal verb is a verb followed by two particles (words that look like prepositions).

come up with = invent or think of

drop in on = visit briefly

Nearly all three-word phrasal verbs are transitive, which means they need an object.

come up with an idea   drop in on a friend

Also, nearly all three-word phrasal verbs are inseparable, which means that the three words stay together and the object comes after the verb and not between the verb and the particle.

YES *He's looking forward to the trip.*

NO *He's looking forward the trip to.*

D Listen to the sentences. Write the three-word phrasal verbs that you hear. 🔊

1. When I _____ my life, I'm happy with my career choices.

2. I would be happy in a job that requires _____ people.

3. I once had a great boss who I really _____ .

4. I try to _____ the amount of water and energy I use.

5. I would like to join a union that _____ employees' rights.

6. If I worked at a hotel, I'd find it difficult to _____ rude customers.

7. I'm _____ starting a career after I graduate.

8. I think it's important to act quickly or you'll _____ opportunities.

E Work with a partner. Discuss whether the statements in exercise D are true for you.

Bubble tents in the Wadi Rum desert of Jordan offer comfort while allowing visitors to feel close to nature.

A Speaking

> ### SPEAKING SKILL Express Approximations
>
> We often need to express approximate numbers, amounts, dates, or times.
>
> *I'm leaving work in **about** 10 minutes. I'll see you **around** 7 o'clock.*
>
> *We need enough food for **approximately/roughly** 20 guests.*
>
> *The meeting will begin at 2:15-**ish/or thereabouts/or so**.*
>
> *I studied for the test for eight hours, **more or less**.*
>
> These expressions are similar in meaning to *almost*:
>
> *This elevator can only carry **up to** 2500 pounds.*
>
> ***As many as** 5000 homes lost electricity in the storm.*
>
> *At least* can be used to mean *more than* or *over*:
>
> *There are **at least** three more seats available on the bus.*

A The talk about hospitality and tourism included a number of expressions for approximating. Listen and write the expressions you hear. 🔊

1. I've been a manager and a director at hotels and resorts all over the world for 30 years _____ .

2. It includes _____ one out of every 10 jobs in the world!

3. It's expanding at _____ 18.5 percent per year.

4. A bachelor's degree takes four years to complete, _____ .

B **PERSONALIZE** Work with a partner. Ask each other these questions. Answer using expressions for approximating.

1. How much vacation time do you have in a year?
2. How far did you travel on your last vacation?
3. How long has it been since you traveled abroad?
4. How many times have you flown in an airplane?
5. How long has it been since you last used social media?
6. How many times a day do you check your phone?
7. How early do you get up on work or school days?
8. How much do you think is a good price for a new phone?
9. How many hours can you use your phone before it needs charging?
10. How often do you speak English outside of class?

PRONUNCIATION Linking with *You* or *Your*

◀) We often link words that end in the sounds /t/, /d/, or /z/ with *you* or *your*. Those sounds are softened and change as follows:

- /t/ sounds like /tʃ/   I see wha**t y**ou mean.
- /d/ sounds like /dʒ/   I'm gla**d y**ou ha**d y**our camera.
- /z/ sounds like /ʒ/   How wa**s y**our trip?

C Mark the linked words in each sentence and check the pronunciation.

		/tʃ/	/dʒ/	/ʒ/
1.	Would you like to check in today?	☐	☐	☐
2.	Excuse me. I'm not sure what you said.	☐	☐	☐
3.	Are you sure he's your tour guide?	☐	☐	☐
4.	Why didn't you book the flight sooner?	☐	☐	☐
5.	Who is going to lead your group?	☐	☐	☐
6.	Why did you cancel the reservation?	☐	☐	☐

D Listen and check your answers to exercise C. Then listen again and repeat the sentences. ◀)

E Practice reading these job interview questions aloud. Be sure to link *you* or *your* correctly.

1. How did you find out about the position?
2. Why does working at the Exotic Breeze Resort interest you?
3. Is your personality a good fit for the position?
4. Can you tell me about your experience in the hospitality and tourism industry?
5. What is your educational background?
6. How would you feel about working nights and weekends?
7. What is your idea of excellent guest service?
8. What would you like to be doing in five years?

F Work with a partner. Review the job advertisement for an activities director in exercise A on page 4. Next write answers to the questions in exercise E above. Then role play a job interview between a hiring manager and a candidate. Take turns playing the roles.

Mint tea is a Moroccan tradition. It ▶ represents friendship and hospitality.

CRITICAL THINKING   Identify and Solve Problems

One of the most important skills employers look for is the ability to identify and solve problems. When identifying problems, it's useful to first consider the rules and principles (i.e., guiding ideas) that people are expected to follow in the situation. A clear rule might be that workers should arrive on time. When solving or dealing with problems, it's important to analyze the situation in a balanced way, taking into account different perspectives, and find a solution that works for everyone.

In the professional world, the word "problems" can be considered a little negative, so you will often hear people say "issues" or "challenges" instead.

Critical Thinking   **G** Read the explanation of ecotourism and the three scenarios. In a group, identify which principles of ecotourism are being broken in each scenario.

> *Ecotourism is a way of conducting tourism with a strong focus on nature conservation, local communities, and sustainability. Effective ecotourism requires that both businesses and customers follow these four principles:*

1. *Reduce the physical and social impacts of tourism.*
2. *Build awareness of local political, environmental, and social situations.*
3. *Direct some of the financial benefits to nature conservation and local people.*
4. *Recognize the rights and beliefs of local people.*

Scenario 1. Tourists staying at a tropical island resort have parties in the forest late into the night, disturbing the animals and often leaving a mess behind. It is a very beautiful natural place that the local people consider special and visit only on certain days. The locals don't complain, though, because they know how important the resort is for their economy and jobs.

Scenario 2. A mountain resort hires workers from the local area. They are paid below the minimum wage, but they say they are happy to have the work. In fact, they often agree to work 60 or 70 hours a week without overtime pay, which is against government regulations.

Scenario 3. A seaside resort was built on a beach where an endangered species of bird lives. To protect the birds, there are laws against using the beach, but the tourists don't know about them. Local people sometimes block the beach, but the police soon arrest them. The police don't want to cause trouble for the resort, which brings a lot of money to the community.

> *Scenario 1 breaks three principles. It breaks principle 1 by not reducing the physical impact of the tourists on the place and the animals.*

H   SOLVE Work in a group. Discuss how to solve the issues you identified in exercise G.

One part of ecotourism is staying in an eco-friendly place with renewable energy sources, such as Zmar Eco Camping Resort & Spa in Alentejo, Portugal.

Video

Sustainable Surfing

handicrafts (n) objects made by hand
longboard (n) a type of board for surfing

locals (n) local people
outsiders (n) people from outside the local culture

▲ Surfing in Papua New Guinea is a big business.

A Watch the video. Choose the correct answers. ▶

1. Why did Sam Bleakley come to Papua New Guinea?
   a. He wanted to find out how people can travel responsibly.
   b. He wanted to start a business there.

2. What has Shane set up in New Guinea?
   a. An international surf contest.
   b. A surf resource management plan.

3. What does Shane hope to provide for tourists?
   a. Large group tours with surf competitions.
   b. Tours with few people in remote areas.

4. How does Shane help locals through his business?
   a. He hires locals and helps communities make money.
   b. He offers classes to help locals set up their own businesses.

B Read the statements and watch again. Choose T for *True* or F for *False*. ▶

	T	F
1. Sam is a professional surfer from Cornwall, England.	T	F
2. Shane was born and grew up in Australia.	T	F
3. The surf school is new so the teachers aren't very good yet.	T	F
4. Shane got the idea for his business from his father.	T	F
5. The surf resource management plan funded a new classroom.	T	F
6. Shane believes that it's OK if businesses make a profit.	T	F

C In Lesson A you learned about careers in hospitality and tourism. With a partner, discuss the pros and cons of working for Shane in his surf resource management business.

B Vocabulary

A Listen and check the words you know. Use a dictionary to help you with any new words. 🔊

automated (adj)	**eliminate** (v)	**luxury** (n)	**monitor** (v)	**obsolete** (adj)
cutting-edge (adj)	**germ** (n)	**modify** (v)	**multiple** (adj)	**undergo** (v)

B **MEANING FROM CONTEXT** Read the advertisement for a security company. Complete the sentences with the correct form of the words from exercise A. Then listen and check your answers. 🔊

ProtectMyEvent
The Event Security Specialists

Hosting events for government officials and company presidents has special problems. You can offer the ¹_____ they expect, but can you provide for their ²_____ security needs? Let us help!

IDENTIFY CRIMINALS FAST

Our entry/exit camera system uses artificial intelligence to identify criminals. It recognizes them even if they ³_____ their appearance with dark sunglasses or makeup.

RECOGNIZE GUESTS' VOICES

Our VoiceCheck system can identify anyone by their voice. It's fast and avoids the need to have important guests ⁴_____ embarrassing ID checks.

PROTECT GUESTS' HEALTH

Our ⁵_____ air filtering systems ⁶_____ 99.99 percent of ⁷_____ from the air.

DON'T FORGET SECURITY OUTSIDE

Our flying camera drones can silently ⁸_____ large areas for up to 12 hours at a time. And don't worry about needing to pay staff to operate them because they're fully ⁹_____.

So remember: Where the rich and powerful meet, be sure the security technology isn't ¹⁰_____. Choose ProtectMyEvent!

C Choose the correct form. Use a dictionary to help you if necessary.

1. After we lost, our team was (elimination / eliminated) from the tournament.

2. I ate at an (automated / automate) restaurant run by robots.

3. The resort we stayed at in India was extremely (luxurious / luxury).

4. The entrance was (modified / modification) to allow easy wheelchair access.

5. During her college years, Nabila (undergone / underwent) an amazing change.

6. The students were (monitored / monitoring) by their teacher during the test.

D Match each word with its synonym.

1. _____ obsolete (adj)   a. change

2. _____ modify (v)   b. several

3. _____ germs (n)   c. watch

4. _____ multiple (adj)   d. advanced

5. _____ monitor (v)   e. out-of-date

6. _____ cutting-edge (adj)   f. viruses

E Replace the words in bold with the correct form of a word from exercise A.

1. What is a task you must do every day that you wish were **done automatically**?

2. What is an example of a technology that is now **no longer in use**?

3. What are some of the things hotels and airlines have to do to control **viruses**?

4. What is a **wonderful and expensive thing** that you experienced on vacation?

5. What is an example of a **very advanced** device that you would like to own?

6. What treatment do people **have happen to them** at the airport before a flight?

7. Do you ever **regularly check** airline ticket prices online when planning a trip?

8. Do you think people should apply for **several** credit cards, or is one enough?

9. Do you think hotels and resorts should **get rid of** plastic straws?

10. In what ways do you **change** your behavior when you go on vacation?

F **PERSONALIZE** Work with a partner. Ask and answer FIVE of the questions in exercise E.

Listening Cutting-Edge Resort Technology

Critical Thinking

A ACTIVATE You are going to hear a conversation between two managers about new technology at their resorts. With a partner, discuss these questions.

1. If you were going on vacation, would you bring your digital devices with you?
2. How could technology improve hotel guests' experiences?
3. What are some of the most cutting-edge technologies hotels or resorts offer?

B MAIN IDEAS Listen to the conversation. Match the technologies with their uses. 🔊

1. _____ touch screens and animation
2. _____ facial recognition technology
3. _____ artificial intelligence monitoring
4. _____ voice recognition technology
5. _____ robot technology
6. _____ virtual reality technology

a. open guest room doors
b. record guests' preferences
c. keep rooms clean
d. give resort tours
e. help guests check in
f. turn devices on and off

C DETAILS Listen again. Choose the correct answers. 🔊

1. At the front desk at the Fairview Seaside Resort, guests' questions are answered by _____.
   a. an animation
   b. a robot
   c. a human clerk

2. Fairview Seaside Resort guests can download an app that allows them to _____.
   a. order food
   b. ask questions
   c. request a taxi

3. Artificial intelligence is used at the Fairview Seaside Resort to monitor customers' preferred _____.
   a. room
   b. airline
   c. activities

4. The high-tech mirrors at the Ocean Vision Resort allow guests to _____.
   a. order clothes
   b. check email
   c. send text messages

5. The Ocean Vision Resort needs ten more employees in the _____ department.
   a. housekeeping
   b. event planning
   c. food preparation

6. Using robots is a partial solution to the Fairview Seaside Resort's _____ shortage.
   a. staff
   b. water
   c. tour guide

D **INFER** Discuss the questions with a partner.

1. How would you describe Hana and Min-jun's relationship based on their conversation?
2. What was Min-jun implying when he said that he couldn't remember his name sometimes?
3. What was Hana implying when she asked Min-jun if he knew about any job openings?
4. What was Hana implying when she said she was in love with her new house?

E **FOCUSED LISTENING** Listen and write the three-word phrasal verbs you hear.

1. It's a system that uses artificial intelligence to chat with the customers and answer almost any question they can _____.
2. Those old white ones we were using were _____.
3. As you know, at Ocean Vision, we make a special effort to _____ each guest and their personal preferences.
4. I _____ seeing you the next time you're back in the area.
5. This resort doesn't _____ our expectations. It's not very nice.

Habitas AlUla in Saudi Arabia aims to fit in to its natural surroundings and have minimal impact on the environment.

B Speaking

See Irregular Verbs and Past Participles in the Appendix.

GRAMMAR FOR SPEAKING   Mixed Conditionals

Mixed conditionals are conditional sentences that mix two different times in one sentence. There are two types.

The first expresses an unreal present situation and its likely but unreal result in the past.

unreal present situation   **unreal past result**

If I **had** a degree in hospitality and tourism, I **would have found** a better job.
simple past   would /could/might + have + past participle

The second expresses an unreal past situation and its likely but unreal result in the present.

unreal past situation   **unreal present result**

If I **had followed** my parents' advice, I **would be** happy today.
past perfect   would + verb

Because these two types of mixed conditionals are used to express how the situation could be different, we often use them to express regrets.

If I **weren't** so busy with school, I **would have accepted** the job offer.
If I **had invested** in Apple when I was in high school, I **might be** rich now!

A Complete the mixed conditionals with the correct form of the verb in parentheses.

1. If I were more adventurous, I _____ (travel) around the world when I was younger.

2. If the train _____ (not stop) for repairs yesterday, I would be in Mumbai by now.

3. If Sofia weren't afraid of heights, she _____ (become) a pilot instead of a doctor.

4. If I _____ (not drink) that cup of coffee after dinner, I would be asleep right now.

5. If my wife _____ (not hate) to fly, we would have booked a flight instead of driving.

6. If Oliver _____ (speak) Arabic, he would have been able to understand our recent visitor from Egypt.

7. If my mother were younger, she _____ (come) to Hawaii with us last summer.

8. If we had more money, we _____ (check) in to that five-star hotel last week.

B **PERSONALIZE** Work with a partner. Use the sentence starters to make mixed conditional sentences that are true for you.

1. If I were incredibly rich, ...
2. If I had known . . . .
3. If I had never . . . .
4. I wouldn't have gone to . . . if . . . .
5. I would never have . . . if . . . .
6. I would be happier today if . . .

C Read and listen to the description of a very special hotel. Then discuss with a partner why you would or wouldn't like to stay here. 🔊

THE FRIENDLY ROBOT HOTEL

During your stay at the Friendly Robot Hotel, you might never see another human being. You're greeted at the door by a cute toy robot. At the front desk, a robot helps you with the self-check-in machine. In the lobby, a robot waste basket asks if you have anything to throw away. Next, a robot luggage cart takes your suitcase to your room. A camera recognizes your face, and the door opens. Inside, a tiny voice-controlled robot welcomes you and turns on the lights if you ask it to. The vending machines have everything you could want, from snacks to pajamas. The hotel owner plans to build hundreds of these robot hotels around the world. He's sure people will love them!

D **RANK** Work with a partner. Read these reviews of the Friendly Robot Hotel. Discuss how many stars you think the guests gave the hotel. Then match the stars to the reviews. | Critical Thinking

a. ★ ★ ★ ★   b. ★ ★ ★   c. ★ ★   d. ★

1. _____ I'm sure the Friendly Robot Hotel will be successful because its use of robots makes it affordable. More staff just means I have to pay higher room rates.

2. _____ The robots had trouble understanding me. I had to repeat myself all the time. Once, the luggage robot didn't stop when I told it to and rolled over my foot. It's not safe to put robots in control of our lives.

3. _____ It was certainly interesting. A unique experience, but a little scary. There's something about robots that makes me uneasy.

4. _____ It's so peaceful living among machines. They never complain or do anything to bother you. I really wish I could set up my home like the Friendly Robot Hotel.

E **PERSONALIZE** Work with a partner. Discuss the questions.

1. Do you think this type of hotel will spread around the world? Explain.
2. Which of the hospitality technologies that you read about are your favorites?
3. Do you think there is a negative side to the growth of technology in the hospitality and tourism industry? Explain.

Review

A   VOCABULARY   Complete the sentences with a vocabulary word from this unit.

1. A big smile, a warm welcome, and kindness are signs of _____.

2. _____ includes reducing waste, resource use, and damage to the environment.

3. It's important to wash your hands often to avoid spreading _____.

4. Translators could lose their jobs if all translation work becomes _____.

B   PRONUNCIATION   Mark the linked words and say the sentences with correct linking. Then check the linking sound you used.

	/tʃ/	/dʒ/	/ʒ/
1. Did you enjoy your stay?	☐	☐	☐
2. Was your room warm enough?	☐	☐	☐
3. Can I get you anything else?	☐	☐	☐

C   GRAMMAR   Complete the sentences with the correct form of the verb in parentheses.

1. You _____ (not be) tired today if you hadn't stayed up late last night.

2. If I had studied more, I _____ (do) better on the test.

3. She would be over the ocean right now if she _____ (catch) her flight.

4. If I _____ (not know) how to drive, I wouldn't have asked you for your car keys just now.

D   SPEAKING SKILL   Read the scenarios. Express an approximation for each.

1. You think 25 percent of reservations are made through the hotel's website, but you aren't sure of the exact number.

2. You know hotel managers make $100,000 but believe the number is often higher.

3. A survey shows that the number of guests who report items missing from their rooms doesn't quite reach 33 percent.

RE-ASSESS   What skills or language still need improvement?

Final Tasks

OPTION 1 Discuss what's important in a job

A **IDENTIFY** Work in a group. Look at the list of aspects people think are important in a job. Discuss which ones a career in hospitality and tourism offers. Give examples.

1. A pleasant work environment
2. Opportunities to learn valuable skills
3. A job with work that feels meaningful
4. Earning a high salary
5. Interaction with others
6. A job that people respect
7. Good work-life balance
8. Job security
9. Opportunities for advancement
10. A flexible schedule

B Which aspects are most important to you and your chosen career or life path? Tell your group and explain.

> *I'm planning to work for an insurance company. I think job security might be the most important aspect to me. I really don't like applying for jobs and going to interviews at all!*

OPTION 2 Give a recruitment presentation for a job

See Unit 1 Rubric in the Appendix.

A **MODEL** Listen to a recruitment presentation for an open position. Take notes in the chart. 🔊

Position	
Qualifications	
Responsibilities	
Benefits	

B **ANALYZE THE MODEL** Listen again. Answer these questions about the model. 🔊

1. How does the speaker introduce the presentation?
2. How is the overall presentation organized?
3. How does the speaker introduce the different sections of the presentation?
4. What does the speaker do at the end of the presentation?

C RESEARCH Follow these steps to prepare your presentation.

1. Find a hospitality and tourism job opening that has information about the job, qualifications, responsibilities, and benefits.
2. Complete the chart below with the job information.

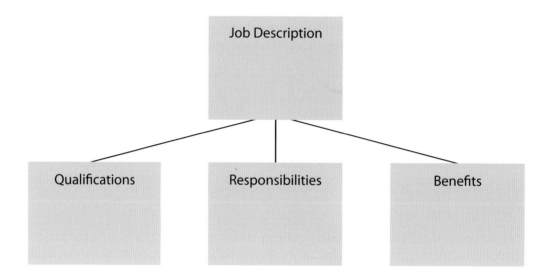

3. Organize the presentation. Include an opening to get your audience's attention and use questions or another technique to move between sections.
4. Prepare appropriate visuals for display during your presentation.

PRESENTATION SKILL   Handle Audience Questions

Questions from the audience can be unpredictable. Here's how to handle them:
- Start by saying "Good question!" to be polite and show interest.
- Repeat the question in your own words. This gives you a little extra time, helps you understand the question, and helps the audience understand it.
- Answer the question as clearly as possible. (If you don't know the answer, say something like, "I'm afraid I don't know. I'll have to get back to you.")
- Check if your answer was understood by asking, "Does that answer your question?"

ONLINE When participating online, people are often more likely to get distracted. So it may be better to break for questions during the presentation rather than wait until the end. You can also keep your audience engaged by asking them to post questions as they come up. Also, if the platform you are using allows participants to virtually raise their hand, you can pause your presentation when they do to answer their questions.

D PRACTICE AND PRESENT Practice with a partner. Give each other feedback before you present. Remember to ask the audience for questions at the end of your presentation.

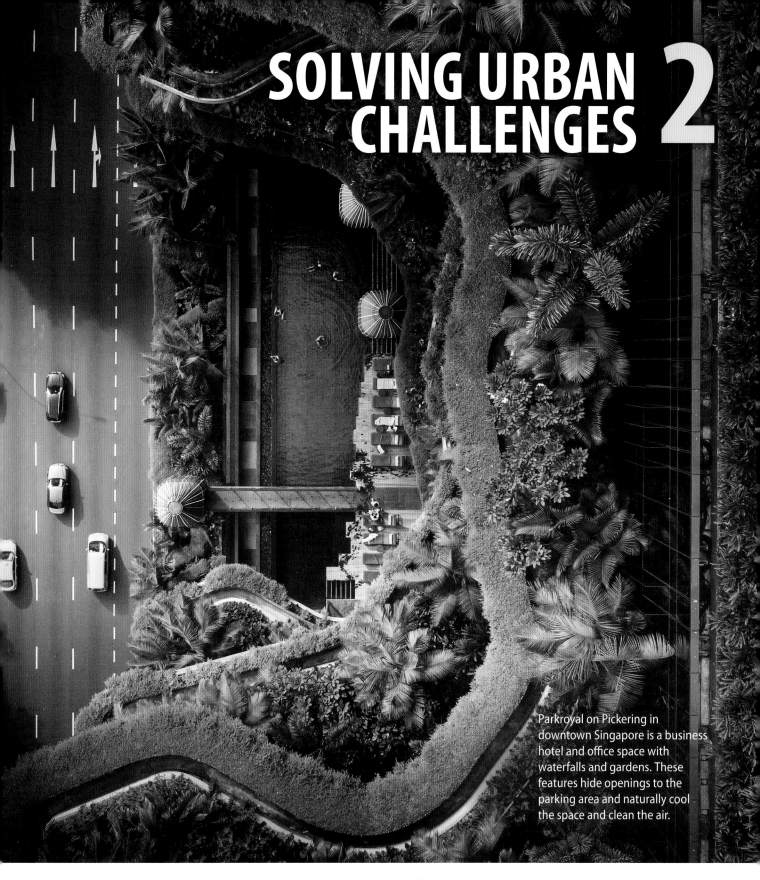

SOLVING URBAN CHALLENGES 2

Parkroyal on Pickering in downtown Singapore is a business hotel and office space with waterfalls and gardens. These features hide openings to the parking area and naturally cool the space and clean the air.

IN THIS UNIT, YOU WILL:

- Watch or listen to a lecture about Venice, Italy
- Watch a video about farming on rooftops
- Listen to a conversation about Singapore
- Discuss how to make your city smarter
  OR Give a pair presentation about laws or rules

THINK AND DISCUSS:

1. What urban challenges do cities in your country face?
2. Why is green space important in a city?
3. What urban challenges does Parkroyal solve?

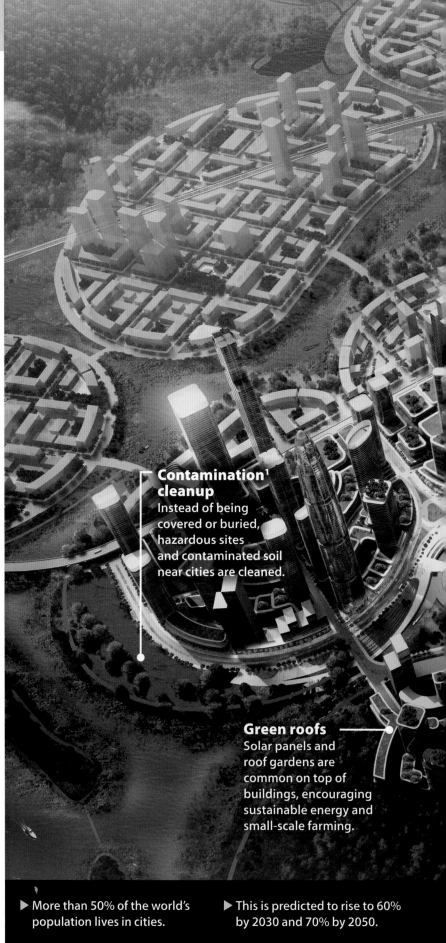

Read the information. Then discuss the questions.

1. How many different ways of making a city smart are shown?

2. Which of these have you seen implemented in cities? Where?

3. Which of these would have the most impact on you? On your city?

4. Given the facts listed at the bottom, what challenges will cities face?

Creating Smart Cities

WHAT MAKES A CITY SMART?

This graphic shows a plan for creating a smart city of the future. Smart cities use information and technology to improve efficiency and create a high standard of living for the community. Smart cities have evolved in response to human and environmental concerns. They focus on sustainability and long-term solutions to environmental problems while addressing the needs of the community.

Contamination[1] cleanup
Instead of being covered or buried, hazardous sites and contaminated soil near cities are cleaned.

Green roofs
Solar panels and roof gardens are common on top of buildings, encouraging sustainable energy and small-scale farming.

▶ More than 50% of the world's population lives in cities.

▶ This is predicted to rise to 60% by 2030 and 70% by 2050.

[1] **contamination** (n) dirt and pollution

Mixed densities
A mix of housing types within each district provides more and different housing options and eases crowding.

Compact neighborhoods
Mixed-use districts provide all services within walking distance of homes and workplaces.

Family life
Open and green spaces, community spaces, and buildings with larger units create happier and healthier families.

Social transit
Regional high-speed rail stations become centers of business and social activities.

Urban farms and gardens
New communities and developments take advantage of advanced technology for urban farming.

Automated recycling
Waste collection and recycling centers are fully automated for faster and more comprehensive reuse of waste.

Rainwater cleansing
Bioswales (absorbent rain gardens) and pools collect and filter rainwater for reuse.

Smart water
Technology maximizes irrigation efficiency in city farms.

Backyard and school gardens
Local, organic, and sustainable farming is part of the curriculum in smart city schools.

▶ Cities occupy just 3% of land but account for 60-80% of energy consumption and 75% of carbon emissions.

▶ Cities and metropolitan areas contribute about 60% of global gross domestic product (GDP).

A Vocabulary

A Match the sentence beginning to its ending to complete the definitions of the words in blue.

1. A **sustainable** solution is ＿＿＿
2. Something that is **affordable** ＿＿＿
3. To **conclude** means ＿＿＿
4. To **regulate** something means ＿＿＿
5. An **innovative** idea is ＿＿＿
6. If you **prioritize** something, you ＿＿＿
7. If a project is **authorized**, ＿＿＿
8. To provide **funds** to a project means ＿＿＿
9. If a building is in need of **renovation**, ＿＿＿
10. An event that occurs **subsequently** ＿＿＿

a. it requires repairs or improvements.
b. to reach a decision after study or research.
c. one that will last or continue for a long time.
d. give it special importance.
e. it receives official approval.
f. happens after something else.
g. one that is new and creative.
h. can be bought at a reasonable price.
i. to control it.
j. to give it money.

B **MEANING FROM CONTEXT** Complete the article with the correct form of a word from exercise A. Then listen and check your answers. 🔊

SOLVING URBAN CHALLENGES

Today's urban areas face a variety of challenges, such as finding environmentally [1]＿＿＿＿＿＿＿＿＿ solutions for housing needs. Some residents of Tokyo, Japan, have found an unusual solution: homes constructed on pieces of land as small as 32 square meters. The cost of these "micro-homes" is very [2]＿＿＿＿＿＿＿＿＿.

Most urban areas also suffer from poor air quality due to pollution and smog[1]. What can these cities do to [3]＿＿＿＿＿＿＿＿＿ pollution from vehicles and factories? One [4]＿＿＿＿＿＿＿＿＿ solution is smog-eating materials for use in roads and buildings. These convert air pollution into harmless chemicals that are [5]＿＿＿＿＿＿＿＿＿ washed off roads and buildings when it rains. The smog-eating material has been used in cities such as Los Angeles and Mexico City, where air-pollution control is [6]＿＿＿＿＿＿＿＿＿. From L.A.'s improved air quality in recent years, we can [7]＿＿＿＿＿＿＿＿＿ that this measure has had a positive effect.

Cities must also find creative ways to build public areas when space is limited. The government of New York City [8]＿＿＿＿＿＿＿＿＿ a project to transform the High Line, an unused railroad line, into an urban park. The [9]＿＿＿＿＿＿＿＿＿ necessary to pay for the [10]＿＿＿＿＿＿＿＿＿ were provided through donations. The High Line has since become one of the city's most inviting public spaces, featuring gardens, a sundeck, and art exhibits.

[1]**smog** (n) a combination of smoke and fog that can harm humans, plants, and animals

VOCABULARY SKILL Word Families

Knowing a word means learning its different forms, or its "family." The more forms of a word you know, the more fluent you will be. Here are examples of word families:

Verb	Noun	Adjective
create	creator/creation	creative
classify	classification	classified

The different forms of a word often have different endings, or suffixes. Here are some common suffixes.

Verb	Noun	Adjective
–ate, –ify, –ize	*–or/–er, –ity, –tion, –ence*	*–d/–ed, –able, –ing, –ive, –al*

C Complete the chart with the correct forms of each word. Use a dictionary to help you. More than one answer may be possible.

	Verb	Noun	Adjective
1.		authorization	
2.	conclude		
3.			innovative
4.		leader	
5.	regulate		
6.	renovate		
7.		identity	

D PERSONALIZE Work in a small group. Discuss if these statements are true for you.

1. It's important to live in a **sustainable** way.
2. When an organization asks me for **funds**, I usually donate.
3. Housing is easily **affordable** where I live.
4. I **prioritize** my studies over my social life.

The High Line adds needed public space in New York City, USA.

A Listening The Impact of Tourism in Venice, Italy

CRITICAL THINKING   Consider Different Perspectives

We all have our own perspective, or way that we see the world. Our perspective is valid but limited to our experiences. For every situation, consider other perspectives.

- *As a bicyclist, I feel that our city should add more bike lanes. Riding a bike in the same lane as a car can be dangerous. Bike lanes would make biking safer. More people would ride bikes, and there would be fewer cars.*
- *As a motorist, I feel that we need more lanes for cars to reduce traffic. Driving in the city takes so much time. We shouldn't add more bike lanes because it will increase traffic.*

Considering different perspectives gives us a more complete understanding of the situation and a more balanced opinion. It's an important part of being a global citizen.

Critical Thinking | **A** Read the title of the lecture. Discuss the possible perspectives of the following with a partner:

- a local business owner
- a tourist
- a resident

LISTENING SKILL   Infer Meaning from Intonation and Stress

🔊 Intonation is how we change the tone of our voice as we speak. Stress is extra loudness and emphasis we put on words. Intonation and stress can change the meaning of what we say. Listen to three examples.

1. *So, we're going to **that** restaurant for lunch.*

That is stressed, and the intonation is bright, indicating that the person is excited about eating at the restaurant.

2. *So, we're going to that restaurant for lunch.*

There is no special stress or intonation as it is a simple statement of information.

3. *So, we're going to **that** restaurant for lunch.*

That is stressed, and the intonation is dark, indicating that the person doesn't want to go to the restaurant.

Critical Thinking | **B** **INFER** Listen to the lecture introduction. Choose the correct answers. 🔊

1. By "a city with such a history," the speaker suggests Venice is a city with a _____ history.
   a. confusing
   b. remarkable
   c. boring

2. By "Now that's an opponent!" the speaker implies the ocean _____.
   a. is difficult to fight
   b. is like a strong person
   c. is easy to control

3. By "but clearly, a more long-term solution is needed," the speaker implies that he is _____ about the situation.
   a. excited
   b. frustrated
   c. confused

C MAIN IDEAS Watch or listen to the entire lecture. Check the THREE main topics. 🔊 ▶

☐ The impact of tourism on city services
☐ How tourists show concern for Venice
☐ The causes of increased tourism in Venice

☐ The effects of tourism on residents of Venice
☐ The drawbacks of visiting Venice as a tourist
☐ The benefits of tourism for Venice

NOTE-TAKING SKILL Use Symbols and Abbreviations

When taking notes, we usually use symbols and abbreviations. There is no correct way to use them. The important thing is to remember what your symbols and abbreviations mean. Good notetakers choose their own abbreviations and use them consistently. Here are some examples.

about/around	~	less/more than	</>	number	#	thousand	K
is/is called/means	=	million	M/mil	positive	+	with	w/
for example	e.g.	negative	neg/-	up/down	↑/↓	without	w/o
cause/lead to	→	month	mo	per/a	/	year	yr

D DETAILS Listen to an excerpt from the lecture. Complete the outline with the numbers, symbols, and abbreviations below. 🔊

50K   =   +   –   36M   #   →   ↓   100K   e.g.

<u>Venice Challenges</u>

  A. acqua alta ^{1}_____ regular floodwaters
     1. residents use boots & raised walkways
     2. Ven. installing barriers in ocean ^{2}_____ stop floods
  B. Tourism: ^{3}_____ & ^{4}_____ aspects
     1. profitable
     2. too many tourists
        a. ^{5}_____ # residents ^{6}_____ from 175K in 1951 to ^{7}_____ now
        b. ^{8}_____ visitors 2019 = ^{9}_____; In summer > ^{10}_____/day

---

E Work with a partner. What other symbols or abbreviations do you see in the notes above? What abbreviations do you use in your notes?

F Were your ideas about different perspectives in exercise A accurate? Discuss with a partner what you learned about different perspectives on tourism in Venice.

G FOCUSED LISTENING Listen to an excerpt from the lecture and write the words that you hear. With a partner, discuss what verb form is used and why. 🔊

  1. Here, grocery stores _____ by expensive souvenir shops.

  2. More and more residents _____ to leave the city.

  3. Many possible solutions _____.

A Speaking

When you want to add information to an argument, you can use these expressions:

In addition,	*Let me add that …*
On top of that,	*Along with …,*
What's more,	*Another point I want to make is …*

When you want to emphasize a point, you can use these expressions:

It's important to note/keep in mind that …	*Let me point out that …*
We need to remember/keep in mind that …	*I'd like to emphasize/stress that …*

A Listen to excerpts from the lecture. Write the language used to add or emphasize information. 🔊

1. _____ these negative impacts of tourism, Venice also suffers from inflation.

2. _____, in popular tourist areas, rent has greatly increased.

3. _____ there is a serious housing problem in Venice.

4. _____ it used to be illegal to convert residential buildings into hotels.

5. _____, in this crazy market, only the very rich can buy a home.

B Explain to your partner what you think about the problems in Venice. Use phrases to add information and emphasize your point.

> *I think that something needs to be done about Venice's tourism problems. We need to remember that Venice is a unique city and needs to be protected for future generations.*

See Forms of the Passive Voice in the Appendix.

GRAMMAR FOR SPEAKING   Passive Voice

In English, transitive verbs (verbs that take an object) can be active or passive.
- **ACTIVE:** *In Venice, tourists **leave** a lot of trash behind.*
- **PASSIVE:** *A lot of trash **is left** behind (by tourists).*

We use the passive voice to emphasize the object, or the receiver, of the action. It is used when the agent, or the doer, of an action is not known or is not important. The *by* phrase is often omitted.

The passive voice is possible in all verb forms. Use the correct form of *be* + the past participle of the main verb.

> *Public parking lots fill up and **are closed**.*
> *More and more residents **are being forced** to leave the city.*
> *Many possible solutions **have been discussed**.*
> *Let's hope the problems **will be resolved** successfully.*

C Work with a partner. Complete the sentences about smart city features. Use the correct form of the verb in the passive voice.

1. In Singapore, vehicle and pedestrian traffic information _____ (collect) electronically.

2. At some Dubai police stations, crimes _____ (report) to a machine rather than to an officer.

3. A planned smart city near Oslo airport _____ (power) only by green energy.

4. In Copenhagen, an app _____ (develop) in 2017 that alerts cyclists to the color of traffic lights.

5. In Boston, repair crews _____ (inform) by drivers online about dangerous holes in roads.

6. In New York City, waste management services _____ (alert) by smart trash cans when they're full.

7. Currently, in New York City, software _____ (test) that can predict future crimes based on crime data.

8. Since 2020, in Barcelona, air quality and noise pollution _____ (monitor) by devices in streetlamps.

D **RANK** Work in a group. Discuss the advantages and disadvantages of the smart city features in exercise C. Then rank them from 1 (most useful) to 8 (least useful).

Critical Thinking

A: I think Singapore's program of collecting vehicle and pedestrian traffic information is a very good idea. More information is always better!

B: I agree. But I'm not so sure about reporting crimes to machines. It's easy to make mistakes when you're upset. I think an officer should be present.

E **BRAINSTORM** Work in a small group. How does tourism impact these aspects of urban life? Could using smart city techniques help? Discuss your ideas.

Critical Thinking

Aspects of urban life	Impacts of tourism and ideas for smart city techniques
public transportation	
culture (arts, restaurants, museums)	
job opportunities for residents	
cleanliness	

F **EVALUATE** Choose a tourist city that you know. What are the pros and cons of tourism there? What are some smart city techniques that might help with the cons? Write your notes in the chart.

City: _____

Pros	Cons and smart city techniques

G Work in a small group. Use your chart in exercise F to tell your group about the impact of tourism in the city you chose and how smart city techniques might help. Explain your ideas and answer questions from the group.

> I chose Muscat, the capital of Oman. It's a beautiful city, and tourists from all over the world visit. Tourists bring lots of advantages but also some problems, like long lines at the airport. I think more smart machines for getting people through customs would help with that.

▼ The Muttrah Souq is one of the oldest marketplaces in Oman and is a popular tourist attraction in Muscat.

Video

Urban Solution: Farming on Rooftops

infrastructure (n) the basic systems and structures that a city or country needs to work effectively

momentum (n) increased speed

pioneer (v) to do something first

core (adj) main, central

alienated (adj) separated, disconnected

▲ Urban rooftop farming in Brooklyn, New York, USA

A   **PREDICT**   The video is about a company working to solve some of the problems of urban life. Look at the title and the photo. Then discuss the questions with a partner. | Critical Thinking

1. What benefits do you think there are to growing vegetables on a rooftop?
2. In addition to growing vegetables, what other types of farming could be done on a rooftop?

B   Watch the video. Check the points that the speakers make. ▶

☐ Rooftop farming is having an enormous effect on cities everywhere.

☐ Ben Flanner discovered his passion for farming when he came to New York City.

☐ The farmers have considered the soil and water.

☐ Rooftop farms connect the community with the production of its food.

☐ The farmers' objective is to provide most of New York City's vegetables.

C   Read the questions. Then watch the video again and answer them. ▶

1. Is rooftop farming practiced on a large scale or a small scale? _____

2. What type of creatures does their apiary business involve? _____

3. How do the stones in the soil compare to a typical rock? _____

4. About how much storm water a year does each farm manage? _____

5. What influence do the farms have on the "urban heat island effect"? _____

D   Work with a partner. In lesson B, you will learn about one of the world's top smart cities, Singapore, where rooftop farming is practiced. Would you and your partner be interested in starting a rooftop farming business? Discuss your feelings and ideas.

B Vocabulary

A **MEANING FROM CONTEXT** Read and listen to the suggestions for travelers. Pay attention to the words in blue. With a partner, discuss if you think the advice is helpful.

CityTraveler	Forum	Flights	Vacation Rentals	About Us

At CityTraveler, we're always looking for good advice on traveling to foreign cities. What suggestions do you have? Post them here!

To get around **linguistic** difficulties, use body language or draw a picture.
See The World 10 minutes ago

Most cities have multiple **ethnic** groups. Experience their culture and cuisine.
ProTourist 17 minutes ago

Avoid standard tours because they mainly show you the **affluent** areas of a city.
Marla424 23 minutes ago

I **highly** recommend electronic translation devices. I never travel without mine!
CitySurfer 28 minutes ago

Double-check the regulations **enforced** by your airline. They can change suddenly!
Frequent Flyer 41 minutes ago

If you make a cultural mistake, relax. It takes a while to **internalize** foreign customs.
Budget Bill 46 minutes ago

Some cities **restrict** activities that others allow. Check the laws and regulations before you go so you'll be sure to **comply** with all of them.
Sunny772 54 minutes ago

Visit places that are **unique** to the city—avoid international stores and restaurants.
GoSolo55 57 minutes ago

Set realistic sightseeing goals so you'll have enough time to **accomplish** them.
Art Of Travel 1 hour ago

The London Eye is unique to the city of London, England.

B Match each word with its definition.

1. _____ linguistic (adj)
2. _____ ethnic (adj)
3. _____ affluent (adj)
4. _____ highly (adv)
5. _____ comply (v)
6. _____ enforce (v)
7. _____ internalize (v)
8. _____ restrict (v)
9. _____ unique (adj)
10. _____ accomplish (v)

a. to limit, often by official rules or laws
b. wealthy
c. to obey an order, rule, or request
d. to make a belief part of your way of thinking
e. relating to people with the same culture and traditions
f. to complete, finish, or achieve successfully
g. existing in only one place or situation
h. having to do with language
i. very; to a great extent; at a high level
j. to make people obey a law, rule, or regulation

C Complete the questions with the correct form of the words from exercise B. Then ask and answer the questions with a partner.

1. What law do you think is the most important to _____ in your community?
2. What rules or regulations are sometimes hard for you to _____ with?
3. What is a tradition that is _____ to your family? To your culture?
4. What things are _____ on your campus? Do you agree that they should be?
5. What is an important value that you have _____? Explain how it impacts you.
6. What is the next important goal that you hope to _____?
7. What types of _____ cuisine do you enjoy? Where can you get them?
8. What are some _____ differences between your native language and English?

D Match each word with its antonym.

1. _____ affluent (adj)
2. _____ highly (adv)
3. _____ affluent (adj)
4. _____ enforce (v)
5. _____ restrict (v)
6. _____ accomplish (v)

a. ignore
b. fail
c. encourage
d. poor
e. poor
f. hardly

E Read the sentences about Singapore. Choose the best collocation for the word in bold. Search the Internet for collocation dictionaries if you need help.

1. Singapore has many **affluent** (neighborhoods / parking lots).
2. Chinese people represent the largest **ethnic** (bunch / group) in Singapore.
3. The use of chemicals in organic farming is (heavily / deeply) **restricted** in Singapore.
4. Singapore's police department is famous for its effective (law / legal) **enforcement**.
5. The public transportation system in Singapore is **highly** (efficient / good).
6. The Singaporean culture values being ambitious and **accomplishing** (intentions / goals).

B Listening The City-State of Singapore

Critical Thinking

A **PREDICT** You are going to hear two students discuss their notes from a lecture about Singapore. With a partner, predict the answers to these questions.

1. Why do you think one student borrowed the other's class notes?
2. Why might the student who borrowed the notes want to discuss them with the student who wrote them?
3. What might the borrower ask the notetaker to do?
4. Look at the photo. Why do you think the Merlion is a symbol of Singapore?
5. Singapore is a city-state. What do you think *city-state* means?

B **MAIN IDEAS** Read the statements. Then listen to the conversation. Choose T for *True* or F for *False.* 🔊

1.	The name *Singapura* means "lion city."	T	F
2.	Singapore is a young country.	T	F
3.	Singapore is rich in natural resources.	T	F
4.	Nearly all the people of Singapore belong to one ethnic group.	T	F
5.	Singapore has a strong economy.	T	F
6.	Being *kiasu* means enjoying life every minute.	T	F
7.	Nick thinks the laws of Singapore are too strict.	T	F
8.	Sofia believes strict laws are a positive thing.	T	F

Merlion Park is a famous Singapore landmark and a major tourist attraction.

C **DETAILS** Listen to an excerpt from the conversation. Complete the notes with the symbols, numbers, and abbreviations below. 🔊

w/o   yrs   →   ½   =   100%   ~   &   =   1st

Singapore

Singapore [1]_____ one of smallest countries in world: [2]_____ 270 sq miles;
[3]_____ urban

Singapore = country [4]_____ many natural resources

People of diff ethnic groups [5]_____ religions, ~ [6]_____ don't speak English at home

Densely populated [7]_____ strong, influential economy

Success partly due to Lee Kuan Yew = [8]_____ prime minister; influential for 50
[9]_____ until 2015

Singaporeans believe in being *kiasu* [10]_____ afraid to lose

D **PERSONALIZE** Discuss these questions with a partner.

1. Are you the type of person who enjoys being *kiasu*? Explain.
2. Do you think that Singapore's laws are too strict or that they're beneficial? Explain.
3. What annoying behaviors that you see in public would you like to be restricted or made illegal where you live?

E **EVALUATE** Work in a small group. Look at this list of regulations in Singapore and the maximum fines and penalties they carry. Discuss what you think the purpose of each regulation is.

Critical Thinking

Regulations and Penalties

1. Selling chewing gum other than for medical or dental purposes ($100,000 or two years in prison)
2. Spitting in public ($1,000)
3. Playing a musical instrument in public (up to $1,000)
4. Connecting to another person's Wi-Fi (up to $10,000 or three years in prison)
5. Forgetting to flush a public toilet (over $150, although rarely enforced)
6. Allowing mosquitoes to breed in your empty flowerpots ($200 minimum)
7. Feeding pigeons (up to $10,000)

F **PERSONALIZE** Discuss with your group whether you think the regulations in exercise E would be a good idea where you live.

Speaking

PRONUNCIATION   Word Stress with Suffixes

🔊 You have learned that different forms of a word often have different endings, or suffixes. Some suffixes can change how the word is stressed.

Noun *–ity, –tion* The stress is placed one syllable before the suffix: *pri**or**ity, authori**za**tion.*

Verb *–ate, –fy, –ize* The stress is placed two syllables before the suffix: ***reg**u**late**, i**den**tify, pri**or**i**tize**.*

Adjective *–d/–ed, –ing, –ive* These do not affect stress; the stress remains where it is on the base word: ***au**thori**zed**, re**lax**ing, in**nov**ative.*

Adverb *–ly* These do not affect stress either: *in**ter**nally, u**nique**ly.*

A Listen to the word pairs and repeat them. Underline the syllable with the main stress in both words. 🔊

1. renovate, renovation
2. regulate, regulated
3. internal, internalize
4. ethnic, ethnicity

5. restrict, restricting
6. compare, comparative
7. diverse, diversify
8. linguistic, linguistically

B Complete the conversation with the words you hear. Mark the stress on those words. Then practice the conversation with a partner. 🔊

A: If you were the mayor of Venice, would you ¹_____ the number of tourists?

B: No. Instead, I'd ²_____ ³_____ tourists.

A: But more tourists would ⁴_____ ⁵_____ more trash, and city services are at the breaking point.

B: I think ⁶_____ on restaurant takeout would solve that problem.

A: I see. And aren't you ⁷_____ about high rents and more Venetians ⁸_____ leaving the city?

B: Yes, but I'd ⁹_____ the ¹⁰_____ of affordable apartments just outside the city.

A: Interesting. Finally, where would you get the ¹¹_____ needed funds for building ¹²_____?

B: I'd ¹³_____ affluent residents and request ¹⁴_____ from them or try more ¹⁵_____ methods of fundraising.

C EXPLAIN Read the statements. Tell a partner whether you agree or disagree and why. Critical Thinking

1. Smoking should be prohibited in all public places, both indoors and outdoors.
2. It's the government's responsibility to provide homeless people with a place to live.
3. Billboards beside the road are ugly and distracting. They should be illegal.
4. In crowded cities, the government should limit the number of cars a family can have.
5. Restrictions on outdoor dining are bad for business.
6. Pets should be allowed in restaurants, shops, and movie theaters.
7. Apartment buildings are more environmentally friendly than houses, so everyone should live in an apartment.
8. All homes should be required to switch to environmentally friendly fuel sources, such as solar, within the next three years.

D EVALUATE Work with a partner. Discuss and decide whether your friend should move to Venice or to Singapore in each situation. Give reasons for your ideas. Critical Thinking

Your friend . . .

1. . . . is an artist.
2. . . . wants to start a business.
3. . . . prefers a relaxed lifestyle.
4. . . . has some health issues.
5. . . . only speaks one language.
6. . . . has several pets.

> *I think if the artist is a painter, then Venice might be the best choice. There are so many museums full of inspiring paintings in Venice and Italy.*

▼ A cat cafe in Seoul, South Korea

Review

How well can you . . . ?	Very well.	OK.	I need improvement.
use the key vocabulary	☐	☐	☐
stress words correctly	☐	☐	☐
use the passive voice	☐	☐	☐
add and emphasize information	☐	☐	☐

A VOCABULARY Use the vocabulary words from this unit to complete the sentences.

1. What are some items that are not _____ for your budget?

2. Why is it important to _____ the number of cars downtown?

3. Who is responsible for _____ rules at your school?

4. What traditions are _____ to your city or town?

B PRONUNCIATION Complete the tasks.

1. Mark where you expect the stress to be on these words:

scarcity   transportation   originate

randomize   creative   specialized

2. Use three of the words above in sentences. Say them aloud, focusing on the stress.

C GRAMMAR Write the active or passive form of the verbs in parentheses.

Recently, the town council [1]_____ (make) many improvements to our town. Last year, a parking garage [2]_____ (build) with over 2000 spaces in the commercial area. Streets [3]_____ (repair), and more streetlights [4]_____ (install). The city also [5]_____ (add) more green spaces for people to enjoy. Finally, more bicycle lanes [6]_____ (create) to make biking safer.

D SPEAKING SKILL Respond to the situation. Add information and emphasize your points.

You are asking your teacher for a better grade. Tell him/her why you deserve a higher grade.

> *I'd like to point out that I did not miss any classes or assignments. On top of that, I . . . .*

RE-ASSESS What skills or language still need improvement?

Final Tasks

OPTION 1 Discuss how to make your city smarter

A IDENTIFY Work in a group. Think about problems in your community. Look at the ideas for creating a smart city below. You may add your own. Then identify which ideas would have a positive impact on those problems. Make some notes.

- bike lanes
- more public parks
- public bike rental program
- better public transportation
- buildings made from green materials

- smart water management
- smog management solutions
- electric vehicle charging stations
- pedestrian-only areas
- _____

B DISCUSS Use your notes to discuss how to make your city smarter. Try to:

- use language to add and emphasize information
- consider different perspectives
- use the passive voice

OPTION 2 Give a presentation about laws or rules

See Unit 2 Rubric in the Appendix.

A MODEL Listen to a pair of students talk about four laws in Venice. Take notes on the laws, the reasons for them, and the different perspectives on them. 🔊

B ANALYZE THE MODEL Listen again and answer these questions about the model. 🔊

1. Did the presenters get and keep your attention?
2. Did each person speak for about the same amount of time?
3. Did they share different perspectives about the laws?

▼ Kayaking on Venice's main waterways was made illegal in 2018.

C **RESEARCH** You and a partner will give a presentation about four laws or rules in a town, city, or country you choose. Follow the instructions.

1. Decide on the town, city, or country you will talk about.
2. Research four interesting laws. Enter the name of your chosen location and one of these search terms or your own ideas into a search engine:
   - unique or unusual laws/regulations
   - rules about using parks
   - laws about building and development
   - laws about selling street food
   - laws about playing music in public
   - rules about making noise
3. When you find interesting laws, take notes on them in the graphic organizer below, including the reason for each law and different perspectives on it.

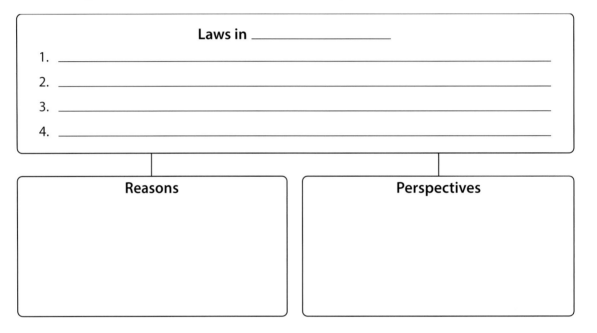

Laws in _____

1. _____
2. _____
3. _____
4. _____

| Reasons | Perspectives |

D **PLAN** Read the information in the Presentation Skill box. Decide how you want to divide the presentation and then finish preparing your presentation.

PRESENTATION SKILL **Present with a Partner**

When dividing up material for a pair presentation, you can try different techniques:
- Divide the material to present in half.
- Take a "tag-team" approach where you take turns presenting different points. This can help keep the audience's attention, but avoid switching back and forth too much.
- Assign different parts of the presentation based on who is best qualified to present each part. It's important to consider the strengths of each presenter. A qualified presenter is more confident and will make a better impression on the audience.

🔊 **ONLINE** If you are using slides to present, it's best to use one set of slides. Each person should know which slides they are responsible for, so the transitions are smooth.

E **PRACTICE AND PRESENT** Practice with your partner. Give each other feedback before you present to the class.

BEAUTY AND APPEARANCE 3

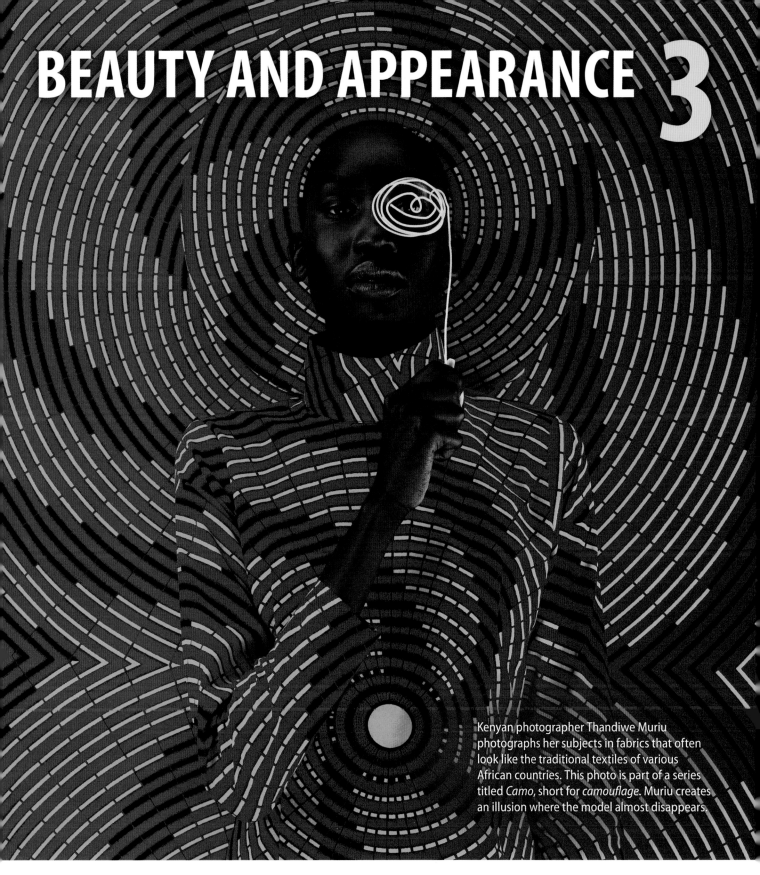

Kenyan photographer Thandiwe Muriu photographs her subjects in fabrics that often look like the traditional textiles of various African countries. This photo is part of a series titled *Camo*, short for *camouflage*. Muriu creates an illusion where the model almost disappears.

IN THIS UNIT, YOU WILL:

- Watch or listen to a news report about beauty
- Watch a video about the future of fashion
- Listen to a conversation about fashion influences
- Discuss clothing influences
  OR Give a presentation about fashion trends

THINK AND DISCUSS:

1. What did you first think when you looked at the photo? Did you see the model?
2. Camouflage is something that you put on so that you cannot be seen or recognized. Who uses camouflage?
3. Does this look like an image you would see in a typical fashion magazine? Why or why not?

Read the information. Then discuss the questions.

1. Do the women in this photo look confident to you? Why or why not?
2. Who do you know who is especially confident? How do they show this?
3. Which of the tips do you already do? Which will you try?

Building Confidence

According to research, confident people are perceived as more attractive. If you want to improve your appearance, try these tips to become more comfortable in your own skin:

 Don't compare yourself to others

 Don't worry about what others think

 Practice positive self-talk

 Exercise regularly

 Smile often

 Focus on your accomplishments

 Explore things that interest you

 Make a list of your positive qualities and read it often

 Eat well

 Stand up straight

Bolivian jewelry and clothing designer Ana Palza designs for *cholitas*, women of Aymara or Quechua descent who maintain their Indigenous culture and traditions. In this photo, the women are wearing Palza's designs at a fashion show in Paris, France.

A Vocabulary

A Match each word to its definition. Use a dictionary if necessary.

1. _____ alarming   a. (v) to have or form a mental picture

2. _____ constitute   b. (v) to change and develop gradually

3. _____ distinct   c. (adj) restricted to a special group

4. _____ envision   d. (n) a proportion, e.g., 2:1

5. _____ evolve   e. (adj) more than is necessary, normal, or desirable

6. _____ excessive   f. (v) to compose or form

7. _____ exclusive   g. (adj) shocking or frightening

8. _____ perceive   h. (adj) chosen without a method or plan

9. _____ random   i. (adj) clear or clearly different

10. _____ ratio   j. (v) to recognize; to be aware of

B **MEANING FROM CONTEXT** Complete the article with the correct form of a word from exercise A. Then listen and check your answers. 🔊

HIGH-FASHION MODELING

High-fashion models' body types differ from those of

¹_____ people on the street. Designers have long

had a ²_____ preference for tall and thin models. However,

images of very thin models in fashion shows and magazines can be

³_____. Some models have a height-to-weight

⁴_____ that is unhealthy. For example, a model might be

around 175 centimeters tall but weigh only 50 kilos.

Fortunately, the fashion business is ⁵_____. Businesses no

longer ⁶_____ hire the thinnest of models. Healthy-looking

models now appear at fashion shows, too. In some countries, there are

even laws against hiring ⁷_____ thin models. Today, designers

⁸_____ their clothes on various body types. This is reflected in the models they choose. As a

result, people are beginning to ⁹_____ models differently. On top of that, their idea of what

¹⁰_____ beauty is starting to change.

C Complete the sentences with the correct form of the word in parentheses. If necessary, use a dictionary.

1. James was _____ (alarm) when he discovered a gray hair on his head.

2. That black hat looks _____ (distinct) better on you than the blue one.

3. The designer said the dress wasn't as stylish as what she had _____ (envision).

4. There has been an _____ (evolve) of workplace fashion from formal to casual.

5. We don't shop at that store because the prices are _____ (excessive) high.

6. Our shopping club offers _____ (exclusive) discounts to members.

7. There is a general _____ (perceive) that Paris is the world capital of fashion.

8. The winners were _____ (random) selected from the audience.

D Work with a partner. Choose the word that forms a collocation with the word in bold. Search the Internet for collocation dictionaries if you're not sure.

1. I never plan what I'm going to wear. I just choose my clothes (at / for) **random**.
2. The **ratio** (for / of) women to men in my class is 2 to 1.
3. The designer is successful because her designs are **distinct** (to / from) most.
4. These beauty products are **exclusively** (for / to) our loyal customers.
5. The increase in extreme dieting is an **alarming** (trend / trending).
6. His small business (gradually / regularly) **evolved** into a great fashion company.
7. Men who wear neckties are **perceived** (in / as) being professional.
8. Those new fashions are **excessively** (beautiful / expensive).

E Work with a partner. Take turns using the collocations in exercise D to say sentences.

> *I don't think it's a good idea to select your college major at random.*

F **PERSONALIZE** Work in a small group. Discuss the questions.

1. What **constitutes** beauty for you?
2. If you knew someone who was **excessively** concerned with physical appearance, what could you say to convince them that attractiveness is not **exclusively** physical?
3. Are there any modern fashion trends that you find **alarming**? Explain.
4. Do you ever try to make yourself look **distinctive**? How?
5. What traits (physical or personality) do you **perceive** as your greatest strengths?
6. What do you **envision** yourself doing in five years?

A Listening Perceptions of Beauty

Critical Thinking | **A** **EVALUATE** Discuss these questions with a partner.

1. Look at the two rows of photos. These photos were shown to people who participated in a study about beauty. Select the photo from each row that you think shows the most beautiful face. Do you and your partner agree?
2. Look at the photos again. According to researchers, most people would choose photos 4 and 9 as the most beautiful faces. Why do you think most people choose these photos?

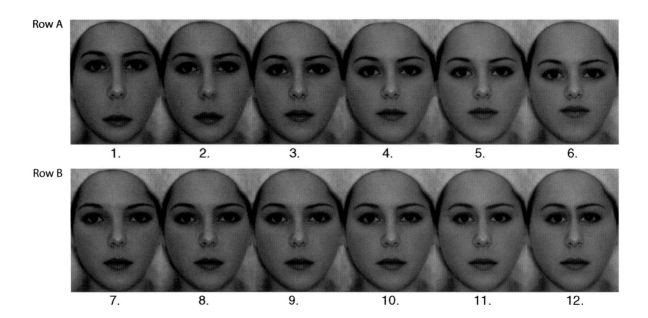

Row A

1.   2.   3.   4.   5.   6.

Row B

7.   8.   9.   10.   11.   12.

B **MAIN IDEAS** Watch or listen to a news report. Match each scientist or group of scientists to their research result. 🔊 ▶

Scientists	Research Results
1. _____ Judith Langlois	a. Men are attracted to signs of health in women.
2. _____ Pamela M. Pallett/ Stephen Link/Kang Lee	b. A well-balanced face is a beautiful face.
3. _____ Victor Johnston/David Perrett	c. The standards of beauty online are similar to those in real life.
4. _____ Don Symons	d. There is a "golden ratio" for the ideal distance between the eyes, the mouth, and the edge of the face.
5. _____ Hellen Egger	e. Men prefer large eyes, full lips, and a small nose and chin.

NOTE-TAKING SKILL Use an Outline

Using an outline can help you organize main ideas and details. You can create an outline while taking notes or afterward to organize your notes. A formal outline looks like the one in exercise C below. Notice how the outline shows the structure of the talk, with roman numerals for main ideas, capital letters for supporting points, and numbers for details.

C DETAILS Listen again and complete the outline. Write one word or number in each blank. 🔊

I. Studies on beauty

  A. Langlois

    1. [1]_____-looking faces are beautiful

    2. a beautiful face is well [2]_____

  B. Pallett, Link, & Lee

    1. discovered the [3]_____ ratio

    2. eyes ◄─► mouth = [4]_____ of length of face

  C. Johnston & Perrett

    1.   Men prefer large eyes, full lips, small nose & [5]_____

  D. Symons

    1. Men attracted to [6]_____-looking women

    2. Signs of health = ability to produce healthy [7]_____

  E. Egger

    1. [8]_____ are used on social media to change appearance

    2. Instagram face = larger eyes, smaller nose, fuller lips

II. Other cultural standards of beauty

  A. Maya: [9]_____ eyes considered beautiful

  B. Africa: [10]_____ considered beautiful

  C. Māori: [11]_____ used to achieve beauty

D PERSONALIZE Discuss the questions in a small group.

1. Do you judge people by their appearance when you first meet them?
2. Do you think beauty affects a person's success in life?
3. How do you think society's standards of beauty are changing?

A Speaking

A Read and listen to the article. Then look at the bar graph. What is the graph about? 🔊

THE GROWING POPULARITY OF COSMETIC[1] SURGERY

If you think the risks of cosmetic surgery are alarming, there's good news! Cosmetic procedures are evolving; many are not particularly dangerous, and some are quite safe. You may be able to get the new look you envision with nonsurgical procedures, such as fillers to help remove lines and laser treatments to remove age spots or scars, which constitute 68 percent of cosmetic procedures in the United States. Once exclusively for the rich and famous, cosmetic procedures are being chosen by more people every year.

There is a distinct difference in the way people in different cultures perceive beauty, but cosmetic surgery is a common choice in many parts of the world. The graph "Top Markets for Cosmetic Procedures" compares the total number of procedures per capita[2] in 14 countries, and the ratio of surgical to nonsurgical procedures.

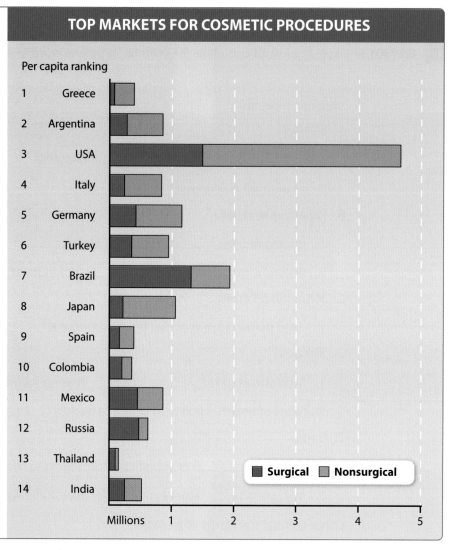

TOP MARKETS FOR COSMETIC PROCEDURES

Per capita ranking

1 Greece
2 Argentina
3 USA
4 Italy
5 Germany
6 Turkey
7 Brazil
8 Japan
9 Spain
10 Colombia
11 Mexico
12 Russia
13 Thailand
14 India

■ Surgical ■ Nonsurgical

Millions 1 2 3 4 5

[1]**cosmetic** (adj) relating to treatment intended to improve a person's appearance
[2]**per capita** (adj) per person relative to the total population

CRITICAL THINKING Interpret a Bar Graph

To understand a bar graph, it's important to study the following features:

- Title: tells you what the graph is about
- Labels: tell you what the bars or numbers represent
- Scale: tells you the unit of measurement
- Color coding/key: shows you what different colors mean

B Work with a partner. Answer the questions about the bar graph.

1. What is the title of the graph?
2. Look at the labels. What do the horizontal bars represent?
3. How many countries have more than a million total cosmetic procedures?
4. Look at the color coding and the key. What do the colors represent?
5. The United States has considerably more cosmetic procedures than other countries. What can you infer from this?
6. What do you find interesting or surprising about the information in the graph?

C Discuss the questions with a partner.

1. Is it a positive trend that cosmetic procedures are now more affordable? Explain.
2. How has technology contributed to the evolution of cosmetic surgery?
3. What are some ways to stay young and healthy looking without cosmetic procedures?

SPEAKING SKILL Paraphrase

When you paraphrase, you express something in a different way. Paraphrasing allows you to restate information that may be new or difficult for listeners to understand. You may use different words or word forms. You may use an example or a description to clarify meaning. You can also paraphrase what you've heard to clarify your own understanding.

> It's said that beauty lies in the eye of the beholder, yet the opposite seems to be true. **What I mean by that is our standards of beauty aren't personal; they're part of the culture we live in.**

Here are some expressions you can use to paraphrase information:

I mean	*Let me put it another way.*
In other words,	*To put it another way,*
That is (to say),	*What I mean by that is . . . .*

D In the news report, the speaker used a number of expressions to paraphrase. Listen and write the expressions you hear. 🔊

1. You often hear, "Beauty is only skin deep." _____, someone can be beautiful on the outside but be mean or unpleasant on the inside.

2. Another saying is, "Beauty is in the eye of the beholder."

   _____, each person's idea of beauty is different.

3. Her research showed that a beautiful face is well balanced.

   _____, if the two sides of a face are highly similar to each other, we consider that face beautiful.

E **INTERPRET** Read these quotations about beauty. In your own words, write what each one means. Then explain each to your partner using an expression from the Speaking Skill box.

1. Beauty is not in the face; beauty is a light in the heart. —Kahlil Gibran

   _____

   _____

2. It matters more what's in a woman's face than what's on it. —Claudette Colbert

   _____

   _____

3. I've never seen a smiling face that was not beautiful. —Author Unknown

   _____

   _____

F You are going to conduct a survey about beauty and fashion. Use the questions below and write two new questions of your own for your survey.

   • Is it better to be beautiful, intelligent, or wealthy?
   • Who is someone that you think is truly beautiful?
   • How often do you shop for new clothes?
   • Are there any fashions today that you think are strange?

   • _____

   • _____

G Interview three classmates. Ask each classmate your survey questions. Take notes on each person's answers. Share your survey results with a small group. What is interesting or surprising about the information you heard? Were your answers different from your classmates'?

People who smile are often perceived as more attractive.

Video

The Future of Fashion

impact (v) to have a direct effect on; to influence

tailored (adj) specially made to fit one person's body

outfit (n) a set of clothes that go together

▲ Technology, such as virtual reality (VR), can reduce waste, making the process of designing fashion more sustainable.

A Watch the video and read the statements. Choose T for *True* or F for *False*. ▶

1. Fast fashion is clothing that people wear for a short time.   T   F
2. People are starting to buy fast fashion less and less.   T   F
3. People on social media want new clothes to show people.   T   F
4. Digital clothing is something that you can wear in real life.   T   F
5. Regina Turbina makes digital clothing that is very expensive.   T   F
6. Digital clothing is better for the environment than fast fashion.   T   F

B Watch again. Are these statements about fast fashion or digital clothing? Write FF or DC. ▶

1. _____ It is only in fashion for a short time.
2. _____ It's a big part of global retail sales.
3. _____ It is specially made for one person.
4. _____ The speaker thinks people buy too much of it.
5. _____ The buyer is sent a photograph of the outfit.
6. _____ It's made within 48 hours.

C In the video, you heard the speaker say, "Technology is everywhere and is now impacting our fashion choices, too." Discuss with a partner how technology impacts your fashion choices.

Vocabulary

A **MEANING FROM CONTEXT** Work with a partner. Listen to and answer the questions on the fashion quiz. Notice the words in blue. 🔊

FASHION ● Quiz

1. Do you prefer **practical** clothes or more **imaginative** designs?

2. How many **influential** fashion designers can you name?

3. Do you prefer to shop for clothes online or in **retail** stores?

4. What are some **mainstream** brands you wear?

5. Are there any **drawbacks** to keeping up with trends in fashion?

6. Do **persuasive** salespeople ever make you spend too much on clothes?

7. Do you think that the power of clothing is **underestimated** by some people? Do you think that a great outfit can improve your day?

8. Which **fabrics** do you prefer to wear?

   denim   silk   wool   cotton

   other: _____

9. Which clothing **textures** do you prefer?

   lightweight   heavy   smooth

   shiny   soft   stiff

   well-ironed   raised patterns

   other: _____

B Are these statements true or false? Write T for *True* or F for *False*.

1. _____ **Practical** clothes require a lot of special care.

2. _____ **Imaginative** designers come up with new ideas.

3. _____ **Influential** people have a strong effect on others.

4. _____ Clothing stores buy their clothes at **retail** prices.

5. _____ **Mainstream** fashions are popular with many people.

6. _____ One **drawback** of expensive clothes is that you don't mind if they get dirty.

7. _____ **Persuasive** ads are good at convincing you to buy something.

8. _____ If you **underestimate** the cost of clothing, you spend less than you expected.

9. _____ **Fabrics** are the materials most clothing is made of.

10. _____ The **texture** of clothing depends on the size you wear.

C Work with a partner. Change the false statements into true ones.

See Word
Families in
the Appendix.

VOCABULARY SKILL Adjective Suffix –ive

The adjective suffix –ive gives the meaning "doing or tending to do."

persuasive = persuading, tending to persuade

attractive = attracting, tending to attract

When adding –ive to a verb, sometimes other changes need to be made.

Verb → Adjective	Rule
affir**m** → affirm**ative**	ends in *m* or *n*: add –ative / –itive
innovat**e** → innovat**ive**	ends in consonant + *e*: drop *e* and add –ive / –ative / –itive
defin**e** → defin**itive**	
persua**de** → persua**sive**	irregular form
repe**at** → repe**titive**	irregular form

Check a dictionary if you are not sure of the form.

D Work with a partner. Use a verb from the box and the suffix –ive to complete these opinions. Use a dictionary if necessary. Then discuss whether the statements are true for you.

addict	alternate	construct	exclude	imagine	impress	inform	restrict

1. I think watching videos on the Internet is _____—once I start, I can't stop!

2. I think winning a soccer game by five points is very _____ .

3. I like science fiction and fantasy movies because they're so _____ .

4. I'm always open to criticism of my work, as long as it's _____ .

5. I'm into _____ fashion because I think it's boring to look like everyone else.

6. I've mostly stopped watching the mainstream news because it's not very

   _____ .

7. I think rules that force students to wear uniforms are too _____ .

8. I often go to _____ clubs where they don't let anyone in wearing jeans.

E Work with a partner. Discuss the appropriate clothes and appearance for the people in the situations below.

1. A candidate at a job interview
2. A guest at a wedding
3. Friends going hiking
4. Friends going skiing

> *I think a candidate at a job interview should wear mainstream business clothes—nothing too wild!*

B Listening Fashion Influences

Critical Thinking

A PREDICT You are going to hear two students discuss fashion influences. With a partner, predict the answers to these questions.

1. Why might they have started talking about fashion?
2. What influences on fashion will they talk about?
3. Given the topic, do you think they will agree or have differences of opinion?

B MAIN IDEAS Number the fashion influences 1–6 in the order you hear them discussed. Two are not mentioned in the listening. 🔊

a. _____ high-fashion designers

b. _____ commercials and advertising

c. _____ salespeople

d. _____ online catalogs

e. _____ celebrities

f. _____ the clothes we already own

g. _____ family members

h. _____ high-tech fitting rooms

C DETAILS Listen again. Complete the statements with *Marcus* or *Nicole*. 🔊

1. _____'s friends feel that the clothes they own are boring.

2. _____ suggests that online catalogs are highly influential.

3. _____ points out that the sense of touch is key when shopping.

4. _____ doesn't trust technology to decide if clothes fit.

5. _____ would feel strange wearing a celebrity's styles.

6. _____ is suspicious of commercials and advertising.

7. _____ thinks the tracking of people's search habits is frightening.

8. _____ feels that companies can have positive effects on society.

LISTENING SKILL Recognize Arguments *For* and *Against*

Most topics of discussion have more than one side, and it's important to be able to recognize arguments for and against something. Listen for these words that:

Signal arguments *for* or *pro*:

benefit	*upside*	*positive*
advantage	*plus*	*point/argument in favor*

An **upside** of fashion today is the use of natural fabrics.

Signal arguments *against* or *con*:

drawback	*downside*	*negative*
disadvantage	*minus*	*point/argument against*

An important **downside** of fast fashion is the waste.

D Listen to an excerpt from the conversation. Match the halves of the sentences you hear. 🔊

1. The drawback to that is _____
2. The problem is _____
3. Their convenience is _____
4. Being able to touch the clothes is _____
5. If they save a lot of time, that's _____
6. The downside is _____

a. a big advantage.
b. a point in their favor.
c. only affluent people can shop there.
d. they're still in the research phase.
e. not experimenting with new styles.
f. a plus.

E Are the sentences in exercise D arguments for or against? Write the sentence numbers.

Arguments *for*: _____

Arguments *against*: _____

F **APPLY** Work in pairs. In the listening, you heard about some ways technology influences fashion choices. In what other ways is technology influencing our ideas about fashion?

Critical Thinking

Fashion designers are influential in determining what styles become popular.

Speaking

PRONUNCIATION Consonant Clusters Across Words

🔊 A consonant cluster is a group of consonant sounds with no vowel sound in between (i.e., *tch*). When a word ending with a consonant or a cluster is followed by a word beginning with a consonant or a cluster, a new consonant cluster is formed across those words.

advertise**ments f**or	wa**tched th**em	bla**nk ch**eck	lu**nch br**eak
pea**rl n**ecklace	sma**rt m**irror	he**lp m**e	retai**l pr**ice

In consonant clusters across words, especially in informal speech, the sounds /p/, /t/, and /d/ are sometimes reduced. Listen to the full and reduced forms of these sentences.

Can you help me?	*Can you hel$_p$ me?*
Is that a smart mirror?	*Is that a smar$_t$ mirror?*
I heard this is on sale.	*I hear$_d$ this is on sale.*

A Read the sentences aloud without pausing between words, paying particular attention to consonant clusters across words. Then listen and check your pronunciation. 🔊

1. I make it a point never to pay retail price.
2. Park Street is a great place to shop for affordable jewelry.
3. The credit card company authorized the payment.
4. Most people wear clothes that conform to certain social standards.
5. Our clothing choices are influenced by internalized values.
6. Different ethnic groups wear distinct styles of clothes.
7. Exclusive shops sell their products to mostly affluent customers.
8. Once I start shopping online, I find it difficult to stop spending money.

B Practice saying the sentences again, this time reducing word-final /p/, /t/, and /d/ sounds in consonant clusters across words.

GRAMMAR FOR SPEAKING Noun Modifiers

Nouns, adjectives, and prepositional phrases can all be used to modify or describe a noun.

Before the noun

Nouns: *a **business** suit; a **fashion** magazine* (Note the singular form—NOT *a ~~fashions~~ magazine*)

Adjectives: ***ripped** jeans; **expensive** shoes; an **exclusive, innovative** design*

(Note: Adjectives are normally placed before nouns: *a **blue business** suit*.)

After the noun

Linking verb + adjective(s): *These shoes **look expensive**. That design **is innovative**.*

Prepositional phrases: *I just read an article **about fashion**.*

C Work with a partner. Put the words and phrases in the correct order to complete the statements. Then discuss whether the statements are true for you.

1. ideas / in my family / fashion / from people

   I often get _____.

2. movies / with famous actors / Hollywood

   I like to watch _____.

3. a direct / flight / book / to my destination

   When I fly, I usually _____.

4. apps / are useful / on my phone / and convenient

   Most of the _____.

5. Scotland / a / vacation / walking / in

   I plan to take _____.

6. phone / friends / calls / long / with old

   I often have _____.

7. websites / attractive / on / advertisements

   I'm easily influenced by _____.

8. with / community / members / children / newer

   Most of the _____ are in favor of the rule.

D Work with a group. Take turns describing people and things you see in the photo. Use noun modifiers in your descriptions.

▼ Our friends often influence our fashion choices.

Review

SELF-ASSESS

How well can you . . . ?	Very well.	OK.	I need improvement.
use the key vocabulary	☐	☐	☐
pronounce consonant clusters across words	☐	☐	☐
use noun modifiers	☐	☐	☐
paraphrase	☐	☐	☐

A VOCABULARY Answer the questions.

1. What's an example of a **persuasive** ad? _____

2. What is the **ratio** of women to men in your family? _____

3. What is one of the **drawbacks** of living in a city? _____

4. Who is an **influential** person in your country or community? _____

B PRONUNCIATION Complete the tasks.

1. Mark the consonant clusters across these word pairs:

   affordable jewelry   distinct styles   lunch break   wear clothes   stop spending   brand new

2. Identify letters in the clusters that can be reduced.

C GRAMMAR Put the words and phrases in the correct order to complete the sentences.

1. for men / a new / of cosmetics / line

   The company introduced _____.

2. clothes / exclusive / designer

   That shop sells _____.

3. without buttons / denim / a used / jacket

   I bought _____.

D SPEAKING SKILL Paraphrase the following sayings.

1. *Don't judge a book by its cover.* _____

2. *The best mirror is a friend's eye.* _____

RE-ASSESS What skills or language still need improvement?

OPTION 1 Discuss and rank clothing influences

A **PERSONALIZE** Work in a group. Look at the results of a survey of where clothing ideas come from. Discuss how much the sources influence you.

Sources of Clothing Ideas		Rank
Already own and like	80.9%	
Store displays	67.5%	
People seen regularly	50.6%	
Catalogs	42.1%	
Family members	42.5%	
Commercials and ads	40.5%	
Fashion magazines	31.0%	
Salespeople	19.4%	
Celebrities	17.2%	

A: I think I get most of my ideas from what I already own and like.
B: Really? Not me. I get most of mine from fashion magazines.

B **RANK** Rank the items in exercise A from 1–9 according to how much the sources influence you. Then share and compare your ranking with the group.

OPTION 2 Present fashion trends

See Unit 3 Rubric in the Appendix.

PRESENTATION SKILL Prepare Visuals for Display

When preparing visuals for a presentation, digital devices are useful, but options such as posters and handouts can be just as effective. Remember that the main point of visuals is to add interest and clarify or support your message. When preparing visuals, ask yourself:

- Is the size of the lettering large enough for everyone to see?
- Is the language clear, correct, brief, and easy to understand?
- Will everyone be able to see the photos and graphics clearly?

🔊 **ONLINE** To share a visual online, you will need to share your screen. You want your audience to focus on you, so don't share your screen for the entire presentation. Share your screen only when the visual supports your message.

A **MODEL** Listen to a pair presentation about fashion trends. Take notes in the chart.

Fashion trend	Description	When did it start?
1.		
2.		
3.		
4.		

B **ANALYZE THE MODEL** Listen again and answer these questions about the model.

1. How does the first speaker introduce the presentation?
2. How is the overall presentation organized?
3. What language do the speakers use as they take turns?
4. How is the information about each fashion trend organized?

C **RESEARCH** Follow the steps to prepare your presentation.

1. Work with a partner. Search the Internet for fashion trends. Choose two trends each that interest you.
2. Research the four trends and take notes in the chart below.
3. Organize the presentation.
4. Prepare appropriate visuals for display during your presentation.

Trend 1

Trend 2

Fashion Trends

Trend 3

Trend 4

D **PRACTICE AND PRESENT** Practice with your partner. Give each other feedback before you present to the class.

GOING GLOBAL 4

According to the World Economic Forum, around 90% of goods are moved using container ships such as these docked in Bangkok, Thailand.

IN THIS UNIT, YOU WILL:

- Watch or listen to a lecture about skills in global business
- Watch a video about being a global citizen
- Listen to a podcast about augmented reality
- Discuss tech skills for the workplace
  OR Give a group presentation about a social media platform

THINK AND DISCUSS

1. Do you know where your clothes and electronic devices are made? Do you know how they get to you?
2. Why do you think container ships are used to transport so many goods?
3. Apart from global business, in what other ways is the world connected?

EXPLORE THE THEME

Read the information. Then discuss the questions.

1. Augmented reality (AR) is the integration of digital information with the user's environment in real time. For example, it can allow you to see how a table would look in your home before buying it. What uses of AR in the pie chart are you familiar with?

2. What are some examples of AR in daily life?

3. Does any of the data in the pie chart surprise you? Explain.

Global Use of Augmented Reality

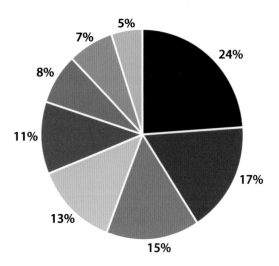

- ■ Industrial & Manufacturing 24%
- ■ Automotive 17%
- ■ Gaming & Entertainment 15%
- ▨ E-commerce & Retail 13%
- ■ Health Care 11%
- ▨ Air & Defense 8%
- ▨ Education 7%
- ▨ Others 5%

An industrial engineer uses augmented reality (AR) to see information about an oil, gas, and fuel transport pipeline. The global AR market is expected to grow 40.9% by 2030.

A Vocabulary

A **MEANING FROM CONTEXT** Read and listen to the article. Think about the meaning of the words in blue. Then write the correct form of each word next to its definition. 🔊

GLOBALIZATION AND SKILLS

Globalization refers to how countries, companies, and people depend on each other more and more in terms of the movement of goods and services, technology, and information. It's a trend that's affecting the skills that are **in demand** in workplaces everywhere. Advanced technologies, a key **component** of globalization, are more **widespread** than ever before, and companies in every business **sector** are **integrating** them into their business processes. This means that technology skills are welcomed throughout the **labor** market. However, while new tech **facilitates** tasks in almost every type of business, it also **inevitably** takes over jobs that humans used to do. Fortunately, **competency** in various uniquely human skills (also called "soft skills") remains highly valuable, and companies will compete to hire and **retain** workers who possess these skills.

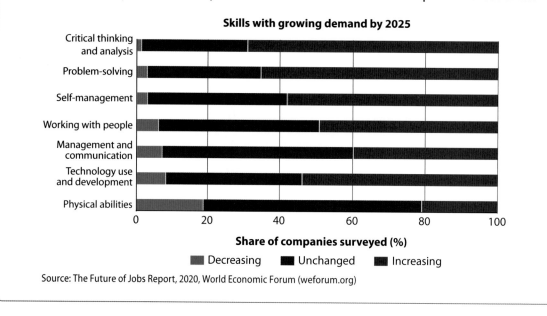

Skills with growing demand by 2025

Share of companies surveyed (%)

■ Decreasing   ■ Unchanged   ■ Increasing

Source: The Future of Jobs Report, 2020, World Economic Forum (weforum.org)

1. _____ (n) an area of a society or economy

2. _____ (v) to make something part of a larger process, system, etc.

3. _____ (adj phr) wanted or needed by many

4. _____ (v) to keep

5. _____ (n) work or employment

6. _____ (n) the ability to do something well

7. _____ (adv) certainly, necessarily

8. _____ (v) to make something easier or more efficient

9. _____ (adj) existing or happening over a large area

10. _____ (n) a part of a larger whole

B **ANALYZE** Work with a partner. Complete the sentences with a skill from the graph in exercise A. Critical Thinking

1. The smallest number of companies think _____ is decreasing in importance.

   a. critical thinking and analysis   b. problem-solving

2. The largest number of companies think _____ will remain unchanged in importance.

   a. self-management   b. physical abilities

3. More than 50% of the companies think _____ is growing in importance.

   a. technology use and development   b. management and communication

4. More companies think _____ is increasing in importance than think self-management is.

   a. working with people   b. problem-solving

VOCABULARY SKILL   Collocations

Collocations are combinations of words that are frequently used together. To check for collocations, use an online collocations dictionary or concordancer, a computer program used to search, access, and analyze language from a corpus. You can expand your vocabulary by learning these combinations. Here are two common patterns.

Noun + noun (The first noun acts as an adjective.)

   labor markets   *business sector*   *human skills*

Adjective + noun

   key component   *advanced technologies*   *remote control*

C Complete each global career tip with the correct collocation.

1. Knowing only your _____ isn't enough these days. Learn a second one.

   a. natural language   b. first language   c. personal language

2. Do your own research to keep up with _____ in your chosen field.

   a. major trends   b. upper trends   c. considerable trends

3. Don't forget that companies often fill their _____ with local talent.

   a. peak positions   b. senior positions   c. elder positions

4. If you hope to work in the _____, do a leadership training program.

   a. managing sector   b. manager sector   c. management sector

5. Develop the ability to adapt to other cultures, as it's part of a global career _____.

   a. skill club   b. skill arrangement   c. skill set

6. Join online discussions related to your field _____.

   a. to interest   b. of interest   c. for interest

D **APPLY** Work in a group. Discuss the career tips in exercise C. Then use the collocations to make your own career tips. Critical Thinking

> *Don't worry if you don't speak English as well as your first language. A lot of successful international businesspeople are still perfecting their English!*

A Listening Skills for Global Business

Critical Thinking **A ACTIVATE** Discuss these questions in a small group.

1. What does it take to be successful in today's globalized business world?
2. You are going to hear a lecture about four skill sets, called "competencies," needed to succeed in business today. Look at the skill sets and discuss what you think each means.

   - personal competency
   - social competency
   - business competency
   - cultural competency

B MAIN IDEAS Watch or listen to the lecture. Match each competency with its TWO key skills. 🔊 ▶

1. personal competency _____
2. social competency _____
3. business competency _____
4. cultural competency _____

a. bridge building
c. emotional intelligence
e. managing chaos
g. practical trust

b. developing leadership
d. time management
f. positive impatience
h. understanding your own culture

C DETAILS Read the statements. Then listen again. Choose T for *True* or F for *False*. 🔊

1. Dr. O'Brian thinks finding a great job today is easier than ever.   T   F
2. Dr. O'Brian researched the four competencies himself.   T   F
3. Emotional intelligence helps us set priorities and keep schedules.   T   F
4. Practical trust keeps managers from doubting workers too much.   T   F
5. Managing chaos is helped by keeping communication lines open.   T   F
6. It's important to develop leadership in oneself as well as in others.   T   F
7. Japanese businesspeople prefer a very direct style of communication.   T   F
8. Bridge building means making connections within a company.   T   F

LISTENING SKILL   Listen for a Summary

After a complex and/or lengthy explanation, speakers will sometimes finish with a short summary. This reminds listeners of the main ideas presented. Listen for these expressions, which introduce a summary.

In sum, ...   *In summary, ...*   *In brief, ...*   *To summarize, ...*

To sum up, ...   *In short, ...*   *In conclusion, ...*   *The bottom line is . . . .*

D Listen to excerpts from the lecture. Then work with a partner to write the summary you hear at the end of each. 🔊

1. _____

_____

2. _____

_____

3. _____

_____

4. _____

_____

E Listen to the summaries and check your answers to exercise D. 🔊

F **PERSONALIZE** Answer the questions with a partner.

1. Which of the competencies is an area of strength for you? Give an example.
2. Which of the competencies would you like to develop? Why?
3. What can you do to improve your cultural competency?

▼ Emotional intelligence is an important part of global competency. Employees with high emotional intelligence can help facilitate group decision making and employee integration.

A Speaking

SPEAKING SKILL Define Terms

When giving a presentation, you may sometimes use specialized terms. Your listeners may not be familiar with these terms, and their meaning may differ from everyday usage. In these cases, you should define the terms using language that your audience will understand. Here are some expressions you can use:

The term ... refers to/means ....   *By ..., I mean ....*

This means ....   *... is defined as ....*

You can also define a term by pausing after you use it and giving a definition.

A Match each term on the left with its definition on the right. Then work with a partner. Practice saying sentences to introduce and then define the terms, using expressions from the Speaking Skill box.

1. _____ coca-colonization
2. _____ postnationalism
3. _____ food miles
4. _____ digital divide
5. _____ soft power
6. _____ digital native
7. _____ emotional intelligence
8. _____ bridge building

a. the ability to make connections across cultures

b. the globalization of American culture through U.S. products

c. a country's ability to convince others to do what it wants without force

d. a person born in the digital age and comfortable with new technology

e. understanding one's own and others' emotions

f. the gap between those who have access to digital technology and those who do not

g. the process by which nations become global entities

h. the distance food is transported from producer to consumer

> *One aspect of globalization is coca-colonization. By coca-colonization, I mean the globalization of American culture through U.S. products.*

Critical Thinking | **B** **DEFINE** Work with a partner. Read the excerpts. Then take turns defining the terms in italics using your own words and the expressions in the Speaking Skill box.

1. I'll start at the individual level with *personal competency*.
2. A skill connected with social competency is what I call *practical trust*.
3. Another critical skill related to social competency is *positive impatience*.
4. In the area of business competency, the skill of *managing chaos* is key.

CRITICAL THINKING   Interpret Data in Charts and Graphs

Charts and graphs are useful because they present data in a clear, visual way. However, it's important to think critically about the information presented. Here are some things you should consider:

- How was the data obtained? Is there enough data to be significant?
- How is the data presented? Is the presentation of data clear?
- What can you conclude from the information presented? Is the overall message clear?

C Examine the graph. Then answer the questions below.

Critical Thinking

25,000 People in 25 Countries Surveyed:
Percentage "Positive" or "Negative"

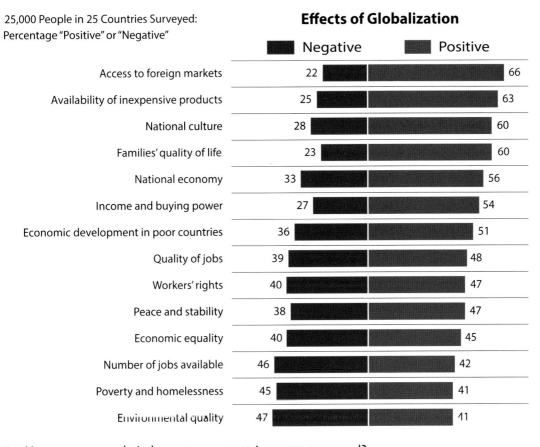

Effects of Globalization

Negative   Positive

Issue	Negative	Positive
Access to foreign markets	22	66
Availability of inexpensive products	25	63
National culture	28	60
Families' quality of life	23	60
National economy	33	56
Income and buying power	27	54
Economic development in poor countries	36	51
Quality of jobs	39	48
Workers' rights	40	47
Peace and stability	38	47
Economic equality	40	45
Number of jobs available	46	42
Poverty and homelessness	45	41
Environmental quality	47	41

1. How many people in how many countries were surveyed?
2. What do the red bars mean? The blue bars?
3. What percentage said globalization has had a positive effect on access to foreign markets?
4. What percentage said globalization has had a negative effect on the quality of jobs?
5. Did more people say that globalization has had a positive or a negative effect on environmental quality?
6. Did you find anything about the graph interesting or surprising?
7. How would you summarize the information in this graph for someone?

D **PERSONALIZE** Work with a partner. Which issues in the chart are the most important for you or your country right now?

An adjective clause provides information about a noun. It tells us 'which one' or 'what kind.' It's a way to combine ideas or sentences.

All the countries removed trade barriers. The countries signed the agreement.

*All the countries **that signed the agreement** removed trade barriers.*

There are two types of adjective clauses. One is essential to the meaning of the sentence, and the other provides extra or non-essential information.

Essential:

*The students **who signed up for the exchange program** will study in Peru this fall.*

*The competency **(that) I think is most important** is personal competency.*

In essential adjective clauses, the pronoun is often dropped when it is the object of the clause.

Non-essential:

*Sarah**, whom you know,** signed up for the exchange program.*

*One global business skill is emotional intelligence**, which Dr. O'Brian talked about**.*

Use *which* instead of *that* and one or two commas with non-essential clauses.

We can also express place in an adjective clause with *where*.

*The students are in Peru**, where they are doing an exchange program**.*

*I live in a city **where there is little crime**.*

E Combine the sentences using an essential or non-essential adjective clause. Use correct punctuation.

1. Most of the electronics are manufactured abroad. I buy the electronics.

   _____

2. I buy vegetables from local farmers. The farmers care about our community.

   _____

3. I don't think countries should export products. The products are essential.

   _____

4. Globalization results in lower prices. Globalization has received criticism lately.

   _____

5. The people need to elect politicians. The politicians will protect the jobs of local workers.

   _____

6. I'd like to see a world. Oil spills don't occur there.

   _____

7. I spoke to Dr. Phillips. Dr. Phillips gave a presentation on global business last week.

   _____

8. I'm planning a trip to Vietnam. Several of my friends have already been there.

   _____

F **PERSONALIZE** Work with a partner. Say whether the first three statements in exercise E are true for you.

What Is a Global Citizen?

respectful (adj) showing appreciation and admiration
embrace (v) to accept as a belief

diversity (n) differences and variety
engage in (v phr) to do or take part in

▲ UNESCO's headquarters in Paris, France. UNESCO's goal is to promote peace through international cooperation in education, arts, sciences, and culture.

A Watch the video. Choose the correct answer to complete the sentences. ▶

1. The questions are being asked to _____.
   a. university students
   b. people attending a conference

2. The speakers seem to be mostly speakers _____.
   a. of English as their first language
   b. of languages other than English

3. The people answered the questions _____.
   a. by giving right or wrong answers
   b. freely using their own ideas

4. According to one speaker, a global citizen _____.
   a. teaches others what global citizenship means
   b. knows their own culture

B Watch the video again. Choose the TWO phrases used to answer each question. ▶

1. What is a global citizen?
   a. building our understanding
   b. to live well with people
   c. living in many countries

2. Why should everyone be a global citizen?
   a. to vote for global leaders
   b. to make our world better
   c. to embrace a concept of diversity

3. As a global citizen, what do you do?
   a. solve problems
   b. go to conferences
   c. respect myself

C **PERSONALIZE** Ask and answer the THREE questions from the video (and in exercise B) with a partner. Then share your answers with another pair.

B | Vocabulary

A | Listen and check the words you know. Use a dictionary to help you with any new words. 🔊

anticipate (v)   capability (n)   enrich (v)   insert (v)   prominent (adj)
application (n)   collaborate (v)   implication (n)   portable (adj)   state-of-the-art (adj)

Critical Thinking | **B** | **ANALYZE** *Augment* means to increase or make larger. Read the "Revealed World" section in the article below. What do you think *augmented reality* means? Discuss your ideas with a partner.

C | **MEANING FROM CONTEXT** Complete the article with the correct form of the words in exercise A. Then listen and check your answers. 🔊

REVEALED WORLD

Imagine bubbles floating before your eyes, filled with cool information about things you see on the street. Science fiction? No, it's augmented reality, and it's changing how the world gets information.

THE WORLD OF AUGMENTED REALITY

Augmented reality (or AR) modifies the reality we see through a smartphone or other [1]_____ device by [2]_____ information in the form of bubbles, images, sounds, or videos. At work, this information gives workers the [3]_____ to accomplish tasks they otherwise couldn't. AR apps for smartphones and AR glasses are now [4]_____ technologies in retail and many other industries. One of the most [5]_____ examples of AR was launched in 2016—Pokémon GO—a game that has [6]_____ the play time of millions of people. Since then, various outdoor games have used AR to allow multiple players to [7]_____ as they hunt for digital objects or creatures. Other [8]_____ of AR technology include software that displays information about restaurants, historic sites, museum exhibits, or where you parked your car. In the years to come, the technology industry [9]_____ that AR will have broad [10]_____, touching nearly every business sector.

D Complete the chart with the correct form of each word. Use a dictionary if necessary.

	Verb	Noun	Adjective
1.	collaborate		
2.		implication	
3.	anticipate		
4.	– – – – – – –		prominent
5.	insert		
6.			enriched, enriching

E **PERSONALIZE** Discuss these questions with a partner.

1. How could an **augmented reality** system help you at work or school?
2. What do you think the **implications** are of children using technology for many hours every day?
3. Which **state-of-the-art** technology products would you like to own?
4. In what ways do you **anticipate** your life will change in the next five years?
5. Who is **prominent** in the world of business these days?

▼ Augmented reality adds another level of information to museum exhibits. Dinosaur bones get a layer of flesh and the ability to move around at the Royal Ontario Museum in Canada.

Listening Global Trend: Augmented Reality

Critical Thinking | **A** **ACTIVATE** You are going to listen to a podcast about augmented reality. Discuss these questions with a partner.

1. The podcasters think that augmented reality might be new to some of their listeners. What do you think they do at the beginning of the podcast?

2. Two experts are on the podcast. How do you think their talk will be organized?

    a. question and answer   b. turn-taking

3. Where might you see an image like the one below?

4. What kinds of information are available in the image?

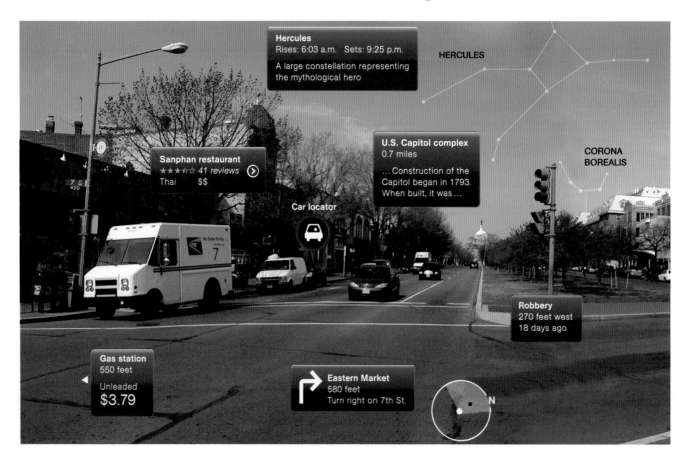

B **MAIN IDEAS** Listen to the podcast. Check the EIGHT areas discussed.

1. ☐ retail shopping   6. ☐ furniture shopping

2. ☐ AR games   7. ☐ self-driving cars

3. ☐ restaurant menus   8. ☐ education

4. ☐ industry   9. ☐ tourism

5. ☐ shipping   10. ☐ public safety

C **DETAILS** Listen again and choose the correct answers. 🔊

1. AR videos for shoe shopping eliminate _____.
   a. the need to try shoes on
   b. the problem of different languages

2. Alex references Facebook and Twitter to show how _____ Pokémon GO was.
   a. popular
   b. profitable

3. Alex points out that Pokémon GO facilitated the globalization of _____.
   a. culture
   b. the Internet

4. Kings of Pool is an AR game that allows people to play pool _____.
   a. on a computer screen
   b. on any flat surface

5. Alex thinks using AR to label machine parts is better than _____.
   a. using physical labels
   b. having a manager explain them

6. Jasmin believes that DHL's use of AR for shipping must _____.
   a. save the company time
   b. cost the company a lot of money

7. Alex mentions that using AR to check how a sofa looks in a room _____.
   a. means fewer mistakes
   b. avoids heavy lifting

8. Jasmin likes the idea of using AR travel guides instead of _____.
   a. going on a group tour
   b. using a paper guidebook

9. Firefighters use AR glasses so that they can _____.
   a. locate burning areas
   b. move through dark places

D **FOCUSED LISTENING** Listen and complete these sentences from the podcast with the adjective clauses you hear. 🔊

1. Augmented reality, or AR as it's often called, is a technology trend
   _____.

2. That is, it's a way of adding something to the reality
   _____.

3. People who work in the warehouses of the shipping company DHL wear AR glasses as they move around and find items _____.

4. More and more firefighters are wearing AR glasses
   _____.

E **PERSONALIZE** Discuss these questions in a small group.

1. Which of the applications of AR mentioned in the podcast is most interesting to you?
2. Which of the AR applications mentioned could best facilitate globalization?
3. Have you ever used an AR application in real life? If so, tell the group about your experience.

B Speaking

PRONUNCIATION Silent Letters

🔊 Silent letters appear in words but are not pronounced. Here are some examples.

Word-initial pairs with silent letters (in parentheses):

kn—(k)nit, (k)now	gu—g(u)est, g(u)ess	ps—(p)sychology, (p)sychiatrist
sc—s(c)ience, s(c)issors	wh–w(h)en, w(h)ite	wr—(w)rite, (w)rap

Word-final pairs with silent letters:

bt—de(b)t, dou(b)t	ue—antiq(ue), uniq(ue)	gh—dou(gh), althou(gh)
mb—tom(b), com(b)	mn—colum(n), autum(n)	te—cigaret(te), brunet(te)

Other silent letters:

g before n in words like foreign

h at the beginning of certain words—(h)our, (h)onest

l before some consonants—ta(l)k, wou(l)d

p in recei(p)t and cu(p)board

A Look at the sentences and mark the silent letters from the Pronunciation box.

1. Why did you put the biscuit dough in the cupboard?

2. You should use a sharp knife to cut the salmon into pieces.

3. Honestly, I doubt I'll have enough money to resign from my job before autumn.

4. I couldn't guess why they asked me to sign my name before entering.

5. I wrestled with the assignment for half a day.

6. This website always uses design techniques that are unique.

7. After talking to the guard, I took my assigned seat and fastened my seat belt.

8. The hotel employee knocked on the foreign guest's door to give him a new comb.

B Listen and check for additional answers to exercise A. Then listen again and repeat the sentences. 🔊

C Work with a partner. Write four sentences that include at least two examples of silent letters. Then ask your partner to say the sentences. Check that your partner's pronunciation is correct.

1. _____

2. _____

3. _____

4. _____

D | **APPLY** Work with a group. Look at these educational technologies and check the ones you have used before. Add your own idea. Share your experiences with your group and discuss how these technologies improve learning, as well as any drawbacks they have. | Critical Thinking

☐ **Virtual Reality** Learn in a computer-generated world in three dimensions!	☐ **E-books** Say good-bye to carrying heavy books around!
☐ **Distance Learning** Learn without leaving the comfort of your home!	☐ **Digital Gamification** Computer games can be used to teach almost any subject.
☐ **Video Conferencing** Feel like you're in the classroom with a 360° camera that captures audio and video from the room.	☐ **Online Quizzes** Frequent online quizzes confirm student knowledge and motivate learning.

Your idea: _____

▼ Tourists visit the Time Tunnel of Qiandao Lake, a visual project using immersive virtual reality technology in Hangzhou, China.

Review

SELF-ASSESS

How well can you . . . ?	Very well.	OK.	I need improvement.
use the key vocabulary	☐	☐	☐
recognize silent letters	☐	☐	☐
use adjective clauses	☐	☐	☐
define terms	☐	☐	☐

A VOCABULARY Write the antonym (opposite) for these words. Use any of the vocabulary from this unit.

1. separate (v) _____

2. unpopular (adj) _____

3. release (v) _____

4. not expect (v) _____

5. old-fashioned (adj) _____

6. work alone (adj) _____

7. rarely found (adj) _____

8. take out of (v) _____

B PRONUNCIATION Mark the silent letters. Then say the sentences, making sure not to pronunce the silent letters.

1. I guess that you knitted this white sweater last autumn.
2. I dropped the scissors while fastening my coat.
3. Honestly, I doubt I'll find my comb in the cupboard.

C GRAMMAR Complete the sentences with an essential or non-essential adjective clause.

1. Recently I met an interesting person _____.

2. I've never played Pokémon GO _____.

3. I like to watch movies _____.

4. I'd like to visit Los Angeles _____.

D SPEAKING SKILL Write a sentence defining these terms.

1. globalization _____

2. augmented reality _____

3. emotional intelligence _____

4. coca-colonization _____

RE-ASSESS What skills or language still need improvement?

Final Tasks

OPTION 1 Discuss the role of new technologies in globalization

A Read the passage about Globalization 4.0.

> Globalization refers to how countries, companies, and people depend on each other more and more in terms of the movement of goods and services, technology, and information. Economists estimate this process is approximately 500 years old. However, the World Economic Forum now speaks of *Globalization 4.0*. This is defined as how the rules of the economy are being changed by modern technologies such as 1) robotic process automation, 2) artificial intelligence, 3) blockchain technology, 4) cyber security, and 5) the Internet of Things.

B **DEFINE** Work in a small group. Each member picks one of the five Globalization 4.0 technologies in the passage and researches a definition for the term.

C **DISCUSS** Share what you learned from your research. Think about how these technologies have changed your country or community. Then discuss how they are affecting globalization.

OPTION 2 Give a presentation about a social media platform

See Unit 4 Rubric in the Appendix.

A Work in a small group. Answer the questions. Then choose one platform to present.

1. What are some of the most popular social media platforms?
2. Which ones do you use the most?

B **MODEL** Listen to three students give a presentation on a social media platform called Quora. Take notes on the description of the platform, its history, how it makes money, its competitors, how it facilitates globalization, and the future of Quora. 🔊

C **ANALYZE THE MODEL** Listen again and answer these questions about the model. 🔊

1. How is the overall presentation organized?

   _____

2. What language do you hear the speakers use as they take turns?

   _____

3. Which new terms do the speakers define?

   _____

4. What examples of summarizing language do you hear?

   _____

D RESEARCH Each group member will research one part of the presentation. Use an outline like this to organize the information.

Social Media Platform: _____

    A. Introduction
        1. A brief description of the platform
        2. A brief history of the platform
    B. The Business Side
        1. How does it make money?
        2. Who are its competitors?
    C. Globalization and the Future
        1. How does it facilitate globalization?
        2. What does the future of the platform look like?

PRESENTATION SKILL Manage Nervousness

It's normal to be a little nervous at the beginning of a presentation. Because the first impression you make on your audience is important, learn to manage any nervousness. First of all, remember to breathe and be as natural as you can. Make an effort to speak slowly and calmly. Memorizing the first few sentences you plan to say can sometimes help. Soon you will feel more comfortable and confident.

E PRACTICE AND PRESENT Practice your presentation, focusing on managing nervousness. Make sure the transitions between the parts of the presentation are smooth and define any new terms. Give your group members feedback on their presentation and then present to the class.

▼ In 2023, 4.76 billion people around the world used social media.

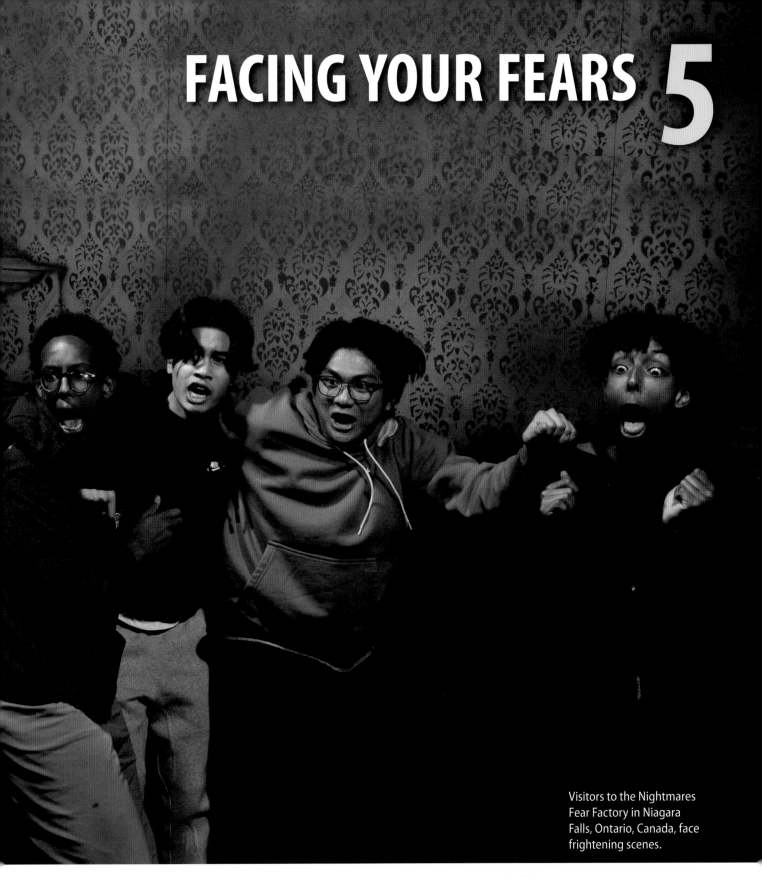

FACING YOUR FEARS 5

Visitors to the Nightmares Fear Factory in Niagara Falls, Ontario, Canada, face frightening scenes.

IN THIS UNIT, YOU WILL:

- Watch or listen to a lecture on science vs. fear
- Watch a video about how fear drove human evolution
- Listen to a podcast about people who overcame fear
- Tell a story about a time you were courageous
  OR Give a pair presentation about a courageous person

THINK AND DISCUSS:

1. What do you think the people in the photo are reacting to?

2. Do you think being frightened is fun? Would you want to experience this house of nightmares?

3. Fears can be big or small. In what ways do you face your fears every day?

Read the information. Then discuss the questions.

1. Which of the fears mentioned are you familiar with?

2. What information in the infographic do you find surprising?

3. Do you know people who have any of these fears, or others?

What Are You Afraid Of?

Nobel-prize winning scientist Marie Curie said "Nothing in life is to be feared, it is only to be understood. Now is the time to understand more, so that we may fear less." Yet almost everyone has a fear of something. In fact, up to 60% of people admit to having at least one fear. Here are some of the most common fears around the globe.

COMMON FEARS

FEAR OF GERMS OR DIRT
This fear can result in over washing your hands, wearing gloves to prevent contact with germs, and taking multiple showers a day.

FEAR OF FLYING
You're more likely to become a professional athlete than to be involved in a plane crash.

FEAR OF SPIDERS
Only 12 out of 40,000 spider species can cause serious harm to adult humans.

FEAR OF REPTILES
Reptiles include snakes, lizards, turtles, alligators, and crocodiles.

FEAR OF PUBLIC SPEAKING
This is perhaps the most common fear of all, affecting around 15 million people. Approximately 10% of people actually love public speaking.

An American crocodile

A Vocabulary

A Match the words with their definitions. Use a dictionary if you need help.

1. _____ alert
2. _____ detect
3. _____ exposure
4. _____ irrational
5. _____ scan
6. _____ scare
7. _____ therapist
8. _____ trigger
9. _____ verify
10. _____ weaken

a. (v) to examine using a piece of equipment
b. (n) someone trained to help with physical or psychological issues
c. (v) to cause to lose energy or power
d. (v) to frighten
e. (v) to confirm the truth of something
f. (v) to cause to happen
g. (n) the state of being in contact with something
h. (adj) not logical or reasonable
i. (v) to discover or notice
j. (adj) quick to notice and react

B **MEANING FROM CONTEXT** Use the correct form of the words from exercise A to complete the article. Then listen and check your answers. 🔊

THE SCIENCE OF HORROR

When something [1]_____ us, it [2]_____ a fear response in a part of our brain called the amygdala. The amygdala sends signals to the brain and body, telling them to be [3]_____ to trouble. However, the amygdala can't distinguish imaginary situations from real-life ones. Scientists have [4]_____ this by [5]_____ the brains of people watching horror movies. But why do people enjoy horror movies at all? It seems [6]_____ to enjoy something you're afraid of. The answer is that people enjoy overcoming fear. In people who watch a lot of horror movies, scientists [7]_____ less fear activity in the brain. This is because repeated [8]_____ to a lot of frightening events [9]_____ the amygdala's fear response. In a way, horror movies are like a good [10]_____ who treats fears and gradually makes them disappear.

C Complete the sentences with the correct form of a word from exercise A.

1. People in love may sometimes follow their heart and act in _____ ways.

2. Every computer should have software that is able to _____ and eliminate viruses.

3. Research shows that _____ to art supports good mental health.

4. I used to get mad often, but my _____ helped me learn to control my anger.

5. That machine _____ passengers to find things they mustn't take on the plane.

6. I drink coffee because I'm a police officer and I need to be _____ at work.

7. You need two forms of ID to _____ your identity to open a bank account.

8. Rising food prices caused support for the once popular president to _____ .

See Word Families in the Appendix.

VOCABULARY SKILL Noun Suffixes –*ist* and –*ant*

The suffix –*ist* is added to some verbs or nouns to refer to a person who performs an action, uses an instrument or device, or works in a certain field.

    therapy → therap**ist**   tour → tour**ist**

The suffix –*ant* is added to some verbs to refer to a person or thing that performs an action.

    apply → applic**ant**   descend → descend**ant**

D Write a word ending in -*ist* or -*ant* that matches the definition. Use the underlined words and a dictionary to help you.

1. _____ someone who <u>participates</u> in an activity

2. _____ someone who works in the field of <u>biology</u>

3. _____ a person who studies the <u>future</u> and makes predictions

4. _____ a person who <u>migrates</u> from one place to another

5. _____ a person who draws <u>cartoons</u> for a living

6. _____ a person who <u>defends</u> himself or herself in court

7. _____ a scientist who does <u>genetic</u> research

8. _____ a person who <u>inhabits</u> a certain region

E **BRAINSTORM** Work with a partner. Brainstorm ideas to answer the questions.

Critical Thinking

What are some . . .

1. . . . things that **scare** you?

2. . . . ways to **verify** someone's identity?

3. . . . ways to **detect** when someone is lying?

4. . . . situations where it's important to be **alert**?

A Listening Science vs. Fear

Critical Thinking | **A** **PREDICT** You are going to hear a lecture on how scientists are working to remove frightening memories from people's minds. With a partner, discuss these questions.

1. What types of fears would you expect to hear about in the lecture?
2. What might cause someone to develop an irrational fear?
3. How might scientists measure whether someone feels fear?
4. One scientist uses "exposure therapy" to treat fears. What might that mean?

B **MAIN IDEAS** Listen to the introduction and choose the sentence that summarizes it best.

a. It's better to avoid fear because it's not a useful emotion anymore.
b. Fear was and is a useful emotion, although some people develop fears that interfere with their lives.
c. Fears such as phobias serve useful purposes, although they can cause problems in life.

C **MAIN IDEAS** Watch or listen to the complete lecture and choose the correct answers.

1. What is the main conclusion of Hauner's experiment on people with a phobia of spiders?

   a. Exposure therapy to treat a phobia of spiders had positive but only short-term effects.
   b. The benefits of exposure therapy to treat a phobia of spiders start after six months.
   c. Exposure therapy to treat a phobia of spiders had immediate and long-lasting benefits.

2. What is the main conclusion of Hauner's experiment with photos of faces and smells?

   a. Frightening memories linked to a smell can be weakened by exposure therapy.
   b. Smells can be frightening, but if a subject sleeps with the smell, it becomes less so.
   c. The fear caused by a photo and electric shock can be increased by adding a smell.

3. What is the main conclusion of the experiment by the team of scientists using money?

   a. A fear linked to a mental image can be erased by rewards given each time the fear comes to mind.
   b. A fear linked to a mental image can be erased by giving the person money to forget it.
   c. Rewarding a person when a fear returns to their mind makes the fear stronger.

Musophobia, or a fear of mice and rats, is one of the United Kingdom's top 10 phobias, affecting 9% of the population.

D **DETAILS** Listen to an excerpt. Number the steps of the experiment in order. 🔊

First experiment (by Hauner with 12 adults with a spider phobia)

a. _____ Participants were asked to touch the tarantula with their hand.

b. _____ A brain scan found high brain activity when participants looked at pictures of spiders.

c. _____ Participants were asked to touch the tarantula with a paintbrush.

d. _____ A brain scan found that they were no longer afraid of spiders.

e. _____ Participants were asked to slowly approach the tarantula.

f. _____ False beliefs about tarantulas were corrected.

E **DETAILS** Listen to another excerpt. Number the steps of the experiment in order. 🔊

Second experiment (by Hauner with healthy adults)

a. _____ The photos were found to cause less fear.

b. _____ A smell linked to a photo was released into the air as they slept.

c. _____ Photos, electric shocks, and smells were used to create a fear in the adults.

d. _____ Participants were asked to view the photos again as she tested their fear response.

F **DETAILS** Listen to another excerpt. Number the steps of the experiment in order. 🔊

Third experiment (by an international team of scientists with 17 volunteers)

a. _____ When the specific pattern was detected, the participants were given money.

b. _____ The fear memory triggered no sweat reaction or fear activity on a brain scan.

c. _____ The brains of volunteers were scanned to identify the specific pattern of activity linked to the fear memory.

d. _____ An image and an electric shock were used to create a fear in volunteers.

G **FOCUSED LISTENING** Listen and complete the sentences with the time words you hear. 🔊

1. _____, she worked with a group of healthy adults without phobias or PTSD.

2. _____ was to place a fear in their brains.

3. _____, when they went to sleep, one of the smells from the experiment was sprayed into the air in their room all night long.

4. _____, she tested the adults again.

5. _____, changes in brain scans verified her findings.

A   Speaking

A **DEFINE** Work with a partner. Decide on the meanings of the words and write them in the chart. Then check your guesses in a dictionary.

Root Words in Ancient Greek or Latin	English Word	Meaning
1. *arachni* (spider) + *phobos* (fear)	arachnophobia	*fear of spiders*
2. *atyches* (unfortunate) + *phobos*	atychiphobia	_____
3. *aero* (air) + *phobos*	aerophobia	_____
4. *claustrum* (closed-in space) + *phobos*	claustrophobia	_____
5. *akros* (highest point) + *phobos*	acrophobia	_____
6. *agora* (marketplace) + *phobos*	agoraphobia	_____

B With a partner, answer the questions.

1. How are phobias different from ordinary fears?
2. Which phobia would be the most difficult to live with?
3. In the listening, you heard about the use of "exposure therapy" to cure arachnophobia. Choose one of the other phobias on the list above. How might a therapist use exposure therapy to cure it?

A giant tarantula on the back of a man in the rainforest

See Common Phrasal Verbs in the Appendix.

GRAMMAR FOR SPEAKING   Separable Two-Word Phrasal Verbs

A two-word phrasal verb has a verb and a particle, a word that looks like a preposition. The addition of the particle often changes the meaning of the verb. Two-word verbs frequently have one-word synonyms.

call off = cancel   *blow up* = explode   *let down* = disappoint

The object of a phrasal verb appears either after the verb or the particle.

*He played with an injury because he didn't want to **let** his team and his fans **down**.*

*He played with an injury because he didn't want to **let down** his team and his fans.*

However, if the object is a pronoun, it appears after the verb and never after the particle.

*He played with an injury because he didn't want to **let** them **down**.*

*Never: He played with an injury because he didn't want to **let down** them.*

C Work with a partner. Say the sentences differently by replacing the words in bold with a separable phrasal verb from the box. Practice putting the object both before and after the particle, as well as using a pronoun.

play up	rule out	see off	pass up
burn down	chop up	calm down	fill out

1. Please peel the potatoes while I **cut** the onions and carrots **into small pieces**.
2. There was a fire in my neighborhood that **destroyed** an old factory.
3. My boss asked me to **go say good-bye to** our Japanese visitors at the airport.
4. I'm eager to start working, but I won't **reject** getting a master's degree.
5. My friends said that I shouldn't **say no to** such a wonderful opportunity.
6. After the argument, it was a long time before I could **make** Lisa **relax**.
7. I'm required to **complete** a very long form whenever I go to the dentist.
8. During the job interview, you should **emphasize** your strong points and successes.

D **APPLY** Work in pairs. Use the phrasal verb in parentheses to say how you would react to these situations.

Critical Thinking

1. You are swimming, and a bird is trying to steal food from your bag on the beach. (scare off)
   I would get out of the water and scare off the bird.
2. You are shopping and see your favorite chips for 80% off. There are six bags left. (buy up)
3. You planned a team meeting after work, but a huge snowstorm is expected soon. (call off)
4. You receive a call from your friend. He's having a bad day and is depressed. (cheer up)
5. You planned to meet your sister for lunch, but she called to say her car won't start. (pick up)
6. You received a job offer today, but you accepted a position yesterday. (turn down)
7. You planned to write a report, but an old friend invited you to dinner. (put off)
8. You see your friend on the street. You just got paid, and you owe her money. (pay back)

| **E** **BRAINSTORM** Work in a group. Some people enjoy the feeling of fear they get from horror movies. But we enjoy other activities for the ways they make us feel, too. Brainstorm activities for each emotional response and write them below. Discuss why it belongs in that category.

Frightened 😨
Watching horror movies
_____

_____

Relaxed 😌
_____

_____

Excited 🤩
_____

_____

Interested 👍
_____

_____

Amused 😄
_____

_____

See Speaking Phrases in the Appendix.

SPEAKING SKILL Respond to Suggestions

When you are trying to reach a group decision, it's important to make your voice heard. When group members suggest ideas that you're not in favor of, politely let them know and then offer an alternative. By doing so, the group will remain in harmony and make the best decision possible. Here are some expressions you can use.

Politely reject suggestions	**Offer alternatives**
I don't really like	*I'd prefer to . . . instead of . . . .*
I'm not a big fan of	*My second choice would be . . . .*
I'm not crazy about	*I think I'd rather . . . .*
I don't care for	*If it were up to me, I'd . . . .*

F Work in a group. Imagine you are deciding what to do this weekend. Each person chooses a different emotion from the chart above and suggests activities from the list of ideas for that emotion. The others react by either accepting or politely rejecting the suggestions and offering alternatives from their list. Finally, agree on one weekend activity.

How Fear and Anxiety Drove Human Evolution

loom on the horizon (v phr) to appear in the distance in a frightening way
hyper-vigilance (n) an extremely high level of caution and attention

neurotransmitter (n) a chemical released by nerve cells
wither (v) to shrink as if drying up or dying
trauma (n) emotional damage caused by a severe shock

▲ Parachuters prepare to jump from a height of 900 meters over Croatia.

A Watch the video. Number the ideas in the order you hear them. ▶

a. _____ Fear and anxiety have been useful in human evolution.

b. _____ How the amygdala increases our attention level

c. _____ The negative long-term effects on reasoning of an over-active amygdala

d. _____ The distinction between the words "fear" and "anxiety"

e. _____ The effect of the world being a more dangerous place long ago

f. _____ The physical effects of an active amygdala when we sense something dangerous

B Watch the video again. Choose T for *True* or F for *False.* ▶

1. The lion is an example of a short-term fear.   T   F
2. Hyper-vigilance was a drawback of anxiety a long time ago.   T   F
3. The release of neurotransmitters improves our focus.   T   F
4. The prefrontal cortex is associated with making decisions.   T   F
5. Fear develops the amygdala but not the prefrontal cortex.   T   F
6. Trauma caused by a highly active amygdala is permanent.   T   F

C In lesson B, you're going to hear about people who overcame fear in their careers. With a partner, discuss this question: What are some ways that fear can hold people back in their careers?

B Vocabulary

A Listen and check the words you already know. Use a dictionary if necessary. 🔊

clarify (v)	exceptional (adj)	motivate (v)	portray (v)	struggle (v)
courageous (adj)	instinct (n)	obstacle (n)	predator (n)	uncertainty (n)

B **MEANING FROM CONTEXT** Complete the interview with the correct form of the words in exercise A. Then listen and check your answers. 🔊

THE BEAR WHISPERER

Reporter: I'm speaking with Eric Roth, the "Bear Whisperer." What ¹_____ you to work with bears?

Roth: I'm unhappy with how the media ²_____ them—as dangerous ³_____ to be avoided. It's my mission to ⁴_____ all the confusion around bears and educate people. I know bears are very gentle animals that are guided by their ancient, predictable ⁵_____.

Reporter: But bears do attack humans sometimes, don't they?

Roth: Yes, but only in ⁶_____ cases. There are millions of bears in the world, and only 40 attacks are reported annually. If you don't show any fear or ⁷_____ around bears, I guarantee you they won't attack. I hope to open my own bear education center here in Alaska to teach people that and much more. Unfortunately, I've been ⁸_____ and haven't made much progress with the project.

Reporter: What ⁹_____ are you running into?

Roth: The government wants me to keep my bears in cages, but I want visitors to walk with the bears as I do and learn what they're really like. I have an idea—let's go meet my bears together right now!

Reporter: No thanks, Mr. Roth. I'm afraid I'm not as ¹⁰_____ as you. But thanks for the interview!

C Complete the chart with the correct form of each word. Use a dictionary if necessary.

	Verb	Noun	Adjective
1.	motivate		
2.	– – – – – – –	instinct	
3.	– – – – – – –	uncertainty	
4.	struggle		
5.	clarify		
6.			portrayed
7.	– – – – – – –	courage	
8.			predatory

D Match each word with its synonym.

1. _____ obstacle (n)   a. represent

2. _____ motivate (v)   b. rare

3. _____ uncertainty (n)   c. excite

4. _____ clarify (v)   d. explain

5. _____ exceptional (adj)   e. brave

6. _____ courageous (adj)   f. hunter

7. _____ predator (n)   g. barrier

8. _____ portray (v)   h. doubt

E Complete the sentences with a word from exercise A.

1. When birds build a nest, they are following a basic _____.

2. We are going to cancel today's picnic due to _____ about the weather.

3. If you're ambitious, you can overcome any _____ on the way to success.

4. If you don't understand the instructions, I'll be happy to _____ them for you.

5. Although movies _____ smoking as "cool," it's an unhealthy habit.

F **PERSONALIZE** Work with a partner. Complete the sentences so they are true for you.

1. I think . . . is an **exceptional** individual because . . . .
2. The most **courageous** person I know is . . . .
3. One **obstacle** to learning a new skill is . . . .
4. Something that **motivates** me to try harder is . . . .
5. Something I **struggle** with in school is . . . .

Listening Victory Over Fear

A **ACTIVATE** Work as a pair. Read the descriptions of three frightened people. What would you tell them?

Someone who . . .

1. . . . has to speak to a large group of people and is too terrified to step on stage.
2. . . . wants to go swimming in the ocean but is afraid of sharks.
3. . . . is about to board a plane for the first time and has discovered they are afraid to fly.

B **MAIN IDEAS** Listen to the podcast and match the person with their way of overcoming fear. 🔊

1. _____ Olivia Husari
2. _____ Gibbs Kuguru
3. _____ Bear Grylls

a. overcame a childhood fear through learning and working.
b. uses a four-step system to remain logical and plan.
c. learned about the brain to keep fear under control.

C **DETAILS** Read the statements. Then listen again. Choose T for *True* or F for *False*. 🔊

1. Olivia Husari used to be afraid of committing errors.	T	F
2. The amygdala tells us to run when there's danger.	T	F
3. Olivia recommends eliminating all fear from life.	T	F
4. Gibbs Kuguru is a geneticist who studies sharks.	T	F
5. Gibbs learned that sharks aren't a danger to humans.	T	F
6. Gibbs suggests avoiding sharks to eliminate danger.	T	F
7. Bear Grylls was once severely injured in an accident.	T	F
8. The "O" in the STOP system stands for "overcome fear."	T	F
9. Bear says we tend to focus on a small area when stressed.	T	F

PRONUNCIATION **Recognize Reduced Vowels in Unstressed Syllables**

🔊 Two reduced vowel sounds in English are /ə/ and /ɪ/. The most common reduced vowel sound is /ə/, called the schwa sound. When you pronounce it, keep your mouth relaxed and half open and your tongue in the middle position and flat. Unstressed *a, e, o,* and *u* are often reduced to the schwa sound:

*A*merican *o*ccur s*u*ggest tunn*e*l

Unstressed *i* and *y* are mostly reduced to /ɪ/ in unstressed syllables:

w*i*thout synon*y*m

/ɪ/ also appears in reduced syllables with various spellings:

b*e*come *e*rase av*e*rage min*u*te

These rules are guidelines, but there are exceptions. The important thing to remember is that /ə/ and /ɪ/ occur in unstressed syllables. And always remember to use your ears!

D Listen to the words. Check the sound of the unstressed syllable. 🔊

		/ə/	/ɪ/				/ə/	/ɪ/
1.	mother	☐	☐		5.	package	☐	☐
2.	begin	☐	☐		6.	music	☐	☐
3.	control	☐	☐		7.	pleasure	☐	☐
4.	biscuit	☐	☐		8.	machine	☐	☐

LISTENING SKILL   Recognize Metaphor

A metaphor is an expression that compares two things that are otherwise unrelated. It aims to describe something in a more creative and impactful way:

> *My son would never do such a thing. He's a little angel!*

The metaphor "He's a little angel" means "He behaves perfectly."

> *I don't recommend following Maria's advice—her head is in the clouds.*

The metaphor "Her head is in the clouds" means "She's an unrealistic dreamer."

We don't generally use *like* or *as* with metaphors. Such comparisons are called similes.

Metaphor: *He's a little angel.*   Simile: *He's like a little angel.*

E **RECOGNIZE** Listen to the short conversations. Write the metaphors you hear. 🔊   Critical Thinking

1. _____

2. _____

3. _____

4. _____

5. _____

6. _____

7. _____

8. _____

F Work with a partner. Compare your answers to exercise E and discuss the meanings of the metaphors.

Speaking

CRITICAL THINKING Recognize Logical Fallacies

Making logical arguments is a key part of academic work. Be careful to avoid arguments that have a "logical fallacy," which is an error in logic or reasoning. Here are three common logical fallacies that you should be able to identify and avoid.

1. An argument against the person rather than the argument:

   Felix says those mushrooms are poisonous, but I know they aren't because he's never studied plants.

2. An argument in which the claim and the conclusions are the same:

   Saturday is our day off because we don't work on that day.

3. Appealing to an anonymous authority:

   I heard somewhere that peanut butter is good for cleaning windows.

Critical Thinking | **A** Work with a partner. Look at the statements. Discuss which type of logical fallacy from the Critical Thinking box they contain. Write 1, 2, or 3.

1. _____ Some people say that drinking lots of water before bed helps you sleep better.

2. _____ Franco said that it's faster to take Center Street, but that can't be true because he doesn't even own a car.

3. _____ I would say I'm afraid of heights because I find high places frightening.

4. _____ They say that it's bad luck to use the same word twice in one sentence.

5. _____ I think the reason Elaf is lucky is because she has good fortune.

6. _____ According to Rahul, the answer to this math problem is 17, but it has to be wrong because he failed math last year.

National Geographic Explorer Gibbs Kuguru researching sharks in the Maldives

B *A scaredy-cat* is a term used for a person who is easily frightened. Take turns asking and answering the questions with a partner.

QUESTIONNAIRE: Are you a scaredy-cat?

1. When you find yourself home alone, what do you do?
   a. I relax and enjoy the peace and quiet.
   b. I make sure the doors and windows are locked tight.
   c. Other: _____

2. If you suddenly look up and see a big spider crawling across the wall, how do you react?
   a. I look around for something to hit it with.
   b. I scream and run into the other room.
   c. Other: _____

3. Your friend invites you to watch a new horror movie. What do you say?
   a. Absolutely! I'll make some popcorn!
   b. Uh . . . maybe. How scary is it?
   c. Other: _____

4. Which type of book would be great to read just before bedtime?
   a. A novel about teen vampires
   b. An adventure story with a happy ending
   c. Other: _____

5. What's your favorite ride at an amusement or theme park?
   a. The fastest roller coaster ride they have
   b. The carousel or merry-go-round
   c. Other: _____

6. How do you feel about walking outside in the dark?
   a. I find the night air so refreshing!
   b. My amygdala is very active.
   c. Other: _____

7. When there's a storm with thunder and lightning, what do you do?
   a. I go outside to see the show!
   b. I hide in my bathtub until it passes.
   c. Other: _____

8. How did answering this questionnaire make you feel?
   a. I enjoyed myself.
   b. I'm glad it's over.
   c. Other: _____

C Join another pair and share your answers. Who among you seems to be the biggest scaredy-cat?

Review

A **VOCABULARY** Complete the sentences with the correct form of any of the vocabulary words from this unit.

1. I need to see your passport to _____ your identity.

2. It's her love of music that _____ her to play the piano.

3. We called the gas company when we _____ the smell of gas.

4. Baby birds follow their _____ and leave the nest once they're able to fly.

5. Just in case someone didn't understand me, let me _____ what I said.

6. I was afraid of thunder when I was a kid, but it doesn't _____ me anymore.

7. My physical _____ taught me some exercises for my back pain.

B **GRAMMAR** Read each sentence. Then say it two more times, first by moving the object of the phrasal verb, and then by using a pronoun instead of the object.

1. My family and I plan to see you and Emilia off at the airport.
2. I would never pass up such an excellent career opportunity.
3. All passengers must fill a customs declaration form out.
4. We had to call the holiday events off due to bad weather.

C **SPEAKING SKILL** Complete the conversation with expressions for responding to suggestions.

A: What would you like to do this weekend? How about going to an art museum?

B: I'm [1]_____ about museums. My second [2]_____ to go to the beach.

A: I don't know. I'm not a [3]_____ the beach. I think [4]_____ go to a concert.

B: Actually, I don't [5]_____ concerts. If it [6]_____, I'd go see a tennis match.

A: Oh! I love tennis! Let's do that then!

RE-ASSESS What skills or language still need improvement?

Final Tasks

OPTION 1 Tell a story about when you've been courageous

A **BRAINSTORM** Think about times in your life when you showed courage. Choose an idea that you remember well enough to tell a story about. Make some notes to help you organize your story, such as what happened that required you to be courageous, when and where it happened, and how you felt.

B Tell the class your story. Share your impressions of each other's stories and ask any questions you have.

OPTION 2 Give a presentation about a courageous person

See Unit 5 Rubric in the Appendix.

A **MODEL** Listen to two students give a presentation. Complete the notes in the timeline.

1998: Amanda Gorman was (1) _____ in Los Angeles, California.

2004: Her (2) _____ and speaking difficulties were (3) _____.

2016: She (4) _____ from high school and was accepted to (5) _____ University.

2021: She read a (6) _____ at the ceremony where Joe Biden became the (7) _____ president of the United States.

B Amanda Gorman read "The Hill We Climb" at the presidential ceremony. Read these lines from her poem and discuss what you think they mean.

"There is always light. If only we're brave enough to see it. If only we're brave enough to be it."

Amanda Gorman reading ▶ her poem at the 2021 presidential ceremony

C | **ANALYZE THE MODEL** Listen again and answer these questions about the model. 🔊

1. How does the first speaker introduce the presentation?

   _____

2. How is the overall presentation organized?

   _____

3. What language do you hear the speakers use as they take turns?

   _____

4. Which two separable phrasal verbs do you hear Juan use?

   _____

D | Work with a partner. Answer the questions.

1. Who are some people that you consider to be courageous in the following areas?

   | Business   Politics   Arts & Entertainment   Education   Other: _____ |

2. What courageous person will you research and give a pair presentation about?

E | **RESEARCH** You and your partner will each research one part of the presentation, either the background or the adult career. You can use a timeline like this to organize the information.

COLLABORATION SKILL Listen Actively

Listening is something we do naturally, but it's often something we do in a passive way. Active listening is especially important when collaborating. Look at the other person and pay attention. Consider what they're saying without making judgments. However, do ask questions if there's anything you don't understand. Finally, confirm that you understand, either by summarizing what the other person said or commenting on it.

📶 **ONLINE** Signals that indicate understanding, such as gestures, eye contact, or nodding, are not as easy to read online as they are in person. Therefore, to show that you are listening actively, look into the camera and not at other participants. Use the "raise hand" feature to ask a question, or type a question or comment into the chat feature to engage with the speaker.

F | **PLAN** Present the information you gathered to your partner. Together, decide what should go into the presentation. Be sure to practice active listening as you discuss what to include.

G | **PRACTICE AND PRESENT** Practice the two parts of your presentation with your partner and give each other feedback. Make sure the transition between the parts of the presentation is smooth and try to include one or more separable phrasal verbs.

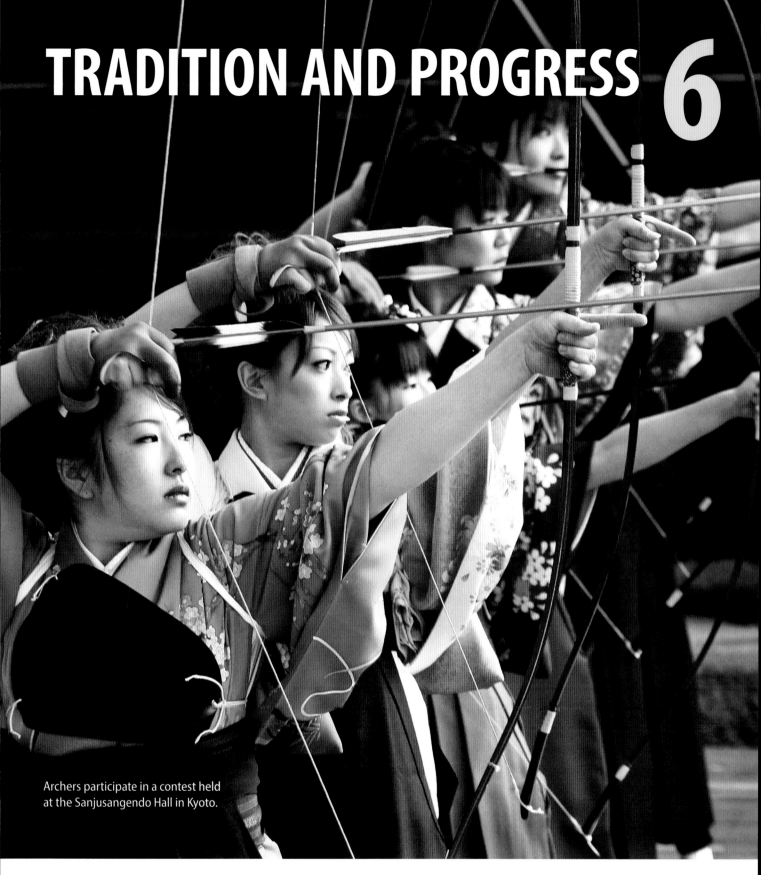

TRADITION AND PROGRESS 6

Archers participate in a contest held at the Sanjusangendo Hall in Kyoto.

IN THIS UNIT, YOU WILL:

- Listen to a presentation about Bhutan
- Watch a video about traditional boat building
- Watch or listen to a lecture about American Indian lands
- Discuss a tradition
  OR Present the results of an interview

THINK AND DISCUSS:

Each year on Coming-of-Age Day in Japan, around 1600 20-year-old archers participate in a contest in Kyoto, which dates back to the 16th century and marks the transition from childhood to adulthood.

1. What coming-of-age traditions are there in your culture?
2. What other traditions mark life transitions?

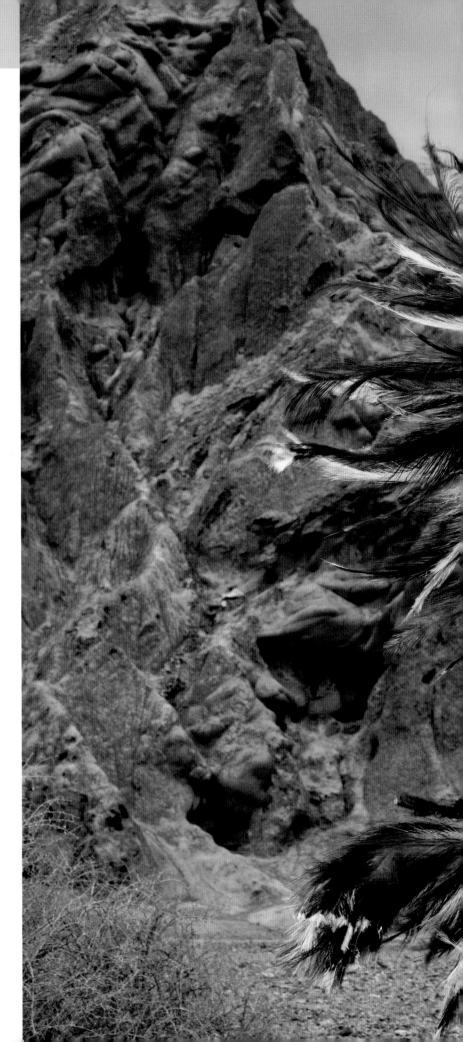

Read the information and discuss the questions.

1. What are some cultural festivals that you are familiar with? How long have they been celebrated?

2. What does Inti Raymi celebrate? How is this celebrated in your culture?

3. In what ways might progress have a positive impact on cultures and traditions? In what ways might it be negative?

Honoring the Past

Change can feel inevitable, yet many cultures manage to hold on to their traditional ways. Ceremonies are ways of honoring the past and preserving cultural identity. In Argentina, the Suris celebrate Inti Raymi or the festival of the winter solstice on the shortest day of the year. The celebration is an essential part of their cultural life and the Nandù feathers are an essential component of their traditional costumes. The tradition has been in place for centuries.

In Jujuy, a remote province in northwest Argentina, a woman wears a feathered costume to represent the Nandù, or sacred bird of the Suris, an Indigenous group of this area.

A Vocabulary

A
MEANING FROM CONTEXT Read and listen to the article. Notice each word or phrase in blue and think about its meaning. 🔊

PRESERVING ANCIENT TRADITIONS: THE HADZA

Hunting and gathering food is a survival strategy that scientists believe humans began to use some 1.8 million years ago. Then around 10,000 years ago, a major **transition** occurred: People learned how to grow crops and domesticate[1] animals, thus starting an agricultural way of life. However, there is a group of people in an **isolated** region of northern Tanzania that rejects the agricultural way of life. Instead, they continue to gather wild plants and hunt animals with bows and arrows that they make by hand. This group, the Hadza, has lived in the Great Rift Valley for 10,000 years and had only limited **interaction** with outside groups until quite recently. The **preservation** of their ancient ways is a priority for them.

The Hadza are nomads[2] who move according to the travel patterns of the animals they hunt. They are **accustomed to** living in temporary huts made of branches and dried grass that can be quickly and easily set up and taken down. It is an interesting **contradiction** that, although the Hadza have very few material possessions, they are happy to share everything they have with others. This **principle**, however, is not followed by local farmers, who are much more **materialistic**. They have **converted** as much as 90 percent of the Hadza's traditional homeland into profitable farmland since the 1950s. If this trend continues, the Hadza may no longer be able to **pursue** their ancient way of life.

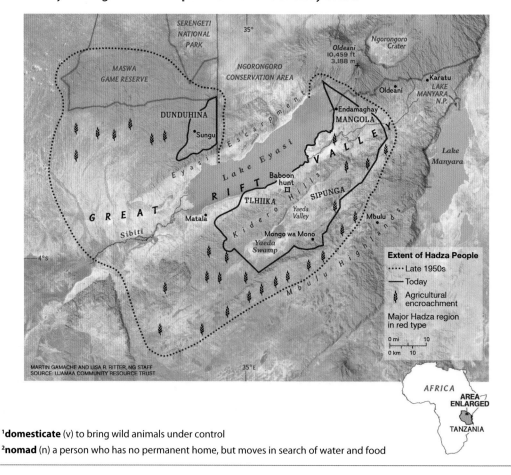

[1]**domesticate** (v) to bring wild animals under control

[2]**nomad** (n) a person who has no permanent home, but moves in search of water and food

B Match each word or phrase with its definition.

1. _____ accustomed to   a. (n) keeping something as it is and protecting it
2. _____ contradiction   b. (n) a situation containing two opposite truths
3. _____ convert   c. (adj phr) used to; familiar with
4. _____ interaction   d. (n) a change from one state to another
5. _____ isolated   e. (v) to change something from one form to another
6. _____ materialistic   f. (n) a guiding rule or idea
7. _____ preservation   g. (adj) remote and difficult to reach
8. _____ principle   h. (v) to follow or carry out (an activity, plan, policy, etc.)
9. _____ pursue   i. (adj) placing great importance on money and possessions
10. _____ transition   j. (n) communication, trade, or cooperation between people

C **PERSONALIZE** Discuss these questions with a partner.

1. How **accustomed** are you **to** speaking English outside of class?
2. What is an important **principle** that you follow?
3. Are you a **materialistic** person? Explain.
4. When is it acceptable to **contradict** someone?
5. What career are you **pursuing** or will you **pursue**?

VOCABULARY SKILL   Collocations: Verb/Adjective + Preposition

---

Some verbs and adjectives are followed by prepositions. When you learn a new adjective or verb, be sure to note whether it usually occurs with a preposition.

Verb + preposition

   participate in, approve of, object to, interact with, interfere with/in

Adjective + preposition

   accustomed to, responsible for, terrified of, content with, involved with/in

Remember that prepositions are followed by nouns or gerunds.

D Choose the correct preposition for each collocation. Use a dictionary if necessary.

1. The Hadza are not shy (about / for) giving interviews, and a great deal of information related (on / to) Hadza customs has been discovered that way.

2. For example, contrary (from / to) popular opinion, the Hadza are not opposed (to / against) development, but rather (for / to) land use that is not sustainable.

3. Fewer and fewer cultures are isolated (from / with) the world.

4. Recent studies have shown that Hadza DNA is distinct (from / to) that of their neighbors.

5. Some people in Tanzania interfere (with / to) the ancient traditions of the Hadza.

A Listening Opening Up Bhutan

Critical Thinking | **A PREDICT** Work with a partner. Look at the image and read the caption. Then answer the questions.

1. Bhutan was isolated from the modern world for many years. Why do you think this is so?
2. What do you think Bhutan is trying to preserve as it opens up to the world?

Paro Taktsang, also known as Tiger's Nest Monastery, is one of the most famous places in Bhutan.

B MAIN IDEAS Watch or listen to the presentation and check the THREE main topics presented by the speaker. 🔊 ▶

a. ☐ Bhutan's isolation and decision to open up to the world

b. ☐ How other countries viewed Bhutan's opening up

c. ☐ A new approach to development by the King of Bhutan

d. ☐ Policies to compete economically with other countries

e. ☐ Why movies made in Bhutan aren't popular abroad

f. ☐ Social and cultural changes after the Gross National Happiness plan began

C DETAILS Listen again. Choose T for *True* or F for *False*. 🔊

1. Bhutan's kings had long wanted to connect Bhutan with the outside world.   T   F
2. The policy of remaining isolated from the world caused problems in Bhutan's public education system.   T   F
3. Bhutan is trying to make its agricultural methods more efficient by clearing land of trees.   T   F
4. The government of Bhutan has placed some restrictions on what the media is allowed to broadcast.   T   F
5. Bhutan has made little progress in the arts since opening up.   T   F

An idea map can provide a clear visual overview of a topic and show connections between ideas. It is a useful note-taking format for a presentation or lecture that describes subcategories of a main topic. Place the main topic at the top of the idea map. Directly connected to the main topic are subtopics; details are then connected to the subtopics.

D   Listen to an excerpt from the presentation. Complete the idea map with information from the presentation. Write only ONE word for each answer.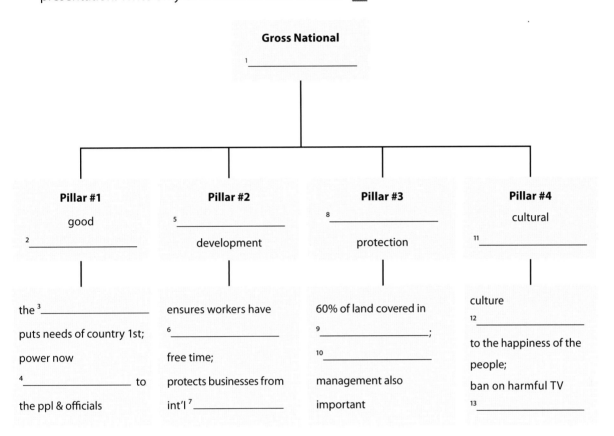

Gross National

1 _____

Pillar #1

good

2 _____

the 3 _____

puts needs of country 1st;

power now

4 _____ to

the ppl & officials

Pillar #2

5 _____

development

ensures workers have

6 _____

free time;

protects businesses from

int'l 7 _____

Pillar #3

8 _____

protection

60% of land covered in

9 _____;

10 _____

management also

important

Pillar #4

cultural

11 _____

culture

12 _____

to the happiness of the

people;

ban on harmful TV

13 _____

E   **BRAINSTORM**   Work in a small group. For each pillar of Gross National Happiness in the idea map, brainstorm additional ideas that Bhutan could try. Then share your best ideas with the class.

Critical Thinking

> *For good government, they could try keeping the taxes low.*

A Speaking

SPEAKING SKILL   Ask Rhetorical Questions

Rhetorical questions are questions that a speaker asks for dramatic effect or to make a point, not to get an answer. Types of rhetorical questions include those used to:

1. Encourage your audience to think about something.

   There were no cars or trucks, no phones, and no postal service. **Can you imagine what life must have been like?**

2. Invite your audience to agree with you, as in tag questions.

   We wouldn't want to lose our sense of culture, **would we?**

3. Provide an answer to a question you think your audience would like to ask.

   So, what is meant by good government? *Well, the king puts the needs of the country first.*

A   Listen and write the rhetorical questions you hear. 🔊

1. In our language, Bhutan is known as *Druk Yul*. In English, that means "Land of the Thunder Dragon." _____? I imagine a dragon jumping from mountain to mountain and making a lot of noise!

2. The second pillar is sustainable development.

   _____? Well, part of it is valuing the contribution of family to society and the economy.

3. Economists use GDP to measure a country's success. But it's not really related to people's happiness, _____?

B   Are the rhetorical questions in exercise A type 1, 2, or 3? Write the correct number.

Question 1: _____   Question 2: _____   Question 3: _____

C   For each item, write a rhetorical question of the type indicated. Then read your questions to a partner.

1. The movie *Castaway* was inspired by a real person named Alexander Selkirk who spent four years isolated on a Pacific island. (Type 1)

   _____?

2. The movie *Super Size Me* is about a person who ate nothing but food from McDonald's for 30 days. (Type 2) _____?

3. I would describe my friend Fernando as a "doomer." (Type 3) _____? It's a very pessimistic person who feels like life has no purpose.

PRONUNCIATION   Long and Short Vowels

🔊 Pronouncing vowels correctly is important. A small change in the pronunciation can change the meaning of a word. Pay attention to these commonly confused vowel sounds.

/ɪ/ (short, relaxed) — /iʸ/ (longer, tongue higher, more tense)

| **hit — heat** | **pill — peel** | **lip — leap** |

/ʌ/ (short) — /æ/ (mouth more open, tongue slightly forward)

| **but — bat** | **tub — tab** | **cup — cap** |

/ɛ/ (short) — /eʸ/ (longer, two smoothly connected sounds)

| **bet — bait** | **pen — pain** | **fed — fade** |

/oʷ/ (mouth rounded) — /ɔ/ (mouth more open, not rounded)

| **so — saw** | **flow — flaw** | **row — raw** |

D Listen and mark the words you hear. 🔊

1. a. sick   2. a. lack   3. a. wreck   4. a. low
   b. seek   b. luck   b. rake   b. law

5. a. ship   6. a. hat   7. a. pen   8. a. Joe
   b. sheep   b. hut   b. pain   b. jaw

E Work with a partner. Take turns saying words from exercise D to your partner. Point to the word you heard your partner say.

F With a partner, take turns reading these tongue twisters as fast as you can. Keep trying until you can say them smoothly.

1. Sheila seeks a sleek ship to take her sick sheep to sea.
2. He has a cat, a bat, and a tub but lacks a cup and a hat.
3. Ben's pen friend said the late train is a pain in the neck.
4. Joe thought he saw the old goat that almost broke his jaw.
5. Peter picked the peppers while Pia peeked at the papers.

A noun phrase appositive describes or gives more information about another noun. It is placed directly after the noun it describes and is set off by one or two commas. Noun phrase appositives often begin with *a*, *an*, or *the*.

> *Sungka, **a traditional game of the Philippines,** was my favorite game when I was young.*
>
> *I want to visit Vanuatu, **an isolated Pacific island where bungee jumping was invented.***
>
> *My friend Jean Pierre was born in Port-au-Prince, **the capital of Haiti.***

Note that a noun phrase appositive adds extra information. If it's removed, a grammatically complete sentence remains.

> *Sungka, a traditional game of the Philippines, was my favorite game when I was young.*

G Work with a partner. Match the words in bold on the left with a noun phrase on the right. Then take turns saying the sentences with the noun phrase appositives added.

1. I always have **baklava** with coffee. _____

2. I love to go see **kabuki** whenever I'm in Japan. _____

3. Be sure to visit the **Tiger's Nest** while you're in Bhutan. _____

4. I was lucky enough to see a **platypus** during my trip to Australia. _____

5. Please bring me back some **yerba mate** when you go to Argentina. _____

6. In Mongolia, I spent a night in a **yurt** before checking in to the hotel. _____

7. I love to listen to the **quena** when I travel in Chile. _____

8. Ancient civilizations used the **abacus** to do difficult math problems. _____

a. a flute they play in the Andes Mountains

b. the traditional circular tent of that country

c. a type of tea made from tree leaves

d. a type of traditional theater with colorful costumes

e. the sweet Greek dessert made with honey

f. a very early form of the calculator

g. one of the most unusual animals in the world

h. an amazing temple on the side of a cliff

▼ A traditional Japanese kabuki performance

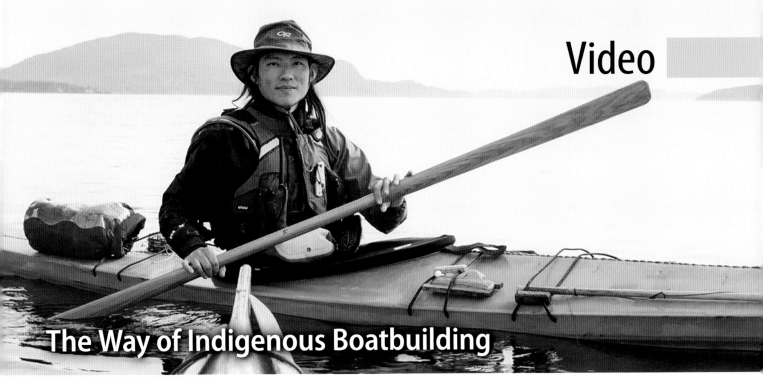

Video

The Way of Indigenous Boatbuilding

Indigenous (adj) native to a particular area
primitive (adj) related to an early level of technology

minimal (adj) at a very low, just adequate level
indefinitely (adv) for an unlimited period of time

▲ National Geographic photographer Kiliii Yüyan explores the San Juan Islands off the coast of Washington state, USA, in a kayak he built.

A Watch the video with Kiliii Yüyan. Choose the FOUR topics discussed. ▶

1. ☐ How animals react when they see kayaks
2. ☐ Kiliii's experience practicing survival skills
3. ☐ The specific methods he uses to construct kayaks
4. ☐ Typical accidents that happen in kayaks
5. ☐ The historical origins of traditional kayaks
6. ☐ Why the kayak is useful

B Watch again. Choose all the correct answers to each question. ▶

1. Which ways of getting food in the wild does he mention?
   a. gathering wild greens   b. catching fish   c. hunting and trapping

2. Which techniques does he use to make kayaks?
   a. traditional techniques   b. Japanese techniques   c. high-tech power tools

3. What materials did Indigenous people use to build the first kayaks?
   a. seal skins   b. wood from trees they cut down   c. wood they found on the beach

4. Which advantages of the kayak does he mention toward the end of the video?
   a. They are easy to make.   b. They can travel long distances.   c. They carry a lot of gear.

C **SYNTHESIZE** Discuss this question with a partner. What do Kiliii Yüyan, the Hadza people, and/or the King of Bhutan have in common?   Critical Thinking

Vocabulary

A **MEANING FROM CONTEXT** Complete the article with the correct form of these words. Then listen and check your answers. 🔊

descendant (n)	**hardship** (n)	**heritage** (n)	**profound** (adj)	**ultimately** (adv)
habitat (n)	**harsh** (adj)	**livelihood** (n)	**thrive** (v)	**undertake** (v)

KEEPING TRADITION ALIVE

National Geographic Explorer Kiliii Yüyan takes unforgettable photographs of the Iñupiaq people. They are an Indigenous group who live along the ¹_____ frozen coast of northwest Alaska. This is the ²_____ of the bowhead whale, which ³_____ in the icy waters. The Iñupiaq people are the ⁴_____ of whale hunters. Whale hunting continues to be a critical part of the community's ⁵_____ and its ⁶_____ . The Iñupiaq feel a ⁷_____ spiritual connection with the whales. They believe that the whales agree to be hunted and give themselves as gifts. Although they now put motors on some boats and use radios, the whale hunters still experience great ⁸_____ , including weeks or even months of waiting in freezing temperatures on dangerous sea ice. After harvesting¹ a whale, as many as 50 people ⁹_____ the nearly impossible task of lifting the 50,000-kilogram animal out of the water—which can take from five to fifteen hours. ¹⁰_____ , the whale is cut up and shared with the entire village.

¹**harvest (v)** to catch or kill an animal for human consumption or use

An Iñupiaq whale hunt photographed by Kiliii Yüyan

B Complete the sentences with the correct form of a word from exercise A.

1. Camels go without water for long periods because their _____ is the desert.

2. French food, French music, and French art are parts of the _____ of France.

3. Things that happen when we are young can have a(n) _____ effect on us.

4. It's amazing that Polynesian explorers would _____ long ocean voyages in such small boats.

5. Some Hawaiians make their _____ from teaching the hula dance to tourists.

6. Indigenous people of Arctic regions are able to endure the _____ climate.

7. The U.S. citizens who took American Indians' land were the _____ of Europeans.

8. Snow leopards _____ in the Himalaya Mountains because they like to climb and do well in cold weather.

9. Travelers from New York to California in 1849 experienced _____.

10. Our flight had five connections before it _____ reached our destination.

C Match each word with its synonym.

1. _____ habitat (n)   a. difficulty
2. _____ hardship (n)   b. source of income
3. _____ harsh (adj)   c. do
4. _____ heritage (n)   d. intense
5. _____ livelihood (n)   e. severe
6. _____ profound (adj)   f. cultural roots
7. _____ ultimately (adv)   g. succeed
8. _____ undertake (v)   h. natural environment
9. _____ thrive (v)   i. in the end

D **CREATE** Complete the sentences with your own ideas. Then discuss them with a partner.   Critical Thinking

1. People **thrive** when . . . .

2. The part of my **heritage** I appreciate the most is . . . .

3. A task that I **undertook** that was too hard for me was . . . .

4. Many young people make their **livelihood** from . . . .

5. An experience that had a **profound** effect on me was . . . .

6. **Ultimately**, my goal is to . . . .

B Listening The Return of American Indian Lands

Critical Thinking

A **PREDICT** You will hear a lecture about American Indian lands. Choose the answers you think are correct.

1. What type of land would you expect to be discussed?
   a. urban   b. rural   c. suburban

2. Which use of land would you expect to be discussed?
   a. cultural use   b. finding oil   c. military use

B **MAIN IDEAS** Listen to the lecture. Complete the main concepts presented with words from the box. 🔊

restoring	forced	business	reservations
giving	buying	point of view	North America

1. The arrival of Indigenous people in _____

2. The American Indian _____ on the land, plants, and animals

3. How the American Indians were _____ off their land

4. A description of American Indian _____

5. The start of _____ opportunities for reservations

6. American Indian tribes _____ back their land

7. Governments _____ land back to Indigenous people

8. The Pueblo and Seminole tribes' projects of _____ their land

C **DETAILS** Listen again and choose the correct information to complete the sentences. 🔊

1. In 1492, the Indigenous tribes of North America spoke approximately ____ languages.
   a. 400   b. 500   c. 600

2. American Indian cultures believe they have a ____ connection with the land.
   a. mainstream   b. spiritual   c. business

3. American Indian reservations were located on ____ land.
   a. poor-quality   b. productive   c. nearby

4. In the 1970s, American Indian tribes received permission to ____ on reservations.
   a. hunt animals   b. restore the land   c. run businesses

5. The Klamath are a(n) ____ tribe that received land back from the government.
   a. Canadian   b. North American   c. Australian

6. Both the Pueblo and Seminole tribes make money from ____.
   a. Hard Rock Cafes   b. movie theaters   c. casinos

LISTENING SKILL   Recognize Repetition and Addition

Speakers often repeat a point to reinforce it:

> In the 1800s, the U.S. government took American Indian land despite legal agreements.
> **Basically,** the government stole American Indian land.

Listen for these expressions that signal repetition:

> In other words, . . .   Put simply, . . .
> Basically (I'm saying that) . . .   That is to say . . .

Speakers may also add information to the discussion:

> In the 1800s, the U.S. government took American Indian land.
> **Not only that,** but the government forced the people to travel to reservations.

Listen for these expressions that signal new information:

> Not only that . . .   I'd also add that . . .   What's more . . .   It's also true that . . .

D   Listen to excerpts. Check whether these statements are repetitions or additions. 🔊

	Repetition	Addition
1. . . . they have a spiritual connection with the land.	☐	☐
2. . . . they have a spiritual connection with the animals and plants as well.	☐	☐
3. . . . reservations weren't easy places to live.	☐	☐
4. . . . many reservations are in the American West.	☐	☐
5. . . . some state governments are giving land back to Indigenous people.	☐	☐

E   **FOCUSED LISTENING** Complete these excerpts with the words you hear. 🔊

1. The land and nature were _____ their heritage.

2. They cover 55 million acres of land, roughly _____ the total land area of the country.

3. In general, the reservations aren't on very good land. _____ it is quite dry.

4. The tribe is using some of its money to modify a _____ its tribal lands.

5. Like the Pueblo Indians in New Mexico, the Seminole in Florida brought back indigenous _____ plants and animals.

Speaking

Critical Thinking | **A** **ACTIVATE** Work in a small group. Read about some New Year's Eve traditions. Discuss which ones you have heard of and any others you know.

NEW YEAR'S EVE TRADITIONS

Lucky Food

Food traditions often represent good luck and happiness in the new year. In the Netherlands, people bring in the new year by eating ring-shaped treats; in Spain, the custom is to eat twelve grapes at midnight; and in Switzerland, it's a tradition to drop ice cream on the floor.

Symbolic Front Doors

Doors also hold special significance for the new year. In China, a red front door signifies happiness and good luck. In Greece, an onion hanging on the front door symbolizes rebirth. In Turkey, sprinkling salt in front of your door brings peace and abundance.

B What is a typical New Year's Eve like for you? Complete the information in the chart.

My New Year's Eve	
Location	
Decorations	
Food and drink	
Activity or ritual	
Other	

C Work with a partner. Discuss how your New Year's Eve celebrations are similar and different and which aspects are traditional or modern.

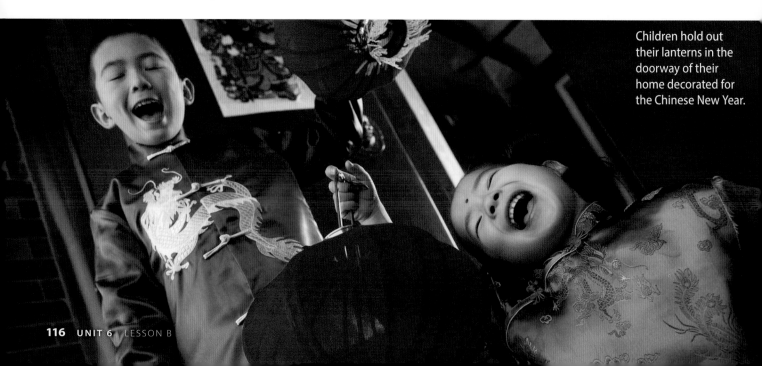

Children hold out their lanterns in the doorway of their home decorated for the Chinese New Year.

CRITICAL THINKING   Express Original Ideas

When you think creatively, you look beyond the normal or traditional way of doing things. It's a good way to solve problems or come up with alternative approaches to situations. Don't be afraid to express your ideas—even ones that are out of the ordinary. By not judging your ideas as they occur to you, you keep your thoughts flowing, which can lead to more innovative thinking.

D Work in a small group. Suggest new traditions for New Year's Eve celebrations that are interesting, fun, or symbolic. Note your best ideas.

Critical Thinking

New Year's Eve Tradition in _____	
Location	
Decorations	
Food and drink	
Activity or ritual	
Other	

E **EVALUATE** Work in a group. Look at this list of new holidays. Discuss them and check whether you think each one is *Real* or *Fake* (four are real and four are fake). Then discuss which ones sound like the most fun to you.

Critical Thinking

Holiday	Country	Activities	Real	Fake
1. International Cheese Day	France	People enjoy trying types of cheese they've never eaten before.	☐	☐
2. National Chewing Gum Day	Singapore	Everyone participates in an all-day gum-chewing marathon.	☐	☐
3. World Bungee Jumping Day	New Zealand	Everyone under 60 enjoys bungee jumping from the country's bridges.	☐	☐
4. World Emoji Day	U.S.	This holiday is celebrated with emoji decorations and costumes.	☐	☐
5. Singles Day	China	On this day, mainly students celebrate being single.	☐	☐
6. National Work Day	Japan	All workers in Japan work two extra hours to show they love their jobs.	☐	☐
7. Public Transportation Day	Monaco	From 1–2 p.m., everyone rides some form of public transportation.	☐	☐
8. Korean Alphabet Day	Korea	To celebrate their alphabet, people take the day off from work or school.	☐	☐

F Check your answers below. Then tell the class your group's score and which ones (if any) you got wrong.

Answers: 1, 4, 5, and 8 are real holidays.

Review

How well can you . . . ?	Very well.	OK.	I need improvement.
use the key vocabulary	☐	☐	☐
differentiate vowel sounds	☐	☐	☐
use noun phrase appositives	☐	☐	☐
ask rhetorical questions	☐	☐	☐

A **VOCABULARY** Use the correct form of any vocabulary from the unit to complete the sentences.

1. Our family had very little _____ with our neighbors in 2020 due to the pandemic.

2. Have you already decided on a career to _____ after you graduate?

3. After moving to Alaska, it took me a few years to become _____ the long, cold winters.

4. Building that artificial island is the largest project our engineering firm has ever _____.

B **PRONUNCIATION** Pronounce these words and mark the vowel sound you used. Then listen and check your pronunciation. 🔊

/ɪ/ /iʸ/   /ʌ/ /æ/   /ɛ/ /eʸ/   /oʷ/ /ɔ/
1. kick ☐ ☐   2. stuck ☐ ☐   3. fake ☐ ☐   4. row ☐ ☐

C **GRAMMAR** Complete the sentences so they are true for you. Add a noun, then a noun and a noun phrase appositive to give extra information.

1. Most weeks I eat _____, _____.

2. I was born in _____, _____.

3. In my free time, I play _____, _____.

See the Speaking Skill on page 108.

D **SPEAKING SKILL** Add a rhetorical question to the sentences (and follow up as necessary) of the type indicated.

1. During my vacation to Kenya, a group of lions walked in front of my motorcycle. (Type 1)
2. We had a wonderful vacation for one week and only spent $200. (Type 2)
3. My mother was a flight attendant and I had the opportunity to travel to wonderful places. (Type 3)

RE-ASSESS What skills or language still need improvement?

Final Tasks

OPTION 1 Discuss a tradition

A In a small group, brainstorm celebrations or festivals other than New Year's that have a long tradition. Think about celebrations that are important in your culture or community. Then agree on one you all know about to discuss.

B Discuss your choice of celebration from exercise A. Use these questions to guide you.

- How old is it and how did it begin?
- What is its purpose?
- Who usually participates in it?
- What decorations, foods, clothing, or activities are traditionally associated with it?
- Has it always been carried out the same way, or have there been changes over the years?
- What personal experiences or memories do you have that are connected with it?

OPTION 2 Interview and present about Gross National Happiness

See Unit 6 Rubric in the Appendix.

A **MODEL** Listen to a presentation about an interview the speaker did on Gross National Happiness using this questionnaire. Write the location and check *Yes* or *No* for each question. 🔊

Gross National Happiness in _____	Yes	No
Pillar 1: Good Government		
1. Is the state of the transportation system satisfactory?		
2. Is the public education system adequate?		
Pillar 2: Sustainable Development		
1. Do most jobs provide enough time off?		
2. Do most jobs pay workers enough to live comfortably?		
Pillar 3: Environmental Protection		
1. Are the levels of pollution, noise, and traffic acceptable?		
2. Are there parks or natural areas available to the public?		
Pillar 4: Cultural Preservation		
1. Do people try to maintain traditions along with new practices?		
2. Do young people value and respect the older generations?		

B **ANALYZE THE MODEL** Listen to the presentation again and answer the questions. 🔊

1. What does the speaker do at the beginning of the presentation?

   _____

2. How is the presentation organized?

   _____

3. How does the speaker introduce each section?

   _____

4. What language does he use to introduce the questions he asked?

   _____

5. How does he finish each section?

   _____

6. What does he do at the end of the presentation?

   _____

C **PLAN** Find someone outside of class from another country or city to interview. Contact them to find out if they are willing. Agree on a place and time to meet for the interview.

D **INTERVIEW** Use the form from exercise A to do your interview. Ask the person to explain their answers and ask follow-up questions about anything you don't understand. Make sure to take notes for your presentation.

E **PREPARE** Create your presentation from your notes. Use the organizational features you noticed in exercise B and insert one or more rhetorical questions.

PRESENTATION SKILL **Speak with Confidence**

When speaking in front of a group, it's important to appear confident. This will give the impression that you know your topic well and that you believe in what you are saying. There are several things that you can do to feel more confident.
- Organize your notes well and practice your presentation at least once.
- Always have good posture and face the audience.
- Use hand gestures, eye contact, and body language and smile when you can.
- Pause between sentences and speak slowly and clearly.

F **PRACTICE AND PRESENT** Practice your presentation on a friend or family member. Then give your presentation to the class.

G **DISCUSS** After everyone has given their presentation, discuss these questions as a class.

1. Which countries or cities seem to have the highest level of Gross National Happiness, and which seem to have the lowest? How does your city or country compare?

2. What was the most challenging aspect of doing the interview? What would you do differently if you interviewed another person?

MONEY IN OUR LIVES

A woman sits in a carriage used for promotional purposes at a gold shop in Hong Kong, China.

IN THIS UNIT, YOU WILL:

- Watch or listen to an interview about money and happiness
- Watch a video about the illusion of money
- Listen to a conversation about money
- Discuss ways to budget
  OR Give a presentation on how to save money

THINK AND DISCUSS:

1. The gold carriage in the photo is worth 60 million HKD (7.7 million USD). How would you feel riding in it?

2. What is your opinion of this kind of interior decoration? What's your emotional reaction to it?

3. What role does money play in your life? How important is it to you?

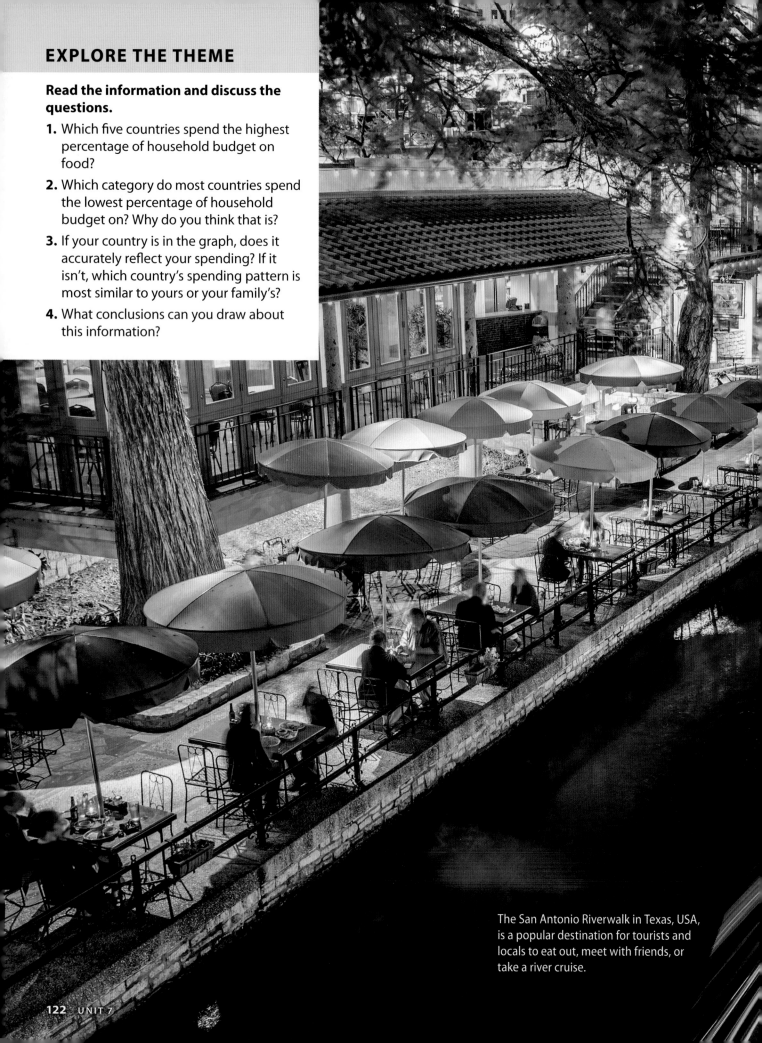

Read the information and discuss the questions.

1. Which five countries spend the highest percentage of household budget on food?

2. Which category do most countries spend the lowest percentage of household budget on? Why do you think that is?

3. If your country is in the graph, does it accurately reflect your spending? If it isn't, which country's spending pattern is most similar to yours or your family's?

4. What conclusions can you draw about this information?

The San Antonio Riverwalk in Texas, USA, is a popular destination for tourists and locals to eat out, meet with friends, or take a river cruise.

Money—How Do We Spend It?

Household Spending Patterns by Percentage

	Housing, Fuel & Utilities	Food	Recreation	Health	Clothing & Footwear	Education
United States	18	7	8	21	4	3
South Korea	16	12	8	12	6	7
Saudi Arabia	20	22	5	2	6	3
Russia	10	31	7	3	9	
Mexico	20	25	6	3	3	2
Japan	25	30	8	4	4	2
India	12	30	2	3	8	2
Canada	24	8	8	4	4	2
Australia	22	8	10	10	4	5

A Vocabulary

A **MEANING FROM CONTEXT** Read and listen to a survey about money. Notice each word in blue and think about its meaning. Then take the survey yourself. 🔊

SURVEY: YOUR VIEWS ON MONEY

	YES	NO
1. Do you admire people who have **accumulated** a lot of wealth?	☐	☐
2. Do you **associate** a high salary with happiness?	☐	☐
3. Do you agree with the **claim** that financial issues affect relationships?	☐	☐
4. Do you **conduct** research before you make a large purchase?	☐	☐
5. Is it important to use your money to **impact** others' lives for the better?	☐	☐
6. Do you generally have a long-term **perspective** on your finances?	☐	☐
7. Does saving money **promote** independence?	☐	☐
8. Is a college degree necessary to have a **prosperous** career?	☐	☐
9. Does having more money increase your sense of **security**?	☐	☐
10. Does saving money contribute to your sense of **well-being**?	☐	☐

B Write the correct form of each word in blue from exercise A next to its definition.

1. _____ (n) a statement that something is true or is a fact

2. _____ (v) to carry out (an activity)

3. _____ (v) to connect in the mind

4. _____ (v) to have a direct effect on

5. _____ (n) a point of view; a way of looking at things

6. _____ (n) confidence about yourself and your situation

7. _____ (adj) successful

8. _____ (v) to gather or acquire gradually

9. _____ (v) to help or encourage to happen

10. _____ (n) a state of comfort, health, or happiness

C Work with a partner. Compare and discuss your answers in exercise A.

Does spending money ▶ increase your sense of well-being?

VOCABULARY SKILL Words with Multiple Meanings

Many English words have more than one definition. When looking up words with multiple definitions, carefully examine the context for clues to the meaning. For example, read this sentence and three possible definitions of *conduct*:

*The scientists **conduct** experiments in the lab.*

1. (v) to organize and carry out an activity
2. (v) to lead or guide someone around a place
3. (v) to transmit a form of energy

Scientists carry out experiments in a lab. They do not guide experiments around the lab, nor do they transmit energy. Therefore, we know the correct definition in this case must be number one.

D Choose the best definition for the **bold** word in each sentence.

1. The movie had a powerful **impact** on me.

   a. an effect
   b. one thing hitting another
   c. the physical effect of a disaster

2. **Security** for the concert will include guards at the entrance and cameras in key locations.

   a. safety; protection from harm
   b. measures taken to protect a place
   c. a certificate proving investment

3. International travel **promotes** global understanding.

   a. to advance to the next grade
   b. to help to grow or develop
   c. to advertise

4. Who will **portray** Nelson Mandela in the new movie?

   a. to draw a picture of
   b. to describe with words
   c. to play the role of

5. When I thought about it from Rita's **perspective**, I realized I was wrong.

   a. an artistic technique
   b. a balanced viewpoint
   c. a point of view

E **PERSONALIZE** Complete the statements. Then discuss your answers with a partner.

1. The three factors that **impact** my **well-being** the most are _____

   _____

2. I feel a sense of **security** when _____

   _____

3. Some products people **associate** with my country are _____

   _____

A Listening Money and Happiness

Critical Thinking

A RANK Read the phrases. How happy does each situation make you? Rank them from 1 (the happiest) to 6 (the least happy).

_____ having money in the bank   _____ earning money

_____ spending money on items you want   _____ receiving money as a gift

_____ giving money to other people   _____ spending money on travel

B MAIN IDEAS Watch or listen to the interview. Then choose the correct answers. 🔊 ▶

1. What did Richard Easterlin try to find out about rising income?

   a. Whether happiness impacts income
   b. How rising income impacts happiness
   c. Whether rising income affects countries more strongly than individuals

2. Which idea did the study by Rachel Thomson and her colleagues support?

   a. More money provides more happiness after financial security is achieved.
   b. Achieving financial security doesn't have a strong effect on happiness.
   c. When financial security is achieved, more money has less impact on happiness.

3. What did Lara Aknin and her colleagues' experiment attempt to demonstrate?

   a. That candy isn't as important as helping sick children in the hospital
   b. That it's better to spend money helping sick children than buying candy
   c. That people are happier when they spend money on others rather than on themselves

4. What did Amrit Kumar conclude based on his experiment?

   a. Greater well-being results from purchasing experiences rather than things.
   b. People spend more money on experiences when their spending is monitored.
   c. Spending money on things instead of experiences results in greater well-being.

5. What did researchers discover about low-income areas of Asia and Oceania?

   a. The poor and rich in these areas are equally happy.
   b. The poor in these areas are being lifted out of poverty.
   c. The poor in these areas are as happy as the rich in wealthy areas.

6. What did the study by Jennifer Aaker and her colleagues show?

   a. The lives of people with lower incomes have more meaning than those of the wealthy.
   b. Happiness comes from meaning for people with lower incomes.
   c. The wealthy can find meaning if they give away some of their money.

C **DETAILS** Listen to excerpts from the interview. Choose the best summary for each. 🔊

1. a. In this study, all the participants were given some money.
   b. Participants whose money went to buy candy for sick children were happier.
   c. Half of the participants didn't want to give candy to sick children.

2. a. The study looked at what over 2600 people bought.
   b. The study focused on people's happiness after a purchase.
   c. The study showed that buying experiences led to more happiness than buying things.

3. a. Sara Miñarro gave a well-being survey to people from low-income areas in Asia and Oceania.
   b. Sara Miñarro and her colleagues studied happy people from high-income areas.
   c. This study found that happiness comes from the living environments in Asia and Oceania.

4. a. Jennifer Aaker and her colleagues went to 123 different countries for her study.
   b. The study found that people who make less money find happiness if their life has meaning.
   c. The study found that people prefer to have purpose in their lives than money.

D **APPLY** In a group, discuss which option in each pair would result in more happiness, according to the research studies you heard. Use *According to . . .* to start your sentences. Then discuss your opinions.

Critical Thinking

- buying yourself a $1000 coat / giving $1000 to a charity
- taking a trip around the world / making an initial payment on a new house
- living on a low salary in a friendly community / living on a low salary in the city

▼ Friends experience a ropes course together at an adventure park.

A Speaking

SPEAKING SKILL Refer to Sources

If you use outside sources to support your ideas, your audience may be more likely to agree with your points. In conversation, if you don't remember or care to mention the specific source(s), a general reference can be used instead. Here are some expressions you can use to refer to sources. Keep in mind that you may be asked to specify which sources you are referring to.

Specific references	General references
According to [source] . . .	*Experts say/tell us (that)* . . .
[Source] mentions/says (that) . . .	*Research has shown/demonstrated (that)* . . .
A study by [source] found (that) . . .	*Statistics/Studies show (that)* . . .

A Listen and complete the excerpts with the specific and general references you hear. Then listen again and repeat. 🔊

1. _____ there are two possible explanations.

2. There was a _____ Rachel Thomson and her colleagues that supports this idea.

3. Actually, _____ that may be true.

4. So, _____ it's better to give than to receive!

5. _____, people without much money can be happy if they feel that their life has a purpose, value, and a positive direction.

B With your partner, role-play a conversation between a college student and a student advisor using the information in the chart. The advisor gives advice using expressions from the Speaking Skill box. Then switch roles.

Student's questions	Research for advisor's answers
Should I get a part-time job on campus?	Working more than 15 hours a week lowers grades.
Should I apply for a credit card?	Article: Cards make people spend more.
Should I quit school and work full time?	People with more education make more money.
Should I get financial advice from other students?	Study: Young people don't always understand money.
Should I blame myself for not saving money?	Two-thirds of college students have little or no savings.

C **INTERPRET** Work with a partner. Study the graph. Then answer the questions below. Support your answers with information in the graph.

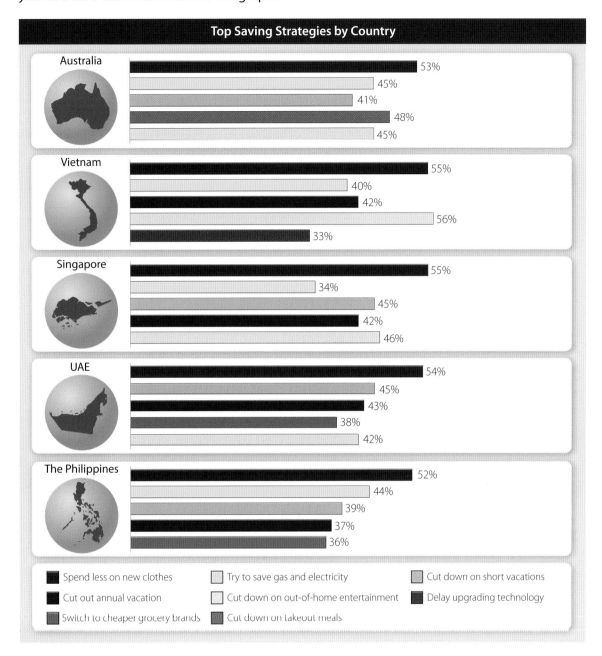

Top Saving Strategies by Country

Australia
53%
45%
41%
48%
45%

Vietnam
55%
40%
42%
56%
33%

Singapore
55%
34%
45%
42%
46%

UAE
54%
45%
43%
38%
42%

The Philippines
52%
44%
39%
37%
36%

■ Spend less on new clothes   □ Try to save gas and electricity   ■ Cut down on short vacations

■ Cut out annual vacation   □ Cut down on out-of-home entertainment   ■ Delay upgrading technology

■ Switch to cheaper grocery brands   ■ Cut down on takeout meals

1. What do the different colors and bar lengths represent?
2. Which country saves the most in each category?
3. What conclusion(s) can you draw from the information?

D **PERSONALIZE** Discuss these questions in a small group.

1. Which of the eight strategies for saving money would be easiest for you? Which would be the most difficult?
2. What other strategies for saving money can you think of?

E You are going to discuss purchases and happiness. To start, write FIVE items, services, or experiences that you have purchased. Then rank them in order from most expensive (1) to least expensive (5).

Purchase	Expense rank	Happiness rank

F Work with a partner. Take turns sharing the purchases on your list in exercise E. Find out if the purchases made your partner happy and why or why not.

Critical Thinking **G** **RANK** Go back to exercise E and rank your purchases in order of the happiness they gave you (1 = most; 5 = least). With your partner, discuss the questions.

1. How did your purchase list and your happiness rankings compare?
2. Does any of the research discussed in the interview on money and happiness support your list and ranking?
3. Considering your purchase list and happiness ranking, what conclusions can you draw about what makes you happy?

CRITICAL THINKING   Prioritize

Prioritizing involves comparing items and deciding how relevant or important each one is in relation to others. It is a key skill for accurate planning and efficient time management. There is usually more than one way to prioritize things, depending on what is most important to you or to people you are working with.

Critical Thinking **H** Write a shopping list of 10 things you need or want to buy in the near future. Work with a partner. Prioritize your list by writing a number from 1 (most important) to 10 (least important) beside each item. As you do, explain your reasons to your partner. Did the information you learned about money and happiness in this lesson influence your choices?

Research shows that spending money on experiences instead of things can make you happier.

Video

The Money Illusion

magician (n) someone who does magic tricks

take out of the equation (v phr) to remove from consideration

worthless (adj) having no value

▲ Every year, millions of tourists throw coins into Rome's Trevi Fountain to ensure they return to the city. About 1.26 million euros are thrown into the fountain each year.

A Watch the video. Choose the correct answers. ▶

1. Eric the magician's main reason for coming to the park is to make people _____ .
   a. give him some money
   b. buy him something to eat
   c. think about the value of money

2. The three people Eric meets probably _____ Eric's paper is real Canadian money.
   a. believe
   b. aren't sure
   c. don't believe

3. Eric seems to change worthless paper into _____ .
   a. fake American money
   b. real American money
   c. real Canadian money

4. Eric tells us that the true value of money _____ .
   a. is in our heads
   b. is what you can buy with it
   c. depends on your country

B Watch again. Are these statements true or false? ▶

1. Eric tells the truth about the climate in Canada.   T   F
2. The man with grey hair recently visited Canada.   T   F
3. Eric said he tried to buy a hot dog in New York.   T   F
4. Eric says he can change the money back to paper.   T   F

C Eric tells us that money is basically just paper, but it actually comes in many forms, some of which you will hear about in lesson B. What are some of the pros and cons of the gradual shift away from paper money to electronic forms of payment?

B Vocabulary

A **MEANING FROM CONTEXT** Read and listen to the personal finance tips. Notice each word in blue and think about its meaning. 🔊

PERSONAL FINANCE TIPS

1. Don't trust yourself to remember to pay your bills on time. Instead, set up a bill pay **reminder** on your bank's website to avoid late fees.

2. If your company offers direct deposit, **deposit** a percentage of your pay into a savings account. Don't include that money in your budget and never **withdraw** any money from your savings account except for emergencies.

3. Banking fees (monthly maintenance fees, ATM fees, foreign **transaction** fees) can add up. You can often avoid these fees by keeping a minimum balance. If that's not possible, consider opening an account with an online bank to save on fees.

4. **Allocate** at least 20 percent of your pay to financial priorities such as paying off debt and building your retirement savings.

5. It's possible to **overdo** saving money in the bank. If you have more than six months' savings in your account, think about investing.

6. College students: Unless you're lucky enough to live in a country where a college education is free, look for sources of financial assistance to help pay for your classes. There are many grants[1] and scholarships[2] available from governments or private organizations if you meet their **criteria**[3].

7. Most people are **reluctant** to borrow money. However, you should consider getting a **loan** if you want to start a business or if you need training to advance your career.

8. Pay off your credit cards in full every month to avoid paying added **interest**.

[1]**grant** (n) money given to someone based on need (e.g., to pay for college or start a business)
[2]**scholarship** (n) money to pay for education given to someone based on academic ability
[3]**criteria** (n) the (irregular) plural form of **criterion**

B Write the correct word in blue from exercise A to complete each definition.

1. _____ is the fee you pay for borrowing money.

2. When you _____ a sum of money, you put it into a bank account.

3. A(n) _____ is an exchange of goods, services, or funds.

4. If you _____ money from a bank account, you take it out.

5. If you _____ something, you assign or give it to a particular person or purpose.

6. A(n) _____ is something that makes you not forget another thing.

7. A(n) _____ is money that you borrow.

8. _____ are standards used to make a decision or judgment.

9. If you are _____ to do something, you would prefer not to do it.

10. If you _____ an activity, you do it excessively.

C **EVALUATE** Work with a partner. Look back at the financial tips in exercise A. Tell your partner which tips you follow or have followed and how well they work or worked. | Critical Thinking

D Choose the best collocation for the word in bold. Use a dictionary or concordancer to help you.

1. I think Andrés forgot to pay me back the money he borrowed, so I sent him a (kind / gentle / soft) **reminder**.

2. With (direct / straight / true) **deposit**, your company deposits your pay into your account electronically.

3. When I receive money from another country, my bank always charges me a **transaction** (tip / expense / fee).

4. My rent is so expensive that I can only **allocate** five percent of my pay (on / to / in) savings.

5. Whenever I go shopping for clothes, I tend to **overdo** (it / itself / its) and buy more than I should.

6. I don't have enough money to buy a car, so I'm going to (take in / take out / take up) **a loan**.

7. I have a lot of money in my checking account, but it hardly (wins / earns / pulls) any **interest**.

8. I need to **withdraw** $100 (from / out / back) my bank account to give as a gift to my nephew.

9. A bank won't give you a loan unless you are able to meet their (loaner / lending / qualify) **criteria**.

10. I won't ask my father for money because I know he'd be (lowly / poorly / deeply) **reluctant** to give me any.

E **CREATE** Look at the pie chart. Then create a pie chart about your own spending. Share your chart with a partner. Discuss how you are similar to or different from the typical American. | Critical Thinking

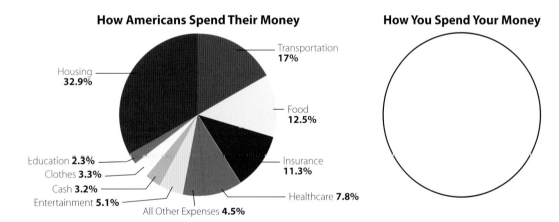

How Americans Spend Their Money

- Transportation **17%**
- Housing **32.9%**
- Food **12.5%**
- Insurance **11.3%**
- Education **2.3%**
- Clothes **3.3%**
- Cash **3.2%**
- Entertainment **5.1%**
- Healthcare **7.8%**
- All Other Expenses **4.5%**

How You Spend Your Money

F **PERSONALIZE** Look at your pie chart. How could you better manage your money? Write FIVE personal finance tips. Use vocabulary from exercise A. Then share your best tip with the class.

_____

_____

_____

_____

_____

B Listening Financial Innovations

A Read the information and discuss the questions with a partner.

FOUR PAYMENT METHODS

Debit Cards: These are directly connected to the money in your bank account. When you use your debit card, money is immediately withdrawn from your account.

Credit Cards: When you use a credit card, you are borrowing money. The credit card company makes the payment for you, and you must pay the money back. If you don't pay the total when you're billed, you must pay interest on the part you don't pay. Also, you can be charged late fees if you don't make your payments on time.

Digital Wallet: This is an app for financial transactions. It stores your debit card, credit card, and/or bank account information so that you can conveniently pay with your smartphone or other mobile device.

Peer-to-Peer Payment Services: These services allow the transfer of funds between individuals and companies or individuals and individuals using a website or app. This means you can use them to make a purchase and also to transfer money to anyone.

---

1. Which of these payment methods do you or your family use?
2. When do you use them?

Critical Thinking

B **PREDICT** Work with a partner. You are going to listen to three coworkers talking about money at lunch. Answer the questions.

1. How might the subject of money come up during a lunch with coworkers?
2. How could the method of payment become a problem when paying for lunch?
3. What other money-related subjects might coworkers talk about at lunch?

C **MAIN IDEAS** Listen and number the topics of conversation in the order you hear them. 🔊

_____ A way to get loans online without banks

_____ Preferred methods of payment

_____ Trouble paying the check

_____ Getting paid by their company

_____ Transferring money internationally

Splitting a restaurant bill is common in the U.S.

D DETAILS Read the statements then listen again. Choose T for *True* or F for *False*. 🔊

1. Noura uses a banking app to deposit checks.   T   F
2. Trang is reluctant to use new payment technologies.   T   F
3. Noura prefers a digital wallet to carrying credit cards.   T   F
4. Trang sends money to her family in Japan.   T   F
5. Yuta is going to give someone money to buy a car.   T   F
6. Peer-to-peer loan criteria are set by banks.   T   F
7. Small peer-to-peer loans can help people in developing countries.   T   F
8. Trang has enough cash to pay for everyone's lunch.   T   F

LISTENING SKILL   Listen for Shifts in Topic

While talking about a topic, speakers sometimes remember a related topic that they want to mention. Recognizing when a speaker is shifting topics will help you follow a talk or discussion. Here are some expressions that signal a shift in topic:

Speaking of [topic], . . .   *By the way, . . .*

Speaking of which, . . .   *That reminds me, . . .*

E Listen to sentences from the conversation. Complete them with the expressions you hear. 🔊

1. _____ , I have to check my bank account.

2. _____ , I just downloaded a digital wallet to my phone.

3. _____ , I'm thinking of taking out a peer-to-peer loan to purchase a car.

4. _____ , I just noticed a sign over there behind the cash register that says, "Cash only."

F **FOCUSED LISTENING** Listen and read an excerpt from the conversation. Underline FIVE errors. Then listen again and correct the errors. 🔊

Noura: Well, it does take a few days to arrive. But, then I just use my banking app to deposit it at home. You know, you just take a picture of the front and back of the check with your phone.

Trang: Really, I've never used my banking app for that.

Yuta: Why not, Trang?

Trang: Well, truly, I'm a little reluctant to adopt new technologies, particularly if they affect my money. Plus, there are so many new types of digital transactions with so many people and companies involved. So certainly, I'm concerned about online security issues.

Speaking

PRONUNCIATION   Aspirated /k/, /p/, and /t/

🔊 The consonant sounds /k/, /p/, and /t/ are strongly aspirated when followed by a vowel sound in a stressed syllable (*e.g., **c**aller, **p**artner, re**t**urn*). *Aspirated* means they are pronounced with a puff of air. These sounds are otherwise only weakly aspirated or not aspirated at all. To test if you are aspirating these sounds, put your hand in front of your mouth. If you can feel a puff of air, you're aspirating them!

A   Listen and repeat these sentences with the sounds /k/, /p/, and /t/. Remember to aspirate the first consonant of each word. 🔊

1. Tony Tuttle took Tanya Taft's ten toys.
2. Kevin Carsten called Kenny King's cat Cathy.
3. Pedro Pardo posted Patricia Patton's party picture.
4. Taki Tanaka took two typing tests Tuesday.
5. Could Karen kindly keep Careem's cola cold?
6. Pilar painted pink paper posters perfectly.

B   Mark the strongly aspirated /k/, /p/, and /t/ sounds in these sentences. Then listen and repeat. 🔊

1. Tanawat paid ten dollars in cash to the kind parking attendant.
2. Camilla's perfect piano playing shocked Carlos's music teacher.
3. Priya was told not to whisper to Carmen during the pop quiz.
4. Kofi purchased a book of popular cartoons to pass the time on the train.
5. Could you please call Peter to tell him to turn in his term paper?
6. Two clever kids took turns painting portraits of people in art class.

GRAMMAR FOR SPEAKING   Modals in the Past

We use modal verbs in the past to speak about possibilities and probabilities.

Should (not) have + past participle: regrets, missed opportunities, and errors in the past

I **should have bought** a car when the prices were lower.

Could/Might (not)/May (not) have + past participle: things you are not sure happened

Miriam **might have left** already—I'm not really sure.

I **may not have paid** my insurance bill this month yet. I'll check my records.

Must (not)/Could not have + past participle: logical deductions about the past

He **couldn't have driven** to work because his car keys are on the table.

Note: In spoken English, the contractions *shouldn't* and *couldn't* are very common.

C Comment on each scenario with a modal verb in the past. Then share your answers with a partner.

1. Sheikha never went to college, but she now realizes that a bachelor's degree is extremely valuable in her profession.
2. It was 4:30 p.m., and Hassan had a question for his boss, but when he went to his boss's office, he found it was locked and the lights were turned off.
3. Brandon got off the airplane, went downstairs to pick up his luggage, and took a taxi home. However, when he opened the suitcase at home, he was shocked to see that the clothes inside it weren't his.
4. Mahesh's car was covered in snow. When it stopped snowing at around 9 p.m., he cleared all the snow from on and around his car. However, the next morning, his car was covered in snow again.
5. Hessa was working for years in a very low-paying job with little future. However, the last time you saw her, she was wearing expensive clothes and driving a brand-new car.
6. Lucas is well-known at work for being a vegetarian and very careful not to eat sweets. However, today you saw him eating a hamburger and ice cream in a restaurant.

D **PERSONALIZE** Complete the statements so they're true for you.

1. When I was younger, I should have . . .
2. When I was younger, I shouldn't have . . .
3. Some of my ancestors could have . . .
4. If I hadn't chosen to study English, I might have . . .
5. If I had stopped going to school, I may have . . .

▼ In some states in the U.S. you can be fined as much as $400 for driving your car when it is covered with snow.

Review

A VOCABULARY Write the missing words in these questions using vocabulary from the unit. Then answer the questions aloud.

1. What is one way that people can increase their _____?

2. When you buy a computer, what _____ do you require it to meet?

3. Do you _____ more money in your bank account than you _____ every month?

4. What lifestyle characteristics do you _____ with success?

5. What are you _____ to spend money on?

B PRONUNCIATION Mark the strongly aspirated /k/, /p/, and /t/ sounds in these sentences. Then say them, making sure to aspirate these sounds.

1. You can't accomplish a task until you attempt it.
2. Tammy keeps polishing her copper pots and pans.
3. Ted couldn't recall where he parked his pickup truck.

C GRAMMAR Use a modal in the past to make a statement about each scenario.

1. Akram was caught in a storm on the way to work and got very, very wet.
2. Zainab asked Richard to go to lunch with her yesterday, but he said, "Not today, thanks."
3. There was a man in the park last week selling new smartphones for half price.
4. Jacob said hello to a person he thought was his friend Mark, but he didn't respond.

D SPEAKING SKILL Restate the sentences by referencing the source in parentheses.

1. The first coins with a person's head on them were made by the Romans. (research)
2. Queen Elizabeth II appeared on the currency of 33 countries. (MoneyNews.com)
3. Bitcoin was first used to pay for two pizzas in Florida in 2010. (experts)
4. Transactions that don't involve cash are increasing globally. (statistics)

RE-ASSESS What skills or language still need improvement?

Final Tasks

OPTION 1 Discuss ways to budget

A Work with a partner. Discuss the question.

Do you use a budget to manage your expenses? Why or why not?

B Read about three budgeting methods. Then discuss the questions with a partner.

BUDGETING METHODS

1. **The envelope system:** First, prepare an envelope for each category of your spending (e.g., groceries, entertainment, gasoline, utilities, etc.). When you are paid, change the money into cash. Put the amount of money you think you'll need during the pay period in each envelope. This will help control your spending as you can only spend the amount in the envelope on each category.

2. **The 50/30/20 budget:** In this system, you allocate 50 percent of your money to necessities, 30 percent to wants, and 20 percent to savings. This relatively simple system saves you time dealing with your finances by focusing on the "big picture."

3. **The "pay yourself first" system:** The first step in this system is to allocate the amount you wish to savings (e.g., for retirement, emergencies, or vacation). Use what is left for your expenses. This is the simplest system and is recommended for responsible spenders who can resist spending money on things they don't really need and who always pay their bills.

---

1. What are the pros and cons of each budgeting system?
2. Which system would be the best for you? Explain.

OPTION 2 Give a presentation on how to save and manage money

See Unit 7 Rubric in the Appendix.

A **MODEL** Listen to the presentation about managing money and complete the chart. 🔊

Source	Tips	Benefits
Student Money website	1.	Saves money
	Pay your rent on time.	2.
	3.	Helps you focus on needs first
Watch Your Money website	4.	Save on movie tickets, bus fare, etc.
	5.	Insurance, gas, repairs are expensive.
	Don't keep cash in your wallet.	6.
Manage Money magazine	Leave credit cards at home.	7.
	8.	It destroys the friendship and your budget.
	9.	It causes stress; other things are more important.

B **ANALYZE THE MODEL** Listen again. Answer these questions about the model. 🔊

1. How does the first speaker introduce the presentation?

   _____

2. What is the structure of the presentation?

   _____

3. Do all three speakers refer to sources?

   _____

4. How do the speakers introduce the next speaker?

   _____

5. How does the final speaker conclude the presentation?

   _____

COLLABORATION SKILL   Collaborate Fairly and Responsibly

To collaborate fairly as a group, divide the work up as evenly as possible so everyone has about the same amount of work to do. Then, to collaborate responsibly, make sure you do your task to the best of your ability. You should also take responsibility for the group's overall work by checking with each other to make sure that everyone understands their task and is able to accomplish it. Finally, make sure the different parts of the work are of similar quality and fit together well.

🔊 **ONLINE** When you are presenting as a group online, make sure your presentation slides are organized so the transition from one speaker to the next is smooth. It's also polite to acknowledge what your co-presenter says. You can say, "As my partner just explained, ..."

C **RESEARCH** You are going to research tips on saving or managing money to present with a group. Each group member will research tips from a different source. Choose THREE tips each to present. Write the source, the tips, and the benefits in a chart like this.

Source	Tips	Benefits

D **PRACTICE AND PRESENT** Use the notes you wrote in the chart in exercise C to practice the presentation with your group. Give each other feedback before you present to the class.

HEALTH AND TECHNOLOGY 8

The R70i Age Suit, developed at Liberty Science Center in New Jersey, USA, simulates the sight, hearing, and mobility of an 85-year-old. Better understanding of the aging process can lead to better health care.

IN THIS UNIT, YOU WILL:

- Watch or listen to a lecture about big data in health care
- Watch a video about biking in the city
- Listen to a podcast about wearable health care technology
- Discuss your city's health
  OR Give a presentation about a health care device

THINK AND DISCUSS:

1. Would you be interested in trying on this age suit? Why or why not?

2. Do you use technology to track your health?

3. What are possible disadvantages of relying on technology for health care?

Read the information and discuss the questions.

1. What advances in medical technology are you familiar with?

2. What health issues do you think could be solved or helped using technology?

3. How would you feel if a robot diagnosed and treated you?

Innovations in Health Care

Innovation and advances in medical technology are at the heart of modern medicine and have led to life-changing treatments and cures for patients around the world. Technology is also transforming the way health care information is accessed and communicated. It has impacted everything from better diagnostic and surgical procedures to preventative medicine and disease management. It has also allowed individuals to take a more active role in monitoring their own health through the development of personal health and fitness trackers and apps.

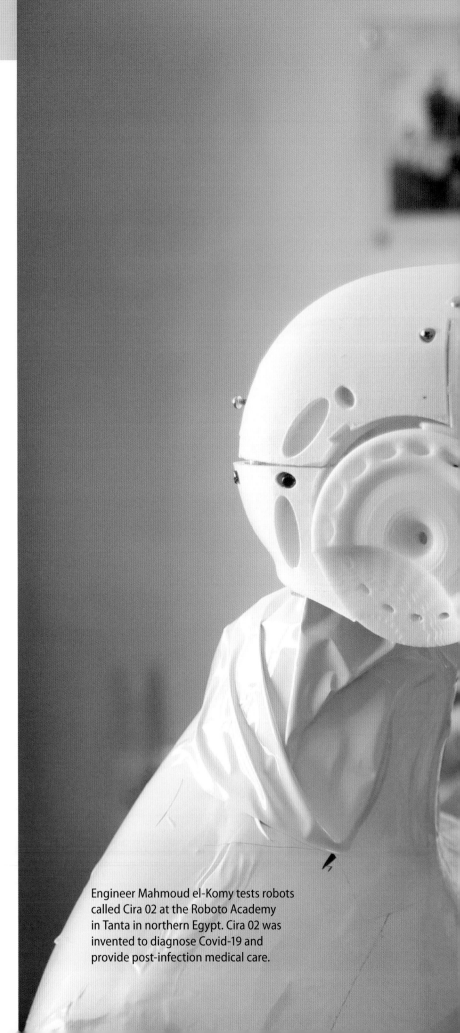

Engineer Mahmoud el-Komy tests robots called Cira 02 at the Roboto Academy in Tanta in northern Egypt. Cira 02 was invented to diagnose Covid-19 and provide post-infection medical care.

Vocabulary

A **MEANING FROM CONTEXT** Read and listen to this information from a health management company. Notice the words in blue and think about their meaning. Then match the words with their definitions. 🔊

HEALTH DATA: MAKE USE OF IT!

The use of technology to manage personal health is **surging**! It's easy to wear a cool device to help you **keep track of** your activity, blood pressure, or body weight. And many of us surf the web for health tips. But the amount of health information available can be **overwhelming**. Maybe that's why so many of us are **hesitant** to take advantage of this information, despite how it can **enhance** our health. Many people have a **tendency** to put off taking care of their health and often wait until a serious problem comes up before they **address** it. With our service, we keep all of your information strictly **confidential**. We analyze your data and send you health reminders. In addition, if you have a problem, we have health professionals you can **consult** for free. They will help to **diagnose** your problem and clarify any other issues you might have. Remember, prevention is relatively cheap when you consider the alternative! Let us help you manage your health data today!

---

1. _____ surge
2. _____ address
3. _____ keep track of
4. _____ hesitant
5. _____ tendency
6. _____ consult
7. _____ confidential
8. _____ diagnose
9. _____ enhance
10. _____ overwhelming

a. (v phr) to monitor
b. (v) to improve something
c. (adj) too strong in effect or too great in amount
d. (n) acting or thinking in a certain way
e. (adj) meant to be kept secret or private
f. (v) to identify a disease or other medical condition
g. (v) to increase very quickly
h. (adj) slow to proceed; somewhat unwilling
i. (v) to seek advice or information from; to refer to
j. (v) to deal with or focus on

PERSONALIZE Discuss the questions with a partner.

1. How do you **keep track of** your finances?
2. Have you ever been **hesitant** to try something new? Explain.
3. What do you have a **tendency** to put off doing?
4. In what situations do you **consult** a dictionary? A grammar book?
5. What is something that you keep **confidential**?

C Complete the chart with the correct form of each word. Use a dictionary if necessary.

	Verb	Noun	Adjective
1.	address		
2.	consult		
3.	diagnose		
4.	enhance		
5.			hesitant
6.	overwhelm	– – – – – –	
7.			surging
8.		tendency	– – – – – – –

VOCABULARY SKILL   Synonyms

Synonyms are words with the same or similar meanings. Learning synonyms enables you to use a greater variety of words and avoid sounding repetitious. It's important to be aware of any differences in meaning and collocations between synonyms. For example, *honest* and *sincere* are synonyms, but we say *honest mistake* and *sincere apology*. You can find examples of usage in a dictionary or by searching online.

D Choose the word or phrase that best completes each sentence. Use a dictionary or other resource to help you.

1. These (surging / expanding) home prices are a sure sign of inflation.
2. You'll never solve your problems unless you (undertake / address) them.
3. Where are your keys? Why is it so hard for you to (keep track of / monitor) them?
4. The actress who played the leading role was (stunningly / overwhelmingly) beautiful.
5. He said he's (doubtful / hesitant) to come with us, but I still think we can convince him.
6. If your blood pressure is too high, you should (consult / refer to) a doctor.
7. I asked the school drama teacher to (diagnose / assess) my daughter's acting skills.
8. In my family, excellent health and long life seem to be genetic (tendencies / habits).
9. Our office supply business is (expanding / enhancing) into several foreign markets.
10. This is a (confidential / private) club—you can only join if invited by a member.

Critical Thinking | **A** **ACTIVATE** You are going to listen to a lecture by a guest speaker about big data in health care. Discuss the questions.

1. Why would a teacher invite a guest speaker to class?
2. What kind of medical data about patients do doctors need?
3. Do you think health data should be kept confidential? Explain.

B **MAIN IDEAS** Watch or listen to the lecture. Which of these points does the speaker make? Put a check in the correct column. 🔊 ▶

	YES	NO
1. The flow of big data can be compared to a wild, fast-moving river.	☐	☐
2. Medical data reported by patients themselves are the most reliable.	☐	☐
3. People worry their health information won't be kept confidential.	☐	☐
4. Doctors need help organizing the overwhelming amount of health data.	☐	☐
5. Once patients leave the hospital, it is no longer possible to keep track of them.	☐	☐
6. In the future, big data will help doctors and take over some of their work.	☐	☐

NOTE-TAKING SKILL   Use a T-Chart

A T-chart can be an effective note-taking tool when a lecture or presentation deals with two sides of a topic (e.g., advantages and disadvantages, challenges and solutions, causes and effects). Placing these aspects on either side of a chart creates a visually clear arrangement that helps both comprehension and memory.

A team of medical scientists reviews data about a patient's health, lifestyle, and environmental exposure to determine the best treatment options.

C Listen to part of the lecture. As you listen, complete the notes related to challenges in the left column. Then listen again and complete the notes related to solutions in the right column. 🔊

Big Data and Health Care	
Challenges	**Solutions**
Big data is like a fast-moving [1]_____ that is difficult for people to use.	We can analyze the [1]_____ and organize it so that people can use it.
Patient data is unreliable because much of it is self-[2]_____.	We can collect [2]_____ data only from measurements and testing.
Patients are hesitant to share their data because it might not be treated as [3]_____.	This issue can be addressed by better data [3]_____ technology.
Doctors require data that is [4]_____ and ready for them to use.	New businesses are able to collect, organize, and analyze data for [4]_____.
Certain patients aren't good at following their doctor's [5]_____.	Big data can identify these patients so that we can [5]_____ them.
It used to be hard to monitor patients in follow-up [6]_____.	Apps allow us to keep track of where they are, whether they're taking their [6]_____, etc.

D **DETAILS** Listen to part of the lecture. Match the companies with their focus. 🔊

1. _____ Hindsait
2. _____ Bering Research
3. _____ PathAI

a. uses big data technology to help identify illnesses.
b. collects data on patients' health in a central location.
c. analyzes patient data to determine potential health problems.

E **FOCUSED LISTENING** Complete the sentences with the verbs you hear. Write no more than THREE words in each blank. Discuss with a partner why the passive is used. 🔊

1. The second issue, the one of keeping data confidential, _____ by better data security technology.

2. Hindsait is a firm that brings health records together so they _____ centrally _____ and searched.

3. Also, I believe big data techniques _____ to diagnose most patients in the future.

4. And these techniques _____ more and more to reading X-rays.

A | Speaking

See Speaking Phrases in the Appendix.

SPEAKING SKILL   Make and Respond to Suggestions

There are many ways to make a suggestion in English:

I have/I've got/Here's an idea. What if we have our meeting at a coffee shop?
What/How about this? We could have a virtual meeting instead.
I know! Why don't we postpone the meeting until next week?

Our response is positive if we like the suggestion, or uncertain if we don't. It's better to avoid negative responses in business or other formal situations.

Positive Response
That's a good/great idea.
I think that (idea) could/might work.

Uncertain Response
I'm not sure how well/if that (idea/plan) would work.
I don't know if that's the best way to go.

After an uncertain evaluation, we often offer a short explanation.

I'm not sure that will work. Coffee shops tend to be a little noisy.

A Work in a group of three. Underline the responses in the conversation and discuss which are positive or uncertain. Then practice the conversation.

A: I've got an idea. What if we organize team vacations to interesting destinations every year?

B: I don't know if that would work. We might not have the budget for that.

C: I know! We could set aside time for teams to play computer games after lunch.

A: I'm not sure that's the best way to go. Not everyone likes to play computer games.

B: Hmm. How about this? We could send teams to help build affordable community housing.

C: That might not be ideal. I don't think our insurance would cover that.

A: You're right. Here's another idea. How about if we sponsor team lunches once a week?

B: I'd say that idea has a lot of potential.

C: Yes, I think that might work. Let's run it by management for approval.

B Work in a small group. Imagine you are a company health care committee deciding on features to include in your health care program. Take turns suggesting the ideas to the group and giving either a positive or an uncertain response with a short explanation.

Reduced Friday hours	Weekly yoga	Bicycle parking area
Walking meetings	Free gym memberships	Healthy food in vending machines
Mental health days	Free fitness trackers	"Take the stairs" days

GRAMMAR FOR SPEAKING   Noun Clauses with *Wh*-Words and *That*

A noun clause functions as a noun in a sentence.

Wh-word noun clauses:
> A new computer system is **what we need**. (subject complement)
> I don't know **why the system crashed**. (object of verb)
> **Why our new system crashed** is difficult to understand. (subject)

The question form is NOT used in noun clauses with *wh*-words.
> I can't remember **who he is**.
> NOT I can't remember ~~who is he~~.

That noun clauses come after:
- *be* + certain adjectives, such as *sure, concerned, interesting, true,* and *worried*.
  I'<u>m sure</u> **(that) we'll see a lot more collaboration in the future.**
- verbs related to thinking, such as *agree, keep in mind, realize,* and *worry*.
  Many people <u>agree</u> **(that) big data has immense potential.**

That is often omitted in noun clauses, especially in speaking.

C Work with a partner. Read the sentences aloud to your partner. Your partner extends the second sentence to include information in the first using a noun clause.

1. Who is the guest speaker today? I didn't ask.

   > *I didn't ask who the guest speaker is today.*

2. Did you know it's possible to become addicted to the Internet? I never realized it.
3. When did Ava come home last night? I'm not sure.
4. Who is the owner of the car parked outside? I don't know.
5. I think the government should pay everyone's college tuition. Many people don't agree.
6. Where is the best place for lunch on campus? I'll ask Mohammed.
7. How is the weather going to be this weekend? I'll check.
8. Children are spending more and more time online. It worries me.

D **PERSONALIZE** With a partner, take turns creating sentences with noun clauses using the sentence starters. Use the topics on the right for inspiration or use your own ideas.

Sentence starters	Topics	
I'm not sure why . . .	vacations	hobbies
Many people think (that) . . .	entertainment	music
I (don't) believe (that) . . .	work	food
Some people may not know who . . .	money	shopping
I think it's amazing how . . .	health care	technology
It's interesting (that) . . .	science	fashion
I really have no idea what . . .		

E **EVALUATE** Work with a partner. Read the chat messages. Discuss which ones view technology in health care positively (+) and which view it negatively (−). Then mark them + or −.

> **This chat stream welcomes your opinions about technology in health care. Please limit your comments to this topic only.**
>
> **HealthNut96** ☐ New technology in health care is great, especially wearable devices. They allow doctors to continuously monitor patients' blood pressure, blood sugar, or temperature.
>
> Remote medical visits using a smartphone are so convenient! It's great not having to drive to my doctor's office in city traffic. **VitaminKing04** ☐
>
> **FitnessFrida** ☐ Medical staff is starting to trust computers too much. Even with this great technology, they should still check that the information they have is correct.
>
> Wearable devices can become an issue when the information they collect isn't kept private. Such information might affect whether someone can get a job or how much their insurance costs. **WeekendBiker55** ☐
>
> **StepCounter89** ☐ Big data and AI are really important in health care. Since they make it possible for more information to be accurately evaluated, medical professionals are making fewer errors than ever.
>
> Your doctor can only diagnose your problem safely if you visit them in person. Remote visits are fast but not complete enough. **WayOfHealth21** ☐

CRITICAL THINKING Synthesize Information

When we synthesize information, we make connections among different ideas. Synthesizing involves using different sources of information to highlight similarities and differences. When we synthesize information, we may gain important insights about the topic, and ultimately a better understanding of it.

F Work with a partner. Discuss these technologies and their positive and negative aspects. Synthesize the information from activity E, what you learned in this lesson's listening passage, and your own knowledge and opinions.

- Wearable medical devices
- Big data in health care
- Artificial intelligence in health care
- Remote visits and monitoring of patients

> **A:** *Wearable medical devices are not only useful for doctors but also for individuals who want to keep themselves in good physical condition.*

> **B:** *Yes, but it's important to remember that the information we get from fitness trackers isn't always completely accurate.*

Biking in the City

proximity (n) how near a thing or place is to another
emit (v) to produce or send out (a sound, signal, etc.)

particle (n) a bit of material smaller than a piece of dust
optimize (v) to make the best or most effective use of

▲ In addition to cars, bikers in cities also need to be aware of pollution.

A Watch the video. Read the statements. Choose T for *True* or F for *False.* ▶

1. The health study is attempting to clarify a question about exercising close to traffic.   T   F
2. Pollution from vehicles on the road is increasing.   T   F
3. Participants wear clothing and gadgets that take measurements.   T   F
4. The larger health study will be complete in two years.   T   F
5. Pollution and smoking can lead to a similar disease diagnosis.   T   F

B Read the questions. Then watch the video again. Take notes as you watch. Write no more than THREE words for each answer. ▶

1. How frequently does the blood pressure monitor take a measurement?

   _____

2. What device do the participants use to log their location?

   _____

3. How long do the researchers have to prove the success of their study?

   _____

4. The planned app would balance less pollution exposure with what other factor?

   _____

C   **ANALYZE** If all the bicyclists in a city wore the monitors used in this study, what data might we get that would interest doctors, city planners, and individual bicyclists?

Critical Thinking

Vocabulary

A **MEANING FROM CONTEXT** Read and listen to this email. Notice each word in blue and think about its meaning. 🔊

From: Human Resources

To: All employees

Subject: Technology and Service Upgrades

Plans to update our office are moving forward! Below is a list of suggestions for new equipment and services that we would like your feedback on. Please rank them from 1 to 8 (1 = most important; 8 = least important) and send this form back to HR by Friday. Your responses will provide valuable **insight** as we set up new programs.

_____ Replace standard keyboards and mouse devices with ergonomic[1] ones to prevent injuries caused by **continually** using the same set of motions to type and move the mouse.

_____ Supply employees with fitness trackers that detect steps taken, calories burned, activity level, etc.

_____ Give employees smart mugs that **track** their beverage **consumption**.

_____ Equip desks with emotion monitors that **notify** employees when their levels of stress and anxiety are high. This will help to **determine** when you need to take a break.

_____ Provide a wearable device that monitors blood pressure, blood sugar levels, heart rate, etc. for employees who request it. It will let you know if any of these levels become **abnormal**.

_____ **Obtain** and install apps on office computers to provide nutritional information about different foods in area restaurants.

_____ Give employees sleep monitors to use at home to check for sleep-related health issues that can impact **productivity** at the office.

_____ Hire a health and fitness specialist for employee consultations. We know new technology can be difficult to use, and we certainly don't want anyone to get **frustrated** with our suggested changes.

[1]**ergonomic** (adj) designed for health and comfort

B Write each word in blue from exercise A next to its definition.

1. _____ (n) use

2. _____ (v) to decide

3. _____ (v) to inform someone about something

4. _____ (adj) different from what is usual and expected, often in a bad way

5. _____ (n) effectiveness of workers at getting things done

6. _____ (v) to get

7. _____ (v) to regularly check the value or position of something

8. _____ (adj) feeling annoyed because a problem cannot be solved

9. _____ (n) a deep understanding of something

10. _____ (adv) occurring again and again

C Choose the word that forms the best collocation with the word(s) in bold. Search the Internet for the collocations if you need help.

1. Unfortunately, the used car that I bought is (steadily / continually) **breaking down**.

2. You should see a doctor if you have (exceptional / abnormal) **blood pressure**.

3. Fresh pineapple is (easily / fluently) **obtained** in Hawaii.

4. By studying history, we can (gain / learn) **insight** into the past of human societies.

5. All the hospitals were **notified** (on / of) the new data privacy legislation.

6. There are legal implications around the **tracking** (of / to) personal data.

7. The new workflow is the reason for our team's (increased / grown) **productivity**.

8. The judges had to look at a photograph to (determine / conclude) **the winner** of the race.

9. I think children's **consumption** (of / in) sugary drinks is much too high.

10. I'm so **frustrated** (with / of) driving to work that I might start taking the train.

D **RANK** Work with a partner. Imagine you work at the company in exercise A. Discuss the importance of the suggestions to you and rank them from 1 to 8.

Critical Thinking

E **PERSONALIZE** Work with a partner. Use the vocabulary words to describe or make suggestions to improve your own work, school, or home life.

> *I want an app that notifies me whenever I make a mistake in English!*

Critical Thinking | **A** **ACTIVATE** Work with a partner. Think of a device, app, or website related to fitness that you have used or know about. Tell your partner about the functions or information it offers and why it is or is not beneficial.

B **MAIN IDEAS** Listen to the podcast. Number the topics of conversation in the order you hear them. 🔊

a. _____ How companies use data to help their workers

b. _____ A reminder not to rely completely on technology

c. _____ The increasing popularity of wearable health care devices

d. _____ How devices help people change their behavior

e. _____ A definition of wearable health care technology

f. _____ How data saves money for insurance companies and customers

C **DETAILS** Listen to an excerpt from the podcast. Complete the sentences with a word or number you hear. 🔊

1. Everyone wants to collect _____ since we live in a digital age.

2. A lot of people are deciding to wear devices that collect _____ data.

3. The data is often sent to the device maker, doctors, and _____ companies.

4. Analyzing the data provides useful insights into how _____ and health are related.

5. In 2030, the global wearable medical device sector is expected to be worth $ _____ billion.

6. In the U.S., only _____ of people use a wearable health care device.

LISTENING SKILL **Listen for Pros and Cons**

Speakers often highlight the pros and cons of different ideas, products, approaches, etc. Listen for words like *pros* and *cons*, *advantages* and *disadvantages*, and *benefits* and *drawbacks*.

> *It's an approach that has its **pros and cons**.*
> *This, too, has its **advantages and disadvantages**.*
> *We should point out the **benefits and drawbacks**.*

To identify when a speaker shifts between discussing pros and cons, listen for transitions that indicate a contrast such as these:

But while . . .	*However, . . .*	*Although/Though . . .*
On the one hand, . . .	*On the other (hand), . . .*	*In contrast, . . .*
But . . .	*Yet . . .*	

D Listen to three excerpts from the podcast. Note the pros and cons in the chart. 🔊

Pros	Cons
1. Insurance companies and their customers using health data to save money	
2. Companies and their workers using health data to improve well-being	
3. Individuals using health data to change their habits	

PRONUNCIATION   Recognize Dropped Syllables

🔊 We sometimes drop a vowel sound after a stressed syllable in words with three syllables or more.

> Maybe it's unattractive, but then, it's not a piece of **jewe̸lry**, is it?
> I was very **inte̸rested** in trying this one out.
> It also analyzes the nutritional profile of the **beve̸rage** you're drinking.
> It's a **myste̸ry** to me how it works.

E One or two words in each sentence have a syllable where the vowel sound can be dropped. Cross out the vowels that are dropped. Then listen to check your answers. 🔊

1. The laboratory was open during renovation.

2. I was able to internalize what I learned in my mathematics class.

3. I find it easy to conform to the corporate culture.

4. I think it's undeniable that broccoli improves your memory.

5. To me, vegetable juice is just cold soup.

6. The drop in sales was disastrous for our restaurant.

7. We're planning to initiate several new projects every year.

8. Did you know that I actually daydream about chocolate?

9. My family takes a two-week vacation every year.

10. Success in business is always a collaborative effort.

B Speaking

A Work in a small group. Look at the graphic below and discuss the questions.

1. Where do most people prefer to attach devices? Why do you think that is?
2. What might be the advantage of a device worn in contact lenses?
3. Where would you prefer to wear a health/fitness device?

Where Do You Wear A Health/Fitness Device?

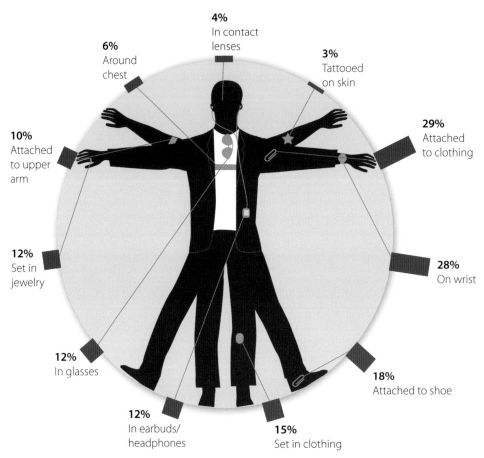

4%
In contact lenses

6%
Around chest

3%
Tattooed on skin

10%
Attached to upper arm

29%
Attached to clothing

12%
Set in jewelry

28%
On wrist

12%
In glasses

18%
Attached to shoe

12%
In earbuds/ headphones

15%
Set in clothing

Critical Thinking | **B** **INTERPRET** Work with a partner. Discuss what these health-related sayings mean.

1. An apple a day keeps the doctor away.
2. A three-color meal is a good deal.
3. Early to bed and early to rise makes a man healthy, wealthy, and wise.
4. Seven days without exercise makes one weak.
5. Laughter is the best medicine.
6. The first wealth is health.
7. A sad soul can kill quicker than a germ.
8. Healthy citizens are the greatest asset any country can have.

C   Work with a partner. Read about health problems caused by technology use and discuss these questions.

1. Have you ever experienced one or more of these problems?
2. How can people avoid them but still use technology?

Texter's thumb	Earbud disease	Texter's neck
A condition due to texting that makes it painful to move your thumb.	An ear infection caused by wearing earbuds all day.	A painful neck due to continually leaning forward to text on a phone.
Carpal tunnel syndrome	**Insomnia**	**Migraine headaches**
Nerve damage in the hands caused by typing a lot.	Trouble sleeping that can be caused by technology use, especially before bedtime.	Extremely strong headaches due to technology use.
Mouse elbow	**Computer vision syndrome**	**Internet addiction**
A painful condition of the elbow caused by using a mouse.	Eye pain or vision problems from looking at a computer screen.	An overwhelming need to be continually online.

D   **CREATE**   With a partner, role-play a patient consulting a doctor about one of the health problems above. The patient describes the symptoms. The doctor diagnoses the illness and makes recommendations. Then switch roles.

Critical Thinking

E   **PERSONALIZE**   Work with a partner. Discuss the questions.

1. Do you think people are more or less concerned about health than they used to be?
2. Which new trend in health care do you think is positive? Are any negative?
3. Do you think the increased use of technology affects the doctor-patient relationship?
4. Would you feel comfortable if robots took care of you instead of nurses?
5. What type of nutritional information should children be taught in school?

Review

A **VOCABULARY** Write the correct form of a vocabulary item from the unit to complete the sentences.

1. I have to limit my caffeine _____ before bedtime or else I can't sleep.

2. The use of educational technology can _____ a child's learning in many ways.

3. I read a great book that gave me some _____ into international politics.

4. I called my bank to _____ them about my change of address.

5. The scientists put a radio collar on the bear so that they can _____ its movements.

6. I'm going to _____ a doctor about the pain in my knee.

B **GRAMMAR** Read what the people said. Then use the sentence starters and noun clauses with *wh*-words or *that* to say sentences.

Sentence starters

1. Maria: "The store closes at 9:00."   Maria told me . . .
2. Rahul: "I need a fitness tracker."   A fitness tracker is . . .
3. Wang Fang: "Li Jun left, but I don't know the reason." Wang Fang doesn't know . . .
4. Agustina: "The market closes at 7. Or is it 8? I can't remember." Agustina forgot . . .
5. Brandon: "I put my keys somewhere, but now I can't find them." Brandon can't remember . . .
6. Angel: "My cat opened the door. I don't know how he did it." Angel doesn't know . . .

C **SPEAKING SKILL** You are discussing how to raise money for a trip. Complete the conversation with expressions to make and respond to suggestions. Use different words in each blank.

A: I ¹_____ ! What ²_____ put on a play and charge admission?

B: I'm not sure ³_____ work. There aren't many good actors in our class.

C: How ⁴_____ ? We ⁵_____ borrow money from a bank.

A: I don't know ⁶_____ go. Banks don't usually lend money for activities such as a class vacation.

B: Here's ⁷_____ . Why ⁸_____ wash cars in the parking lot for money?

C: ⁹_____ a lot of potential. Let's go to the school office and ask for permission!

RE-ASSESS What skills or language still need improvement?

Final Tasks

OPTION 1 Discuss your city's health

A Work in a small group. Read this definition of a healthy city. Then discuss whether your city or town fits the description.

> The World Health Organization defines a healthy city as one that is continually creating and improving physical and social environments in order to support personal health.
> A healthy city enables residents to support each other in daily activities and to reach their maximum potential.

B With your group, discuss how your city is doing in the areas listed below. Then decide on the area that is most important for your city to improve.

- air / water / noise pollution
- parks / green space
- sports / exercise facilities

- public transportation cost / availability
- food prices / quality
- health care costs / availability / quality

> *I'd say the air and water in this city are clean, but the noise pollution is terrible both day and night.*

OPTION 2 Present on a wearable health care device

See Unit 8 Rubric in the Appendix.

A **MODEL** Listen to a presentation about a wearable health care device. Take notes in the chart. 🔊

Product name:	
Use:	
General description:	
Information tracked:	
Other features:	
Pros:	
Cons:	

B **ANALYZE THE MODEL** Listen again. Answer these questions about the model. 🔊

1. How was the presentation divided among the three speakers?

   _____

2. What language do the speakers use to introduce the next speaker?

   _____

3. What transition language is used between the pros and cons?

   _____

4. How did the final speaker end the presentation?

   _____

C **PLAN** Briefly scan the web to find ideas for wearable health care devices that are new and innovative. Then discuss the possibilities with your group. Use language for making and responding to suggestions. Agree on ONE product for your presentation.

D **RESEARCH** Look for information about the product on the company's website or another site. Find reviews online to get pros and cons. Take notes in the chart.

Product name:	
Use:	
General description:	
Information tracked:	
Other features:	
Pros:	
Cons:	

PRESENTATION SKILL   Engage Your Audience

Here are some suggestions to help you engage your audience.
- At the beginning of your presentation, ask some questions that can be answered by a show of hands. (*How many of you wear a fitness tracker?*)
- As appropriate during your presentation, ask for one or more volunteers to assist you or to provide an example for a point.
- Focus on how the points you are making can benefit your audience. When you do, check if they agree.
- Use rhetorical questions to encourage your audience to think about something, to invite them to agree with you, or to ask questions you think your audience would like to ask.

📶 **ONLINE** In addition to using the tips above, you can further engage your audience by having good lighting, making sure your camera is at eye level, and using a good quality microphone.

E **PRACTICE AND PRESENT** Practice with your group. Try to use one or more of the tips in the Presentation Skill box to engage your audience. Give each other feedback before you present.

THE MYSTERIOUS MIND 9

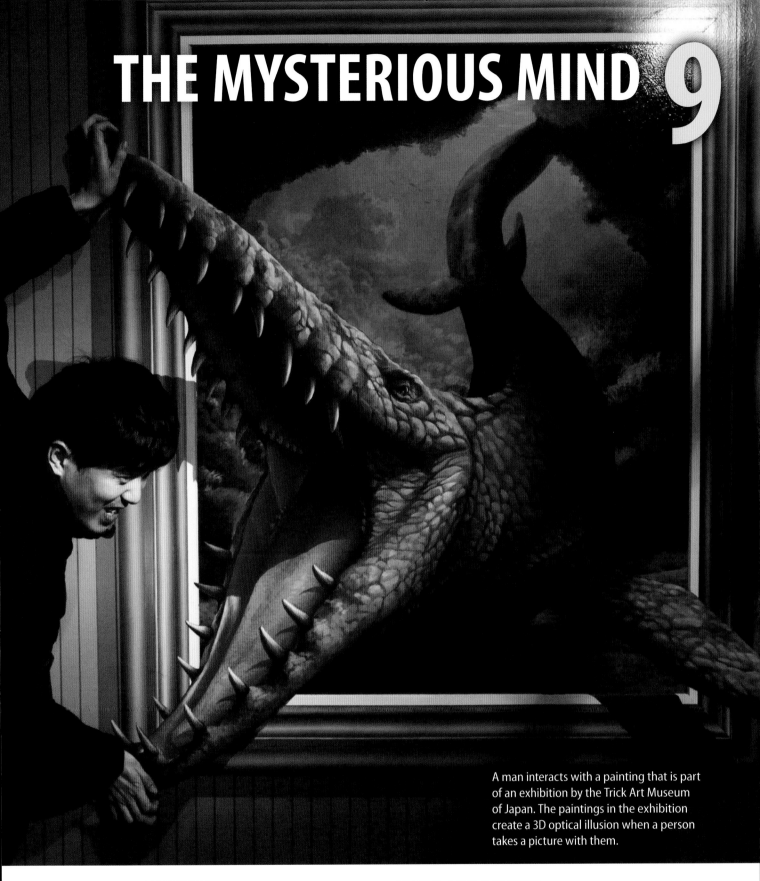

A man interacts with a painting that is part of an exhibition by the Trick Art Museum of Japan. The paintings in the exhibition create a 3D optical illusion when a person takes a picture with them.

IN THIS UNIT, YOU WILL:

- Watch or listen to a lecture about the history of intelligence
- Watch a video about memory and stress
- Listen to a conversation about memory
- Discuss your learning style
  OR Give a presentation about "study/learning hacks"

THINK AND DISCUSS:

1. What is unusual about the art in the photo?
2. What are other examples of things that can trick the mind?
3. Read the title. What do you think you will learn about in this unit?

Read the information and discuss the questions.

1. What qualities do you think are needed to be a good chess player?

2. What areas do you want to become an expert in? Why?

3. Do you agree that more than practice may be needed to become the best at something?

Becoming an Expert

Some scientists believe that with effort and 10,000 hours of practice, anyone can achieve expertise in almost any skill. Others believe that superior cognitive ability, such as general intelligence or memory, is needed to master a skill. Results from 19 studies of chess players with more than 1700 participants showed that the "smarter" the player, the higher the level of chess skill. Another study, which included 500 participants, compared chess players' and non-chess players' ability to solve cognitive tasks. Chess players' performance was significantly superior. So while practice is a necessary component of success in chess and other fields, it may not be enough to become the best.

Tanitoluwa Adewumi moved to the U.S. from Nigeria in 2017 at the age of six. He learned to play chess by joining the club at his public school in New York. He also studied on his own, solving up to 500 puzzles per week. He quickly began winning chess tournaments. At age ten, he became a national master.

A Vocabulary

A **MEANING FROM CONTEXT** Read and listen to the information. Notice each word or phrase in blue and think about its meaning. 🔊

A NEWER THEORY OF INTELLIGENCE

For many years, traditional intelligence tests were thought to assess **actual** intelligence. However, some people are concerned that these tests might be **biased** in favor of Western cultures. There are also concerns about determining intelligence on the **basis** of just one test score and fears that a poor score might harm a child's **self-image**. In the 1980s, such concerns led Professor Howard Gardner of Harvard University to create his theory of multiple intelligences. The central **concept** is that there are at least eight ways of being intelligent. They are presented below.

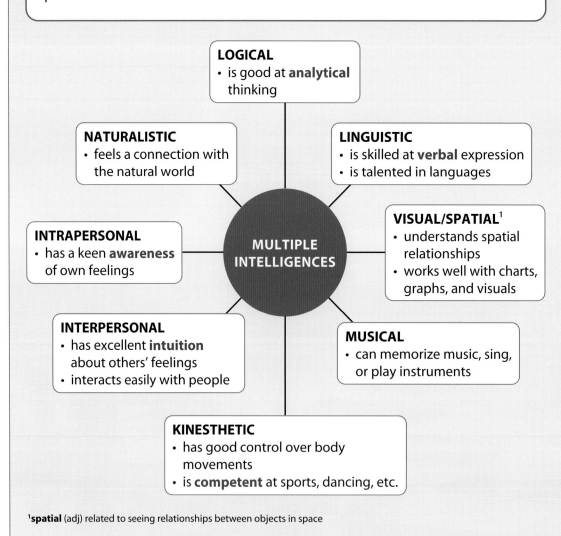

LOGICAL
- is good at **analytical** thinking

NATURALISTIC
- feels a connection with the natural world

LINGUISTIC
- is skilled at **verbal** expression
- is talented in languages

INTRAPERSONAL
- has a keen **awareness** of own feelings

MULTIPLE INTELLIGENCES

VISUAL/SPATIAL[1]
- understands spatial relationships
- works well with charts, graphs, and visuals

INTERPERSONAL
- has excellent **intuition** about others' feelings
- interacts easily with people

MUSICAL
- can memorize music, sing, or play instruments

KINESTHETIC
- has good control over body movements
- is **competent** at sports, dancing, etc.

[1]**spatial** (adj) related to seeing relationships between objects in space

B Write each word in blue from exercise A next to its definition.

1. _____ (n) knowledge that something exists

2. _____ (n) an idea or theory

3. _____ (adj) tending to unfairly favor one (thing, group, etc.) over another

4. _____ (adj) existing in reality or as a fact

5. _____ (n) a person's sense of their own value

6. _____ (adj) related to words and their use

7. _____ (adj) using logical reasoning; logical

8. _____ (adj) having the skill necessary to do something

9. _____ (n) knowing something by feeling

10. _____ (n) the support or foundation for an idea

See Word Families in the Appendix.

VOCABULARY SKILL   Adjective Suffixes –al, –tial, and –ical

The suffixes –al, –tial, and –ical are used to create adjectives from nouns.

- With many nouns, the suffix –al is added directly with no changes in spelling.

  logic**al**   nutrition**al**   verb**al**

- With some nouns, adding –al or -tial involves slight changes in spelling.

  concept**ual**   bene**ficial**   substan**tial**

- Some adjectives are formed by adding the suffix –ical with other spelling changes.

  analy**tical**   hypothe**tical**   ecolog**ical**

C Complete each question with the correct form of the word in parentheses. Use the suffix –al, –tial, or –ical. Use a dictionary as needed.

1. Which of your _____ (education) experiences has been most useful to you?

2. Do you have a _____ (mathematics) mind?

3. Which of your teachers has been the most _____ (influence) in your life?

4. Do you prefer books that are _____ (history) or ones that are _____ (biography)?

5. What is one _____ (practice) strategy you use when preparing for a test?

6. Do you like to drink black, green, or _____ (herb) tea while you study, or something else?

7. Which recent _____ (technology) advances are you interested in?

8. What do you think it means to be a _____ (vision) learner?

D **PERSONALIZE** Work with a partner. Take turns asking and answering the questions in exercise C.

A Listening A History of Intelligence

Critical Thinking **A** **PREDICT** You are going to hear a lecture about the history of intelligence. Discuss the questions with a partner.

1. How long ago do you think scientific research into intelligence began?
2. What do you think are some methods of measuring intelligence?
3. How might assigning an intelligence score to a child affect him or her?

B **MAIN IDEAS** Watch or listen to the lecture. Match the people and concepts with the descriptions. 🔊 ▶

1. _____ Sir Francis Galton
2. _____ Charles Spearman
3. _____ Alfred Binet
4. _____ IQ
5. _____ Howard Gardner
6. _____ Animal intelligence
7. _____ Artificial intelligence

a. is measured using practical puzzles.
b. can perceive its environment and act by itself.
c. measured intelligence as mental speed.
d. developed the theory of multiple intelligences.
e. proposed a "g" factor based on several abilities.
f. designed a test to find students who needed help.
g. was associated with success but also has had critics.

C **DETAILS** Listen to part of the lecture. Choose the correct answer. 🔊

1. Spearman believed the "g" factor was based on _____, math, and spatial skills.
   a. spelling
   b. verbal
   c. analytical

2. Alfred Binet developed a test with the goal of finding _____.
   a. intelligent children
   b. brain-damaged children
   c. children who needed help learning

3. IQ is your _____ divided by your actual age, multiplied by 100.
   a. mental age
   b. grade
   c. math ability

4. An IQ score from _____ is considered average.
   a. 80 to 90
   b. 90 to 109
   c. 100 to 110

5. Criticism of putting students with similar IQs together began _____.
   a. in the 1970s
   b. in the 1960s
   c. when IQ testing started

6. Teachers who expect less of students with lower IQs might be satisfied with _____.
   a. low IQ scores
   b. lazy students
   c. lower performance

7. Children who know their IQs are lower than others' might _____.
   a. get a negative self-image
   b. feel relief
   c. tell their parents

8. IQ could be biased in favor of people from _____.
   a. good schools
   b. intelligent families
   c. Western cultures

D **FOCUSED LISTENING** Complete the sentences with the words or expressions you hear. What do these expressions signal? 🔊

1. But, Spearman thought this "g" factor _____ a combination of several abilities, including verbal, math, and spatial skills.

2. This could _____ teachers being satisfied with low performance.

3. Also, if children realized their IQs were low, it might _____ a negative self-image.

4. This could _____ them not to try their hardest—or even to give up.

CRITICAL THINKING   Identify Premises and Conclusions

A simple argument has a premise and a conclusion. A premise is a claim or assumption, and a conclusion is a judgment based on the premise. It is what the person wants you to believe. Together, a premise and a conclusion form an argument.

Premises are often signaled by *since* or *because*.

premise   conclusion
Since *it might result in a negative self-image, a child shouldn't be told their IQ is low*

Conclusions are often signaled by *so*, *that's why*, *which is why*, or *therefore*.

premise   conclusion
People with a positive self-image tend to be successful; **therefore,** *we should help build children's self-esteem.*

Note that the conclusion can sometimes come before the premise.

conclusion   premise
A child shouldn't be told their IQ is low **because** *it might result in a negative self-image.*

It's important to be able to identify the premise and conclusion in order to judge whether an argument is valid.

E Listen to the sentences. Write *P* beside the premise and *C* beside the conclusion. 🔊

Critical Thinking

1. a. _____ Some students need extra support in the classroom.
   b. _____ A test should be given to identify slower learners' needs.

2. a. _____ She is more likely to have career success.
   b. _____ She has a high IQ.

3. a. _____ The teacher didn't encourage the students to do better.
   b. _____ She knew their IQ scores were low.

4. a. _____ IQ is too narrow a concept.
   b. _____ Howard Gardner proposed his theory of multiple intelligences.

F Work with a partner. Come up with TWO or THREE of your own arguments containing a premise and a conclusion. Then share them with the class.

A Speaking

> ## SPEAKING SKILL   Express Causal Relationships
>
> There are many ways to express causal, or cause and effect, relationships:
>
> | Cause before effect | Cause after effect |
> |---|---|
> | *...result(s) in...* | *...is/are a/the result of...* |
> | *...lead(s) to...* | *...is/are due to...* |
> | *...is/are responsible for...* | *...result(s) from...* |
>
> | cause | effect |
> |---|---|
>
> *Damage to the left brain often **results in** speech problems.*
>
> | effect | cause |
> |---|---|
>
> *His speech problems **are the result of** damage to the left brain.*
>
> We also use *if* and *when* clauses to show cause and effect.
>
> | cause | effect |
> |---|---|
>
> *If the left brain is damaged, a person often has speech problems.*

A Work with a partner. Use the sentence starters to make sentences.

Causes first	Effects first
Playing a lot of online games . . .	Headaches . . .
Reading a lot of books . . .	Dental problems . . .
Going to the gym frequently . . .	Good grades . . .
If you work very hard . . .	Car accidents . . .
Improving your English . . .	Peace of mind . . .
Bad economic conditions . . .	Forest fires . . .
When you get a college degree . . .	Having a successful career . . .

B Work in a small group. Discuss possible causes and effects for each of the situations related to psychology and write them in the chart.

> *Being self-confident is usually a result of having successful or positive experiences.*
> *I think it can lead to more leadership opportunities.*

Situations	Causes	Effects
1. Being self-confident		
2. Computer game addiction		
3. A positive outlook on life		
4. Anxiety		
5. Strong social connections		

▲ A full moon over Tokyo, Japan

C **EVALUATE** Work with a partner. Discuss these popular ideas related to psychology and the mind. Choose T if you think they are *True*, F if you think they are *False*, and U if you're *Unsure*. Critical Thinking

1. Playing classical music to babies increases their level of intelligence.   T   F   U
2. Human beings normally use only 10 percent of their brain.   T   F   U
3. People with opposite personalities find each other attractive.   T   F   U
4. When the moon is full, there is an increase in crime and crazy behavior.   T   F   U
5. Repeating new words is the most effective way to learn them.   T   F   U
6. If you let yourself occasionally show a little anger, you will avoid getting very angry.   T   F   U

D Now read the explanations below and check your answers from exercise C. With your partner, discuss any facts that surprise you.

1. Two recent studies determined that playing classical music to babies produces no clear measurable effect on their intelligence.
2. Although the entire brain isn't used all the time, modern brain imaging techniques have shown that all parts of the brain are regularly active and no part is left unused.
3. Research has shown that people are more often attracted to people with whom they share various similarities.
4. Physics tells us that the pull of the moon has almost no effect on our brains, and studies show that there is no more crime during full moons than at other times.
5. Research has shown that effective vocabulary learning is the result of encountering new vocabulary in various meaningful ways and not the result of simple repetition.
6. Recent scientific studies show that people who allow themselves to show their anger actually become angrier, which leads to negative consequences.

E **ANALYZE** Work in a small group. Read about four psychological experiments. Discuss the question below each one giving reasons for your answer.

1. Participants are shown a short video of six people passing basketballs back and forth. Three of the people are wearing white, and three are wearing black. The participants are asked to count the number of passes between the people wearing white. At one point during the video, a person dressed in a gorilla costume walks through the people passing basketballs.

   Question: How do you think the participants reacted?

2. In a subway station in Washington, D.C., world-famous violinist Joshua Bell played his 3.5 million-dollar violin during rush hour for people walking by. He had recently played in Boston at $100 a ticket, but in the station, he put his open violin case in front of him to collect donations.

   Question: How do you think the people in the station reacted?

3. In a 150-seat movie theater, all the seats except two in the middle are taken by people who look like members of a motorcycle gang. They are, in fact, paid actors. A real couple walks into the theater. The experiment is repeated with several couples.

   Question: What do you think most couples did?

4. Three groups of people were given simple word problems. Group 1 had words like *polite*, *patient*, and *courtesy*. Group 2 had words like *bother, disturb*, and *bold*. A third group had random words. They were then told to go talk with the experimenter, but they found him deep in conversation with someone.

   Question: How do you think the behavior of the people in the groups differed as they waited to talk to the experimenter?

F **SYNTHESIZE** Now listen to the results of the experiments and take notes. What conclusions can you make about human psychology based on each experiment? Discuss your ideas with the class. 🔊

G Work with a partner. Discuss the questions about intelligence.

1. Who is a person you think is intelligent? Why?
2. Do you think intelligence is just one factor, or are there multiple intelligences?
3. Which animals do you think are the smartest?
4. Are people with higher intelligence happier than those with lower intelligence?
5. Besides studying, what can you do to prepare yourself to do well on a test?
6. Would you volunteer to have a chip put into your brain to increase your intelligence?

Your Memory Under Stress

time constraints (n) time limits
set off (v) to cause something to happen, such as an alarm ringing

hormones (n) substances that control processes in the body
combat (v) to fight or work against

▲ Aggressive animals can cause stress.

A Watch the video. Complete the main ideas with the words you hear. ▶

   1. The video begins with a game requiring you to _____ the location of images.

   2. Next, there is an explanation of how the game was made to feel more _____ .

   3. Then, Ben Bailey talks about the _____ of being nervous in front of an audience.

   4. After that, there is a description of the stress _____ triggered by the amygdala.

B Watch the video again and answer the questions. ▶

   1. What are the three items you are asked to find in the game? _____
     _____

   2. What percent of those surveyed couldn't find all three items? _____

   3. What body part feels bigger under the stress of public speaking? _____

   4. What do the hormones in your blood do to your senses?
     _____

C In lesson B, you will hear a conversation about memory. Ask a partner these questions.

   1. How many items did you match in the memory game in the video? Was it difficult?

   2. Do you think a good memory is as important as it used to be now that nearly everyone has access to the Internet?

A **MEANING FROM CONTEXT** Read and listen to the blog post. Pay attention to the words in blue. Then match the letter of the words in blue with their definitions below. 🔊

THE ANIMAL MIND

Do animals think and feel like we do? In the early 20th century, British psychologist C.L. Morgan claimed that animal behavior could only be interpreted in terms of lower mental faculties[1]. This view (a) **stemmed from** the ideas of 17th-century thinkers. At that time, it was (b) **customary** to see animals as living machines. The animal mind was seen as (c) **inferior** to ours in every way.

There has since been a (d) **radical** change in the way scientists view the animal mind. We no longer see all animal behaviors as (e) **innate**. Animals can learn. There have been (f) **unprecedented** discoveries of language abilities in parrots and apes. In one experiment, chimpanzees demonstrated (g) **superior** memory skills; they were able to (h) **memorize** numbers on a screen faster than their human opponents.

As scientists' understanding of the animal mind continues to (i) **deepen**, it is becoming clear that various characteristics once thought to be uniquely human are not. This is leading some to ask serious (j) **ethical** questions about the treatment of animals and their rights.

[1] **faculty** (n) power, capability

1. _____ (adj) accepted as usual practice
2. _____ (v) to expand or make stronger
3. _____ (adj) related to good and bad behavior
4. _____ (adj) less effective
5. _____ (adj) natural, not learned

6. _____ (v) to learn and remember
7. _____ (adj) extreme or severe
8. _____ (v) came from
9. _____ (adj) more effective, better
10. _____ (adj) never seen before

B Match each word or phrase with its **opposite** meaning.

1. _____ unprecedented
2. _____ superior
3. _____ customary
4. _____ stem from
5. _____ radical
6. _____ ethical
7. _____ inferior
8. _____ deepen
9. _____ innate
10. _____ memorize

a. strange or unusual
b. of lower status or importance
c. having happened before
d. dishonest; immoral
e. forget
f. decrease; weaken; lighten
g. of higher status or importance
h. acquired or learned
i. modest or balanced
j. end in

C Complete the chart with the correct form of each word. Use a dictionary if necessary.

	Verb	Noun	Adjective
1.			customary
2.	deepen		
3.	– – – – – – –		inferior
4.	memorize		
5.			radical
6.	– – – – – – –		superior

D Choose the word that forms the best collocation with the word in bold. Search the Internet for collocation dictionaries if you need help.

1. Research involving people must follow strict **ethical** (guidelines / assignments / indications).
2. The jacket was of **inferior** (character / feature / quality), so it fell apart when I washed it.
3. Human babies have an **innate** (ability / habit / performance) to learn languages.
4. The problem was so serious that it required a **radical** (reflection / solving / solution).
5. He has trouble making friends because of his **superior** (sentiment / attitude / mood).
6. Among her colleagues, a handshake is the **customary** (addressing / greeting / receiving).

E Work with a partner. Discuss the questions.

1. What are some **innate** abilities in animals?
2. What makes one school **superior** to another?
3. What kinds of pets are **customary** where you live?
4. What **ethical** questions do doctors sometimes face?

B Listening The Brain and Memory

Critical Thinking **A** **ACTIVATE**   You are going to hear a conversation between two college friends about memory. Discuss the questions with a partner.

1. Why might two college students be talking about memory?
2. Would you say your memory is above or below average? Explain.
3. What do you know about how human memory works?

B **MAIN IDEAS**   Listen to the conversation. Check the topics you hear discussed. TWO are not discussed. 🔊

1. ☐ a condition that gives people incredibly accurate memory ability
2. ☐ a part of the brain that is key to long-term memory formation
3. ☐ a disease that slowly destroys a person's memory
4. ☐ a man who had part of his brain removed
5. ☐ two types of memory called declarative and procedural
6. ☐ a drug that can greatly increase a person's memory
7. ☐ a method that can improve your memory

LISTENING SKILL   Recognize Definitions

When speakers use words that they think their audience might not know, they often provide a definition. Listen for phrases like these:

> A mnemonic device **is a term that describes** a method to strengthen memory.
> A mnemonic device **is the name of** a method to strengthen memory.

Sometimes a definition comes immediately after the term in an adjective clause or an appositive:

> The fear response is regulated by the amygdala, **which is a primitive part of the brain.**
> The fear response is regulated by the amygdala, **a primitive part of the brain.**

In conversation, a definition is often introduced using *In other words* or *I mean.*

> I had a sensation of déjà vu. **I mean** the feeling of having had the same experience before.

C   Listen to excerpts from the conversation. Complete the sentences with the words you hear. 🔊

1. _____ describes a rare memory condition.

2. _____ a part of the brain that's really important for memory function.

3. A short-term memory is formed in the cerebral cortex. _____ the layer of cells around the outside of the brain.

4. Not only that, but he also helped demonstrate the difference between declarative memory and procedural memory, _____ two distinct types of memory.

D **DETAILS** Listen to the last part of the conversation and complete the outline. Write no more than THREE words in each blank. 🔊

1. The method of loci

    A. Began in ancient Greece; a way to remember [1]_____

    B. How it works

        a. Picture a path that [2]_____.

        b. Look at a list of words and [3]_____ for each.

        c. Put those [4]_____ at places along the path.

        d. Later, you [5]_____ walking along the path.

        e. The images will [6]_____ the words.

PRONUNCIATION **Recognize Reduced Function Words**

🔊 Function words show grammatical relationships in a sentence. They include prepositions, pronouns, possessive adjectives, and articles. Function words are not usually stressed. Often, the vowel sounds are reduced to a schwa sound (/ə/), and certain consonants (*h, r, d*) may be dropped. Notice the reduced pronunciation of the underlined function words.

Prepositions:	*We went <u>to</u> the center <u>of</u> town <u>for</u> the lesson.*
Pronouns/Possessive Adjectives:	*Did <u>you</u> give <u>him his</u> award for winning <u>your</u> contest?*
Conjunctions:	*She writes well <u>and</u> studies hard <u>but</u> has a poor memory.*
Articles:	*Give me <u>the</u> test again. I have <u>an</u> hour.*

E Underline the function words that you think are reduced in these sentences. Then listen and repeat to check your answers. 🔊

1. It's a part of the brain that's really important for memory function.
2. I have a huge history exam next week, and I have to memorize a ton of information.
3. Having a good memory isn't an innate skill, you know.
4. In your mind, you need to imagine a path that you know well.

F Practice the conversation with a partner. Reduce the function words. Then switch roles.

A: Hey! How are you doing?

B: Um, I'm a little depressed. Can you tell?

A: Yeah, I knew something or other was wrong. You know, I know a great doctor. Do you want her number? I highly recommend her!

B: No, it's nothing to worry about. It always happens in January and February.

A: Oh, the winter blues! My mom tends to get that. But she sits under a special lamp for half an hour a day and says it really helps.

B: Really? What's her email? I want to ask her about her lamp and maybe buy one, too.

B Speaking

A RECALL Work with a partner. Each person tries to memorize one of the lists of words in one minute. Then close your book and say the words to your partner in the correct order. Record how many words you were able to recall.

Word list A		Word list B	
1. committee	6. mountain	1. weekend	6. profit
2. married	7. pollution	2. goal	7. laboratory
3. roof	8. midnight	3. urban	8. purple
4. flour	9. flame	4. fork	9. advertise
5. friendship	10. printer	5. anniversary	10. battery

B APPLY Now you will apply the method of loci that you heard about in the listening. Follow the instructions.

1. Use your partner's list from exercise A. Think of an image to represent each word. Draw a simple sketch of each image beside the word to help you remember the image.

2. Imagine a path you know well and choose ten locations along it. It can be a path in your home, city or town, school, or classroom.

3. Imagine following the path and placing the images in order at each location. Repeat this three times.

4. Close your books. Imagine following the path again and tell your partner each word represented by the images.

5. Did the method of loci improve your results? Discuss with your partner.

C PERSONALIZE Work in a small group. Discuss the questions.

1. What are your earliest childhood memories?

2. How do you use technology to assist your memory?

3. Have you ever had déjà vu, the feeling that you have already experienced something although you can't remember where or when?

4. What techniques do you use to help you remember English vocabulary?

5. What do you do when you meet someone whose name you have forgotten?

GRAMMAR FOR SPEAKING   Subject-Verb Agreement with Quantifiers

When using quantifiers, be sure to check that the subject agrees with the verb.

- With *all, a lot, some, a few, both,* and *most + of +* a plural count noun, use a plural verb.

    Some of the **methods** <u>work</u> surprisingly well.
    All of the **questions** <u>were</u> incredibly difficult.

- With *all, a lot, some,* and *most + of +* a noncount noun, use a singular verb.

    Most of the **information** <u>was</u> inaccurate.
    A lot of the **advice** from experts <u>is</u> difficult to follow.

- With *one, none, each, neither,* and *every one + of +* a plural count noun, use a singular verb.

    One of the most famous **case studies** <u>was</u> in 1953, in Connecticut.

D Work with a partner. Take turns using quantifiers from the Grammar for Speaking box to make sentences with the following topics.

> *Some of the parrots I've seen in YouTube videos speak surprisingly well.*

abilities that animals have	methods for memory improvement	my friends
learning styles	the people I know	my memories
standardized English tests	the students in the class	advice from my advisor
the lessons in this unit	my parents	information about the brain

The method of loci, which involves imagining a path, creating images for words, and picturing them on the path, can improve your memory.

Review

How well can you . . . ?	Very well.	OK.	I need improvement.
use the key vocabulary	☐	☐	☐
use correct subject-verb agreement with quantifiers	☐	☐	☐
express causal relationships	☐	☐	☐

A **VOCABULARY** Say the sentences. Replace the words in bold with a unit vocabulary item.

1. To become a writer you should have excellent **word-related** skills.
2. On Valentine's Day, it is **accepted practice** to give candy to someone you care about.
3. My brother is **skilled** at both basketball and football.
4. I believe that eating meat is wrong from **a moral** perspective.
5. I had trouble understanding the **ideas** we learned in class today.
6. Our company's success **is due to** the hard work of our employees.
7. I got the latest version of the software, but the previous one was **better**.
8. Running a marathon in under two hours was **never done before**.

B **GRAMMAR** Complete the sentences with a verb in the singular or plural form.

1. Every one of that shop's ice cream flavors _____ delicious.
2. Neither of my parents _____ ever been to China.
3. None of the students _____ class to be canceled tomorrow.
4. A few of my classes _____ held online this semester.
5. Both of my sisters _____ careful track of their spending.
6. Most of the people in the building _____ with the recycling rules.

C **SPEAKING SKILL** Use an expression from the Speaking Skill box to show a causal relationship for each topic.

1. Careless driving . . .
2. Many forest fires . . .
3. Too much salt . . .
4. A poor memory . . .
5. Headaches and eye problems . . .
6. The common cold and the flu . . .

RE-ASSESS What skills or language still need improvement?

Final Tasks

OPTION 1 Discuss your learning style

A Psychology tells us that different people prefer to learn in different ways. Look at these seven learning styles. Which do you prefer? Choose Y for *Yes*, N for *No*, or NS for *Not Sure*.

Learning Style	Description	Preferred		
1. visual	take in information best by seeing it	Y	N	NS
2. audio	receive information best through sound	Y	N	NS
3. verbal	focus best on words—written, spoken, or recorded	Y	N	NS
4. physical	eager to move the body when learning	Y	N	NS
5. logical	like numbers, rules, logic, and solving problems	Y	N	NS
6. social	prefer group work and interacting with others	Y	N	NS
7. solitary	focused and productive in individual activities	Y	N	NS

B Work in a small group. Compare your learning style preferences from exercise A. For each group member, consider their preferred learning styles and discuss ideas for studying effectively.

> A: *Since Sung-min is a visual learner, I think studying grammar charts would be a good idea.*
> B: *Yes, and for vocabulary, flash cards with pictures might be good.*

OPTION 2 Give a presentation on "study/learning hacks"

A **MODEL** Listen to a presentation about "study hacks"—clever ways to help you study more effectively. Take notes in the chart. 🔊

See Unit 9 Rubric in the Appendix.

Study hack	Description	Benefits
1.		
2.		
3.		
4.		

B **ANALYZE THE MODEL** Listen again. Answer these questions about the model. 🔊

1. How does the speaker open the presentation?

   _____

2. How is the presentation organized?

   _____

3. What cause-and-effect expressions does the speaker use?

   _____

4. How does the speaker close the presentation?

   _____

C **RESEARCH** Work with a partner. Go online and research FOUR "study hacks" or "learning hacks." Take notes in the chart describing the hacks and their benefits.

Study/Learning hack	Description	Benefits
1.		
2.		
3.		
4.		

D **PRACTICE AND PRESENT** Practice with your partner. Make sure to include some cause-and-effect expressions when you talk about the benefits. Give each other feedback before you present. Then present your study or learning hacks to the class.

PRESENTATION SKILL **Use Gestures and Facial Expressions**

Gestures can be very useful in a presentation. Keep your hands and body mainly in a neutral position until you want to make a gesture. Here are some appropriate gestures:

- Use your hands and fingers to show size, speed, location, or numbers.
- Raise or lower your shoulders to express doubt or sadness, raise or open your arms to show strength or openness, and use your face to show a variety of expressions.
- Raise your hand and say, "Raise your hand if . . ." to get your audience involved.

🔊 **ONLINE** Online, facial expressions and gestures are possible, but they might be difficult for your audience to see. You can use emojis to express yourself on most online platforms. There are a lot of emojis to choose from for facial expressions and gestures.

Chef Joseph Yoon founded Brooklyn Bugs in New York with the goal of increasing appreciation of edible insects through education. Here we see crickets, Manchurian scorpions, Japanese hornets, black ants, Japanese wasps, silkworm pupae, palm weevils, and locusts from his collection.

IN THIS UNIT, YOU WILL:

- Watch or listen to a lecture about genetically modified foods
- Watch a video about food waste
- Listen to a conversation about food prices
- Discuss ways of saving money on food
  OR Have a debate about a food-related issue

THINK AND DISCUSS:

1. The people at Brooklyn Bugs call themselves "Edible Insect Ambassadors." Why might insects need people to promote them in a positive way?

2. How would you feel about eating the insects in the photo?

3. Why might eating insects be part of the future of food?

Read the information and discuss the questions.

1. The greens in the photo require 95 percent less water than outdoor plants. But what other resources are needed for indoor farming?
2. Which of the statistics about water, energy, and food surprises you most?
3. What are some ways to reduce your own food waste?

Water, Energy, and Food

The population of the planet continues to increase. It's expected that by 2050, our food demand will increase by 60%. In order to feed the world, we need creative solutions for growing food that will lead to: less pollution, less energy use, less water consumption, and less food waste.

70%
of freshwater resources are used for agriculture

30%
of food produced to feed people is wasted or lost

23%
of total net greenhouse gas emissions are created by agriculture-related activities

30%
of global energy is used for food production

The world's largest indoor vertical farm, operated by Aerofarms, is in Newark, New Jersey, USA. It grows vegetables year-round on shelves made from recycled plastic bottles. Aerofarms says they get 390 times more vegetables than outside farms.

866.610.BLUE 51482

A Vocabulary

A **MEANING FROM CONTEXT** Read and listen to the article about the world's food supply. Notice each word in blue and think about its meaning. 🔊

WHY PUT SEEDS IN A BANK?

The world's population is now over eight billion people and growing, and the pressure on world food suppliers is more **intense** than ever. Many large farms now grow only a small number of crops, such as corn, wheat, soybeans, or rice. Scientists **alter** the **genes** of some of these crops to make them more productive. This type of agriculture is known as "monoculture," and it is practiced on a large **proportion** of farmland around the world. This highly productive farming method has given us a global crop **surplus** in the past. But it has also greatly reduced the number of vegetable varieties grown by farmers. Some have even disappeared.

When farmers grow a large variety of crops with different **traits**, a single disease can't do much damage. However, when the crops are all the same, it's possible for one disease to destroy them all. If this happened to any of today's popular monoculture crops, it would be a disaster for the food supply.

To save vegetable varieties from extinction, many experts **advocate** storing seeds in seed banks. At last count, there were over 1700 seed banks around the world. If a disease ever destroys all the monoculture crops, the seeds inside these seed banks would be **invaluable**. They could be **distributed** to farmers to replace ruined crops with healthy and productive ones **resistant** to the disease.

B Write the correct form of each word in blue from exercise A next to its definition.

1. _____ (n) part of a total amount or number

2. _____ (v) to deliver or give out

3. _____ (adj) high in energy or degree

4. _____ (adj) extremely useful

5. _____ (n) an amount greater than what is needed

6. _____ (n) characteristics passed on from generation to generation

7. _____ (adj) having the strength to fight against a threat

8. _____ (v) to modify

9. _____ (v) to publicly recommend something

10. _____ (n) part of a cell passed between generations that controls characteristics

VOCABULARY SKILL Concordancers

You can find collocations by searching online for "concordancer," choosing one of the options, and then entering a word or phrase. The concordancer will then search its database and present all the sentences containing that word or phrase. If you examine the words to the right and left, you'll be able to see which words frequently occur with it. Studying these concordance lines will help you use words correctly.

C Read these sample lines from a concordancer and answer the questions.

to government resources proved **invaluable** to private sector corporations
portable stoves that have proven **invaluable** for preparing food in environments
those early years of orchestra participation were **invaluable** to her career in the

1. What verb is a strong collocation with *invaluable*? _____

2. What prepositions are used after *invaluable*? _____

the finance office reported a budget **surplus** mainly due to reduced spending
second year in a row that we have a **surplus** of wheat, which we can use to
export activity has led to a large trade **surplus** of more than 10 billion dollars

3. What preposition is a strong collocation with *surplus*? _____

4. What nouns form collocations with *surplus*? _____

companies that will widely **distribute** the movie in Asia and North America
contract allows us to legally **distribute** free software to customers who need
should be careful to fairly **distribute** food aid to individuals and families who

5. What adverbs are used with *distribute*? _____

6. What preposition is a strong collocation with *distribute*? _____

some diseases that will become **resistant** to previously effective treatments
so it seems they have an attitude **resistant** to any new approaches to the problem
are known to have become more **resistant** to disease than other GM corn varieties

7. What preposition is a strong collocation with *resistant*? _____

8. What verb is a strong collocation with *resistant*? _____

D PERSONALIZE Complete the statements and discuss your answers with a partner.

1. The most **intense** weather I have ever experienced was . . .

2. I think **altering** the **genes** of plants . . .

3. A large **proportion** of my friends . . .

4. My best personality **traits** are . . .

A | Listening   Genetically Modified Foods

Critical Thinking   **A**   **PREDICT**   You are going to listen to a lecture about genetically modified (GM) foods. With a partner, predict the answers to these questions.

1. How long have humans been modifying the genes of crops and animals?
2. Are GM foods currently available in supermarkets?
3. About how many GM food crops are currently being grown in the world?
4. What are are some concerns people might have about GM foods?

B   **MAIN IDEAS**   Watch or listen to the lecture. Check the FOUR main topics the speaker discusses. 🔊 ▶

1. ☐ Genetic modification past and present
2. ☐ GM plants and animals on the market
3. ☐ Illnesses caused by eating GM foods
4. ☐ Concerns people have about GM foods
5. ☐ Why some countries ban GM foods
6. ☐ Genetic modification success stories

NOTE-TAKING SKILL   **Use the Cornell Method**

The Cornell method of note-taking is a three-step note-taking method. Your paper should be set up with a narrow column on the left to label main points, a wide column on the right for taking detailed notes, and section at the bottom for a summary.

Step 1: Take detailed notes as you listen.

Step 2: After listening, write main points or questions for the different parts of your notes in the column to the left of your notes.

Step 3: Write a short summary of the notes at the bottom of your paper.

The advantage of the Cornell method is that it keeps your notes organized and turns them into an efficient study sheet.

▼ The AquAdvantage salmon (in back) and a non-GM Atlantic salmon

C Listen again and complete the notes section below. Write only ONE word or number for each answer. You will complete the summary section in exercise D. 🔊

GM FOODS

Main points	Notes
Genetic modification	Genetic modification = altering ¹_____ of plants, animals. Done for 1000s of yrs. Selective breeding = choosing plants or animals w/wanted traits, breeding them to strengthen traits. Genetic modification = ²_____, more exact way to get wanted traits. Inserting genes from diff. species into others also possible.
GM foods on the market	GM foods sold since mid- ³_____. 90% soy, corn, sugar beets GM. 22 crops in 41 countries. More productive, resistant to insects and disease, last longer, ⁴_____ better. Only couple of animals so far: One is a ⁵_____. U.S. gov. says safe to eat. 20 animals waiting for gov. OK.
Concerns about GM foods	People think GM foods aren't natural. Worried about future ⁶_____. If GM salmon escape ➔ affect natural salmon. Large companies could control food supply, prioritize profit over people. Some groups have ⁷_____ GM crops.
GM crop success stories	India: GM cotton ➔ Resistant to bollworm. Now farmers grow 4 ⁸_____ as much. Nearly all cotton in India now GM. Africa: GM corn ➔ 100+ varieties sent to 13 countries. Needs less ⁹_____. Now produce 20–30% more. Hawaii: Virus in papaya found in 1950s ➔ production fell ¹⁰_____ by 1990. Hawaiians developed GM virus-resistant papaya. GM papaya now ~90% of all papaya grown in Hawaii.

Summary

Genetic ¹_____ has a history of thousands of years. The old way was selective breeding. Now, newer genetic modification ²_____ give plants and ³_____ wanted traits. Modern GM foods have been sold in supermarkets since the mid-1990s. 22 GM ⁴_____ are grown in 41 countries. Only a couple of GM animals have been ⁵_____ by the government. People are ⁶_____ about the future consequences of producing GM food. They worry large companies might get too much ⁷_____ over the food supply and prioritize ⁸_____ over people. GM success stories include insect-resistant cotton in India, drought-resistant corn in Africa, and virus-resistant papaya in Hawaii.

D Now complete the Summary section in the notes in exercise C with words from the box.

approved	concerned	crops	techniques
animals	control	modification	profits

A Speaking

SPEAKING SKILL   Concede and Refute

In a discussion or debate, you want to be able to defend or support your position. You also need to listen carefully to the other speaker. When they make a good point, you can agree, or **concede**, that the point is a good one. Then you can disagree, or **refute**, by providing evidence against it.

opponent's point

A: *Research shows that GM crops are perfectly safe to eat.*

concession   refutation

B: *While that may be true, the research has been limited.*

Here are some ways to concede and then refute and return to your position.

You have a good point, but…

Although I agree that …, I would argue that…

I see what you're saying; however, ….

A Work with a partner. Partner A reads the A statements. Partner B concedes and refutes. Then Partner B reads the B statements and Partner A concedes and refutes.

A: *Some computer scientists believe AI will become smarter than humans someday.*

B: *Although I agree that AI is smart, it will never equal humans in terms of emotional intelligence.*

A statements:

1. Education should be free for both public school students and college students.
2. Violent video games should be banned.
3. Students should be allowed to use cell phones in class.

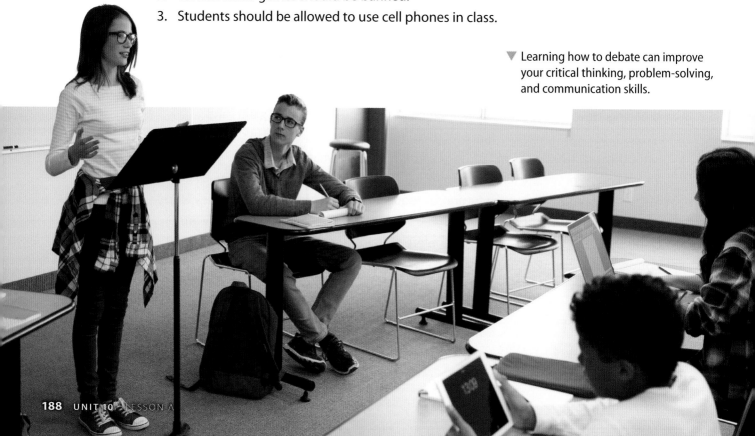

▼ Learning how to debate can improve your critical thinking, problem-solving, and communication skills.

B statements:

1. School uniforms should be required from elementary school to high school.
2. All cars made in the future should be self-driving.
3. Nuclear energy should be our primary source of electricity.

B Work with a partner and take turns making statements with the sentence starters below. Your partner either agrees with your idea or concedes and refutes.

1. A lot of people are worried that robots will . . .
2. Critics of fossil fuels warn that . . .
3. Children who grow up speaking two languages are . . .
4. Advocates for animal rights say that zoos . . .
5. Conservationists warn that . . .
6. Supporters of plastic surgery believe that . . .
7. Vegetarians feel that . . .
8. People who grow monoculture crops are concerned that . . .

C Work with a partner. Role-play a conversation at a grocery store between roommates. Suggest the grocery items in the chart below. Take turns giving your opinions using the positives and negatives and your own ideas.

A: How about we get some of this fruit juice? It looks really fresh.

B: I'm not sure. Experts say it has as much sugar as soda.

A: Yeah, some juice does. But I'm pretty sure that it contains a lot of vitamins.

Grocery item	Positives	Negatives
fruit juice	contains a lot of vitamins	can have as much sugar as soda
tomatoes	may fight some kinds of cancer	tomato farm workers not always well paid
GM salmon	safe to eat	might escape into the environment
beef	high in protein	raising beef often harms the environment
organic apples	100 percent natural	go bad faster than conventional apples
chocolate	good for your heart	you can become addicted to it

D Discuss the questions with a partner. Support your answers with reasons.

1. If a natural vegetable and a GM variety were both available in your supermarket, which would you choose and why?
2. The U.S. government has recently said that a California company's laboratory-grown chicken is safe to eat. It is made without killing chickens. Would you be interested in trying it?
3. The World Economic Forum recommends people eat more insects. Would you like to add them to your regular diet?
4. The online food delivery business is growing very fast. Do you think this is a positive or negative trend?
5. If you had to choose just one type of food to eat for the rest of your life, what would you choose and why?
6. What concerns do you have about the future of food?

CRITICAL THINKING Categorize

When you categorize, you group things with similar characteristics together into the same category. For example, food can be categorized as meat, fruit, vegetable, dairy, or grain. Once you understand the characteristics of each group, you can put items in the appropriate category. Categorizing is an important learning skill because organized information is easier to understand and remember.

Critical Thinking | **E** Read about three methods of breeding or growing and modifying crops. Then decide if the crops and animals described below were created by selective breeding (SB), interspecies cross (IC), or genetic modification (GM). Write the appropriate abbreviation. Then discuss your answers with a partner.

BREEDING BETTER CROPS

Selective breeding	Interspecies cross	Genetic modification
Good traits are identified in separate individuals of the same species, which are then bred to combine those traits.	Good traits are identified in members of different but somewhat similar species, which are then bred for those traits. This is also called *crossbreeding*.	Either a species' existing genes are modified or genes from one species are inserted into a different species to produce a new trait (e.g., inserting a gene from an insect-resistant tomato plant into a bean plant).

1. _____ The tangelo fruit is the result of breeding the grapefruit and the tangerine. It has characteristics of both species and is extremely popular.

2. _____ GloFish® are brightly colored red, green, and orange fish sold as pets. They were created by inserting genes from a colorful jellyfish into black and white zebrafish.

3. _____ Since the 1930s, the yield of corn plants has greatly increased because farmers have bred the most productive plants of the same species in each generation.

4. _____ To wipe out dangerous mosquito populations, scientists "programmed" their genes to make them die before becoming adults. The young bred from "programmed" and wild mosquitoes also die early.

5. _____ Wheat has been improving for over 10,000 years because farmers have selected the healthiest and largest plants of the species they planted to pass on their genetic characteristics to future generations.

6. _____ When two distinct but similar species of strawberry were bred, the wild South American strawberry and the North American strawberry, the result was the pineberry, a fruit that looks like a white strawberry but tastes like a pineapple.

Food-Waste Rebel

disposable (adj) created to be thrown away
commodity (n) a product that can be bought and sold

longevity (n) how long something can last
blemish (n) a small mark that harms the appearance

▲ National Geographic Explorer Tristram Stuart is creating a more sustainable food system. His organization collects food that would go to waste and uses it to cook free meals.

A Watch the video and read the statements. Choose T for *True* or F for *False*. ▶

1. The mountain of bread represents the food we eat.   T   F
2. People used to eat chicken less often than they do now.   T   F
3. Big corporations spend billions of dollars to make us eat less.   T   F
4. Stuart wishes fruit and vegetables on sale looked better.   T   F
5. Stuart wants us to demand markets stop wasting food.   T   F

B Watch again. Choose the correct answers. ▶

1. How much of the world's food is wasted each year?
   a. one quarter   b. one third   c. one half

2. What has happened to the price of food over the last 40 years?
   a. It's gone down.   b. It's gone up.   c. It hasn't changed.

3. How much more food do we buy than we need per week?
   a. 5 percent   b. 10–15 percent   c. 20–30 percent

4. What does the image of a tree being cut down represent?
   a. falling prices   b. clearing land for agriculture   c. wasting wood

C Discuss the questions with a partner.

1. Stuart says, "Food is land, food is forests . . ., food is water, food is labor, food is love." What do you think he means?
2. How can GM foods help increase the food supply and reduce waste?

A Read and check the words you already know. Look up those you don't know in a dictionary.

call for (v)	disastrous (adj)	exceed (v)	output (n)	scenario (n)
coincide (v)	evident (adj)	inadequate (adj)	restriction (n)	stick to (v phr)

B **MEANING FROM CONTEXT** Read the article and complete each sentence with the correct form of a word from exercise A. Then listen and check your answers. 🔊

THE NEXT "GREEN REVOLUTION"

For much of human history, farmers ¹_____ patterns of agriculture that weren't very efficient. Then came an increase in agricultural ²_____ in the late 1900s, which is sometimes referred to as the "Green Revolution." During this period, four important farming technologies ³_____ to allow agricultural production to move beyond the ⁴_____ that had held it back for centuries.

The four technologies are:
- irrigation, a technology that brings water to crops;
- chemical pesticides to help kill or control insects;
- fertilizers, which give plants what they need to grow; and
- development of smaller plants that produce as much food as larger plants.

Unfortunately, it has now become ⁵_____ that we can no longer depend on agricultural production rates to continue to increase as they have in the past. This puts us in a dangerous situation. The problem is the rising global population, which will most likely ⁶_____ nine billion by the year 2050. Many are now ⁷_____ a second "Green Revolution" that will help the world avoid a future nightmare ⁸_____ with excessively high food prices, ⁹_____ food supplies, and their ¹⁰_____ consequences.

To grow more food we will need innovative solutions, such as this hydroponic farm run by robots.

C Match the words with their definitions. Use a dictionary if needed.

1. _____ evident (adj)   a. to happen at the same time
2. _____ call for (v phr)   b. to go beyond
3. _____ coincide (v)   c. not enough
4. _____ exceed (v)   d. obvious
5. _____ inadequate (adj)   e. the amount of production
6. _____ restriction (n)   f. terrible
7. _____ output (n)   g. a situation
8. _____ stick to (v phr)   h. to demand
9. _____ scenario (n)   i. a limit
10. _____ disastrous (adj)   j. to continue doing

D Choose the best collocation for the word or phrase in bold. Use a dictionary or concordancer if necessary.

1. The funds for the seed program were (darkly / emptily / hopelessly) **inadequate**.

2. When we came home, it was (rapidly / urgently / immediately) **evident** we'd been robbed.

3. The winner shouted, "This **calls for** (celebrate / a celebration / celebrations)!"

4. During the drought, the government placed (sharp / severe / mean) **restrictions** on water use.

5. The merits of the plants **exceeded** (expected / expectations / expecting).

6. A flood destroying the crops would be a worst- (model / state / case) **scenario**.

7. The rabbits got into my garden with **disastrous** (conclusions / results / products).

8. The tribal ceremony **coincides** (with / as / to) the beginning of the corn harvest.

9. Multiple storms were the reason for the (low / bare / cheap) **output** of farms that year.

E With a partner, make sentences with FIVE collocations from exercise D.

> *The choice of restaurants in my neighborhood is hopelessly inadequate.*

F **PERSONALIZE** Discuss the questions with a partner.

1. Are you the type of person who **sticks to** something or gives up easily? Explain.
2. What kinds of **restrictions** has the government of your city or country **called for** in recent years and why?
3. Have you ever had a restaurant experience when the food, the service, or something else was **inadequate**? How about an experience that **exceeded** your expectations?
4. Does your taste in music **coincide** with your parents'?

Listening Rising Food Prices

Critical Thinking | **A** **ACTIVATE** Discuss the questions with a partner.

1. Study the bar chart. What are some possible reasons for the difference between the percentage of income spent on food in the United States and in Singapore and the other countries shown?

2. What percentage of your income do you or your family spend on food? Is the percentage increasing or decreasing?

3. What are some reasons for changes in food prices?

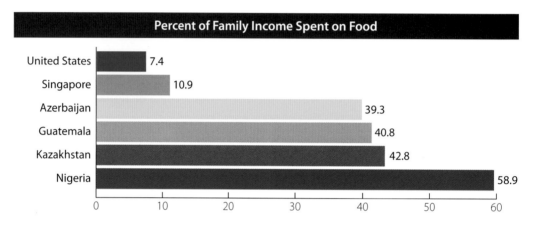

Percent of Family Income Spent on Food

United States	7.4
Singapore	10.9
Azerbaijan	39.3
Guatemala	40.8
Kazakhstan	42.8
Nigeria	58.9

B **MAIN IDEAS** Listen to a conversation about food issues. Then read the statements. Choose T for *True* or F for *False*. 🔊

1. Emily says there are multiple factors affecting food prices.   T   F
2. Economic success in certain countries is affecting food prices.   T   F
3. The habit of eating meat and dairy pushes grain prices down.   T   F
4. Some experts predict parts of Africa and Asia will become deserts.   T   F
5. Scientists say we must increase farmland by cutting down forests.   T   F

LISTENING SKILL   Recognize References

We use pronouns and other words to refer to something we have already said. It allows us to avoid repeating nouns or ideas. For example:

I had to pay seven dollars for eggs. I've never had to pay <u>that much</u> for <u>them</u> before.

In the second sentence, "that much" refers to *seven dollars*, and "them" refers to *eggs*.

By choosing plants or animals with good traits and breeding them together, we can strengthen those traits. Humans were doing <u>this</u> with corn, cattle, and dogs long before the discovery of genes.

In the second sentence, "this" refers to *choosing plants and animals with good traits and breeding them together*.

Recognizing references will help to improve your listening comprehension.

C Listen to the excerpts. What do the words in bold refer to? Write the answers below. 🔊

1. Yeah, I **did**, Emily, but I didn't get any rice.

   _____

2. I hope you **do** since I'm planning to make sushi on Friday.

   _____

3. Really? What makes you think **that**?

   _____

4. Oh yeah. So, as I was saying, now that these new middle classes find themselves moving up in the world, and **they** have more financial freedom, they're choosing more expensive foods such as meat and dairy products.

   _____

D **DETAILS** Preview the questions. Then listen again to the conversation. Take notes as you listen. Write no more than THREE words or a number for each answer. 🔊

1. What does Emily believe is the basic cause of rising food prices?

   _____

2. For how long does Emily estimate food prices have been rising unusually fast?

   _____

3. About how much cultivatable farmland has been lost in the past 40 years?

   _____

4. What kinds of foods do middle classes tend to eat more of?

   _____

5. How much meat can be produced with 3.2 kilograms of grain?

   _____

6. About what percent of their calories do humans get from grain?

   _____

7. What have some governments called for to ensure people have enough food to eat?

   _____

8. Where do scientists suggest increasing the quantity of food grown?

   _____

E **ANALYZE** Discuss the questions in a small group.

Critical Thinking

1. What are some trends in food prices that you've noticed? What changes in the availability of food have you noticed?

2. Where are the vegetables and fruits you eat grown? Where is the meat raised? Do you make purchasing decisions based on where the food items come from?

3. How has your diet changed over the years? Have your food choices been affected by your income or lifestyle?

B Speaking

GRAMMAR FOR SPEAKING   Noun Clauses as Subject Complements

A subject complement follows a linking verb (e.g., *be, feel, seem*). It defines or describes the subject of the sentence. In these sentences, the subject complement is a noun clause.

> The problem was (**that**) *Lucas didn't bring enough money to buy rice.*
>
> My mother felt (**that**) *we shouldn't have ordered so much food.*

- *That* is often omitted in speaking.
- Other introductory words for noun clauses are *what, why, whatever,* and *how.*

> Today's lunch is **whatever** *we have left in the refrigerator.*
>
> "Don't be late for dinner!" was **what** *my mother shouted to me as I left the house.*

A Underline the noun clause subject complements. Then practice the conversation with a partner.

A: I'm having an outdoor potluck party on Saturday, and you're invited!

B: A potluck party? So the guests bring the food, right?

A: That's right! So the food for the party will be whatever the guests decide to bring.

B: OK, I'll go! And I know what to bring. Chicken wings are what I do best.

A: That sounds perfect! And I've hired a band. My hope is that everyone enjoys dancing.

B: You said an outdoor party, right? Aren't you worried about the weather?

A: My biggest concern is that it will rain. But there's only a 20 percent chance.

B: Are you inviting everyone with a group email? That's how I usually do it.

A: No, I sent out a group text. Only Sean can't come. His excuse was that he has to study for a test.

B: That's too bad. But I have a feeling it's going to be a great party. I can't wait!

B Work with a partner. Complete this conversation between a police officer and a driver with noun clause subject complements. Practice the conversation and then switch roles.

Driver: What seems to be the problem, officer?

Officer: The problem is [1]_____.

Driver: Really? How fast was I going?

Officer: My guess is [2]_____. And didn't you see the stop sign?

Driver: Is there a stop sign back there?

Officer: Yes, there is. The fact is [3]_____.

Driver: Oh. Sorry. My poor night vision is [4]_____. Actually, new glasses are [5]_____. These are very old.

Officer: I see. I'm afraid I'm going to have to write you a ticket.

Driver: I understand. Officer, how far is the next gas station?

Officer: My guess is [6]_____ about a mile away.

Driver: I just noticed I'm low on gas. With these old glasses, it's hard to see how much is left.

Officer: Here's your ticket. Good night! And drive carefully!

PRONUNCIATION Recognize Reduced Auxiliary Phrases

🔊 Auxiliary phrases with modals or other helping verbs are commonly reduced. The vowels in *to* and *have* reduce to schwa (/ə/), and certain consonant sounds are changed or dropped. Listen to these examples.

have to → /ˈhæftə/	*should have* → /ˈʃʊdə v/	*must have* → /ˈmʊstə v/
has to → /ˈhæstə/	*would have* → /ˈwʊdə v/	*may have* → /ˈmeʊyə v/
want to → /ˈwvnə/	*could have* → /ˈkʊdə v/	*might have* → /ˈmaʊdə v/
going to → /ˈgvnə/	*shouldn't have* → /ˈʃʊdnə v/	
ought to → /ˈɔdə/	*wouldn't have* → /ˈwʊdnə v/	
supposed to → /sə ˈpoʊstə/	*couldn't have* → /ˈkʊdnə v/	

Note: In casual speech, the /v/ sound is often dropped from *have*. For example, *should have* sounds like *shoulda* (/ˈʃʊdə/).

C Read the sentences and underline the auxiliary phrases. Then listen and repeat the sentences. Notice the reduced phrases. 🔊

1. I could have told you it was going to rain.
2. They must have raised the price again.
3. I'll have to get some next time.
4. I shouldn't have told you that.
5. Someone really has to do something about it.
6. I would have brought home lamb for dinner.
7. And I certainly wouldn't have had any trouble buying rice!
8. We're going to be in trouble.

D With a partner, practice the conversation using reduced auxiliary phrases. Then switch roles.

A: Did you check out the farmers' market on Sunday? The vegetables were amazing.
B: I didn't know about it. But I couldn't have gone anyway. I was studying for a test.
A: How did you do on the test?
B: I could have done better, but I was tired. I shouldn't have stayed up so late.
A: You know what might have helped? Blueberries from the farmers' market.
B: Blueberries? I don't know how those would have helped.
A: Well, they're supposed to be really good for the brain.
B: Really? You should have told me that before the test. I love blueberries!

▼ Studies have shown that blueberries increase blood flow to certain areas of the brain, which improves memory and focus.

Review

A **VOCABULARY** Write the correct form of a vocabulary item from the unit to complete the sentences.

1. Tuan can't operate that machine correctly because his training was _____.

2. If you don't want to get a speeding ticket, make sure not to _____ the speed limit.

3. Insects were a huge problem for farmers before they planted insect-_____ crops.

4. Scientists can produce the traits they want in any plant by _____ its genes.

5. My country has _____ on food exports.

B **PRONUNCIATION** Underline the auxiliary phrases in the sentences. Then pronounce them using the reduced form.

1. I want to pay for lunch, but I can't find my wallet. I must have lost it!

2. Mohammad couldn't have gone home yet. He would have told us first.

3. I know I'm not supposed to drive so fast. I should have checked my speed.

4. You didn't have to buy such an expensive gift. You shouldn't have spent so much!

C **GRAMMAR** Complete the sentences with appropriate noun clause subject complements.

1. Something I'd really like to know is _____

2. Being a hard worker and having a positive attitude are _____

3. An important life lesson I've learned is _____

4. A great thing about being a student is _____

D **SPEAKING SKILL** Concede each point and then refute by providing evidence against it.

1. With so many electronic devices, I'm concerned paper books may disappear.

2. It's important to buy a house when you're young so you don't waste money on rent.

3. We should all think of ourselves as global citizens, not citizens of just one country.

RE-ASSESS What skills or language still need improvement?

Final Tasks

OPTION 1 Discuss ways of saving money on food

A Rising food prices are a problem in many countries. Look at the list of ways people deal with it. With a partner, think of two more ways and add them to the list.

Ways to spend less on food
1. Stop eating in restaurants.
2. Never go shopping when you're hungry.
3. Look for money-saving coupons before you go shopping.
4. Buy products that are on sale because of their expiration date.
5. Buy cheaper store brands instead of well-known ones.
6. Check your receipt carefully for mistakes.
7. Compare prices at different stores.
8.
9.

B With your partner, discuss the ways to spend less on food. Use these questions to guide your conversation.

1. Which of the ways have you used in your daily life? Which of the ways have you seen other people in your community use?
2. Which ways would be easy or difficult for you?

OPTION 2 Have a debate about a food-related issue

See Unit 10 Rubric in the Appendix.

A **MODEL** Listen to two people having a debate. Take notes in the chart. 🔊

Debate question:

"Pro" Arguments and Responses	
Argument 1:	Response:
Argument 2:	Response:

"Con" Arguments and Responses	
Argument 1:	Response:
Argument 2:	Response:

B **ANALYZE THE MODEL** Listen again. Answer these questions about the model. 🔊

1. What does Hamad explain to the audience at the beginning?

   _____

2. What words do the speakers use to concede?

   _____

3. What do the speakers do after they concede?

   _____

C **PLAN** With a partner, choose ONE of these questions about food consumption and eating habits to debate, or use your own idea. Then think of or research "pro" and "con" arguments and their responses and write them in a chart like the one below.

- Should we all be vegetarians?
- Should people eat more insects?
- Should fast-food restaurants be banned?
- Should the government regulate what we eat?
- Your idea: _____

Debate question:

"Pro" Arguments and Responses	
Argument 1:	Response:
Argument 2:	Response:

"Con" Arguments and Responses	
Argument 1:	Response:
Argument 2:	Response:

PRESENTATION SKILL Follow Debate Rules

Participants in a debate often have strong opinions about the subject. That's a good thing, but remember that a debate is a formal argument and it's important to follow the rules.

1. Don't interrupt others when they're speaking. Wait your turn.
2. Remember that time is limited, so don't speak for too long.
3. Speak loudly and clearly so everyone can understand you.
4. Make your point with logical arguments and/or evidence.

📶 **ONLINE** When online, don't debate in a sitting position. Arrange your webcam and microphone so you can stand instead. It will make your voice sound stronger and give you more energy.

D **PRACTICE AND PRESENT** Practice with your partner. Give each other feedback before you present. Then present your debate.

Appendix

I. SPEAKING PHRASES

Giving An Opinion *I think…* *I believe…* *In my opinion/view…* *If you ask me,…* *Personally,…*	**Asking for an Opinion** *What do you think?* *What's your opinion?* *What are your thoughts?* *How do you feel about…?* *Do you have anything to add?*
Showing Interest *Really?* *Wow!* *That's funny/interesting/incredible/awful!* *Seriously?* *No kidding!*	**Giving a Tip or Suggestion** *You/We should/could/shouldn't…* *I suggest (that)…* *Let's…* *How about… + (noun/gerund)* *Why don't we/you…*
Agreeing **Disagreeing** *I agree.* *I disagree.* *Right!* *I'm not sure about that.* *Good point.* *I don't agree.* *Exactly.* *That's a good point, but I disagree.* *Absolutely.*	**Asking for Repetition** *I'm sorry?* *Excuse me?* *Could you repeat that?* *Could you say that again?* *Sorry, I didn't catch that.* *Sorry, I missed that.*
Clarifying *What do you mean?* *What does that mean?* *Do you mean…?* *Could you explain that?* *I'm not sure I understand.* *I'm not sure what you mean.*	**Checking Others' Understanding** *Do you understand?* *Is that clear?* *Are you following me?* *Do you have any questions?*
Rephrasing *In other words,…* *To put it another way,…* *What I mean to say…* *The point I'm making is…*	**Interrupting** *Excuse me./Pardon me.* *I'm sorry to interrupt…* *Can I stop you for a second?* *I'd like to add something.*
Taking Turns *Can/May I say something?* *Could I add something?* *May I continue?* *Let me finish, please.*	**Supporting/Praising Others** *That's a great/excellent idea.* *You make a great point.* *Well done.* *That's fantastic.*
Introducing a Topic *I'm/We're going to talk about…* *My topic is…* *I'm/We're going to present…* *I plan to discuss…* *Let's start with…*	**Listing or Sequencing** *There are many types/kinds of/ways,…* *First/First of all/The first point, idea/To start/To begin,…* *Second/Secondly/The second point…* *Next/Another/Also/Then/In addition,…* *Last/Finally/The last point…*

Giving an Example	Repeating and Rephrasing
The first example is . . . *For instance, . . .* *For example, . . .* *. . . such as . . .* *. . . like . . .*	*What you need to know is . . .* *I'll say this again . . .* *So again, let me repeat . . .* *The most important point is . . .*
Defining	**Talking about Visuals**
. . . , which means . . . *What that means is . . . .* *In other words, . . .* *Another way to say that is . . . .* *That is . . .*	*This graph/infographic/diagram shows/explains . . .* *The line/box/image represents . . .* *The main point of this visual is . . .* *From this we can see . . .*
Concluding	**Participating in a Meeting**
To sum up, *In conclusion,* *In summary,*	*Welcome, everyone. The purpose of today's meeting is . . .* *Today's meeting is to discuss . . .* *Let's move on to the next item.* *Let me share my screen. Can I share my screen?* *Can you see my screen?* *You can post your questions in the chat box.*

II. PRONUNCIATION GUIDE

Vowel and Consonant Symbols

Vowel Sounds

Key Word	Symbol
1. **e**at, d**ee**p	/i^y/
2. **i**t, d**i**p	/ɪ/
3. l**a**te, p**ai**n	/e^y/
4. l**e**t, p**e**n	/ɛ/
5. c**a**t, f**a**n	/æ/
6. b**ir**d, t**ur**n	/ɜr/
7. c**u**p, s**u**ffer*	/ʌ/
about, symb**o**l	/ə/
8. h**o**t, st**o**p	/ɑ/
9. t**oo**, n**ew**	/u^w/
10. g**oo**d, c**ou**ld	/ʊ/
11. r**oa**d, n**o**te	/o^w/
12. l**aw**, w**a**lk	/ɔ/
13. f**i**ne, r**i**ce	/a^y/
14. **ou**t, n**ow**	/a^w/
15. b**oy**, j**oi**n	/ɔ^y/

Consonant Sounds

Key Word	Symbol	Key Word	Symbol
1. **p**ie	/p/	13. **sh**oe	/ʃ/
2. **b**oy	/b/	14. mea**s**ure	/ʒ/
3. **t**en	/t/	15. **ch**oose	/tʃ/
4. **d**ay	/d/	16. **j**ob	/dʒ/
5. **k**ey	/k/	17. **m**y	/m/
6. **g**o	/g/	18. **n**o	/n/
7. **f**ine	/f/	19. si**ng**	/ŋ/
8. **v**an	/v/	20. **l**et	/l/
9. **th**ink	/θ/	21. **r**ed	/r/
10. **th**ey	/ð/	22. **w**e	/w/
11. **s**ee	/s/	23. **y**es	/y/
12. **z**oo	/z/	24. **h**ome	/h/

*The vowel sound/symbol in *cup* and *suffer* is used in stressed words and syllables; the vowel sound/symbol in *about* and *symbol* is used in unstressed syllables.

Source: *Well Said: Pronunciation for Clear Communication*, Fourth Edition, National Geographic Learning/Cengage Learning, 2017.

III. GRAMMAR/VOCABULARY REFERENCES

Irregular Verbs and Past Participles

Base Verb	Simple Past Verb	Past Participle	Base Verb	Simple Past Verb	Past Participle
become	became	become	know	knew	known
begin	began	begun	lead	led	led
bet	bet	bet	leave	left	left
bite	bit	bitten	lend	lent	lent
break	broke	broken	let	let	let
bring	brought	brought	lose	lost	lost
build	built	built	make	made	made
buy	bought	bought	mean	meant	meant
choose	chose	chosen	meet	met	met
come	came	come	pay	paid	paid
cost	cost	cost	put	put	put
cut	cut	cut	quit	quit	quit
dig	dug	dug	read	read	read
draw	drew	drawn	ride	rode	ridden
drink	drank	drunk	run	ran	run
drive	drove	driven	say	said	said
eat	ate	eaten	see	saw	seen
fall	fell	fallen	sell	sold	sold
feed	fed	fed	send	sent	sent
feel	felt	felt	set	set	set
fight	fought	fought	sing	sang	sung
find	found	found	sit	sat	sat
fly	flew	flown	sleep	slept	slept
forget	forgot	forgotten	speak	spoke	spoken
forgive	forgave	forgiven	spend	spent	spent
freeze	froze	frozen	stand	stood	stood
get	got	gotten	swim	swam	swum
give	gave	given	take	took	taken
go	went	gone	teach	taught	taught
grow	grew	grown	tell	told	told
hear	heard	heard	think	thought	thought
hide	hid	hidden	understand	understood	understood
hit	hit	hit	wake	woke	woken
hold	held	held	wear	wore	worn
hurt	hurt	hurt	win	won	won
keep	kept	kept	write	wrote	written

Forms of the Passive Voice

	Active	Passive
Simple Present	People **waste** food every day.	Food **is wasted** every day.
Future	Millions **will see** the movie.	The movie **will be seen** by millions
Simple Past	The city **closed** the restaurant.	The restaurant **was closed**.
Present Perfect	The professor **has read** and **addressed** all the comments.	All the comments **have been read** and **addressed**.
Infinitive	Someone **has to clean** the house.	The house **has to be cleaned**.
Modal	They **should put** a light here.	A light **should be put** here.

Verbs Followed by Gerunds or Infinitives

Verbs Followed by Gerunds	Verbs Followed by Gerunds or Infinitives	Verbs Followed by Infinitives
appreciate mention avoid mind can't help miss consider practice discuss quit dislike recommend enjoy regret finish suggest imagine understand keep	begin need* can't stand prefer continue remember* forget* can(not) stand hate start like stop* love try (in past form tried)* *The meaning changes between use of gerund and infinitive. He stopped eating. (He is not eating now.) He stopped to eat. (He stopped doing something in order to eat.)	agree offer appear plan ask pretend choose promise claim refuse decide seem demand tend expect try hope want learn

Vocabulary Notebook Template

A vocabulary notebook is a way to keep track of the words you are learning.
There are many ways to organize a vocabulary notebook. Here is one way:

Word & part of speech	Definition or synonyms	Antonyms	Example sentence
unique (adj)	unlike anything else; special	common, ordinary	My name is unique; I don't know anyone else who has it.

You many also want to include a translation, other word forms, collocations, etc. Note what's helpful for you to remember the words.

Common Phrasal Verbs

Phrasal Verbs with *Away*	Examples
do away with	They **did away with** (put an end to) the computer class requirement.
give away	Please don't **give away** (reveal) the plot of the movie. I haven't seen it yet.
go away	Please **go away** (leave me alone). I need quiet to study.
pass away	My cat **passed away** (died) last week. I'm still very sad.
turn away	We were **turned away** (refused entrance) because we didn't have tickets.

Phrasal Verbs with *Off*	Examples
call off	They **called off** (cancelled) the concert due to bad weather.
lay off	The company had to **lay off** (dismiss, fire) employees when business slowed.
put off	He **put off** (postponed) studying all semester so he failed the final exam.
take off	The business **took off** (grew quickly) after appearing on social media. Our plane **took off** (left) on time.

Phrasal Verbs with *On*	Examples
decide on	Who will **decide on** (choose) where we're going for lunch?
go on	Please **go on** (continue). I want to hear the rest of your idea.
hold on	If you can **hold on** (wait) for a minute I am sure I can find what you need.
take on	He can't **take on** (undertake) more work now. He's too busy.

Phrasal Verbs with *Out*	Examples
break out	The disease **broke out** (started suddenly) two years ago.
leave out	He **left out** (didn't include) his sources for his research paper.
look out	**Look out**! (Be careful!) There's a car coming. Don't cross the street yet.
stand out	He **stood out** (was noticeable) as the only person not in a uniform.
try out	She **tried out** (tested) the new phone but preferred her old one.

Phrasal Verbs with *Up*	Examples
come up	I'll be there unless something **comes up** (arises, happens) at work.
follow up	It's important to **follow up** (pursue, investigate) when you don't hear back from someone.
give up	Never **give up** (quit) on your dreams.
take up	I'd like to **take up** (start) photography.

Word Families: Stems, Prefixes, and Suffixes

Use your understanding of stems, prefixes, and suffixes to recognize unfamiliar words and to expand your vocabulary. The stem is the root part of the word, which provides the main meaning. A prefix comes before the stem and usually modifies meaning (e.g., adding *re-* to a word means "again" or "back"). A suffix comes after the stem and usually changes the part of speech (e.g., adding *-ion*, *-tion*, or *-ation* to a verb changes it to a noun). Words that share the same stem or root belong to the same word family (e.g., *event, eventful, uneventful, uneventfully*).

Word Stem	Meaning	Examples
ann, enn	year	anniversary, millennium
chron(o)	time	chronological, synchronize
flex, flect	bend	flexible, reflection
graph	draw, write	graphics, paragraph
lab	work	labor, collaborate
mob, mot, mov	move	automobile, motivate, mover
port	carry	transport, import
sect	cut	sector, bisect

Prefix	Meaning	Examples
dis-	not, opposite of	disappear, disadvantages
in-, im-, il-, ir-	not	inconsistent, immature, illegal, irresponsible
inter-	between	Internet, international
mis-	bad, badly, incorrectly	misunderstand, misjudge
pre-	before	prehistoric, preheat
re-	again; back	repeat; return, rearrange
trans-	across, beyond	transfer, translate
un-	not	uncooked, unfair

Suffix	Meaning	Examples
-able, -ible	worth, ability	believable, impossible
-en	to cause to become; made of	lengthen, strengthen; golden
-er, -or	one who	teacher, director
-ful	full of	beautiful, successful
-ify, -fy	to make or become	simplify, satisfy
-ion, -tion, -ation	condition, action	occasion, education, foundation
-ize	become	modernize, summarize
-ly	in the manner of	carefully, happily
-ment	condition	assignment, statement
-ness	state of being	happiness, sadness

IV. VOCABULARY INDEX

AW = Academic word

Unit 1	Page	CEFR level
automated AW	12	OFF
come up with	4	B2
cut down on	4	B2
cutting-edge	12	C1
eliminate AW	12	C1
germ	12	C1
hospitality	4	C1
luxury	12	C1
modify AW	12	C1
monitor AW	12	C1
multiple	12	C1
obsolete	12	C1
outgoing	4	C1
prestigious	4	C1
rate	4	C1
recruit	4	C1
rewarding	4	B2
sustainability AW	4	C2
the norm AW	4	C1
undergo AW	12	C1

Unit 2	Page	CEFR level
accomplish	32	C1
affluent	32	C1
affordable	24	C1
authorized	24	C1
comply AW	32	C1
conclude AW	24	C1
enforce AW	32	C1
ethnic AW	32	C1
funds AW	24	C1
highly	32	C1
innovative AW	24	C1
internalize AW	32	OFF
linguistic AW	32	C1
prioritize AW	24	OFF
regulate AW	24	C1
renovation	24	C1
restrict AW	32	C1
subsequently AW	24	C1
sustainable AW	24	C1
unique AW	32	B2

Unit 3	Page	CEFR level
alarming	44	C1
constitute AW	44	C1
distinct AW	44	C1
drawback	52	C1
envision	44	OFF
evolve AW	44	C1
excessive	44	C1
exclusive AW	44	B2
fabric AW	52	C1
imaginative	52	C1
influential AW	52	C1
mainstream	52	C2
perceive AW	44	C1
persuasive	52	C1
practical	52	B2
random AW	44	C1
ratio AW	44	C1
retail	52	C1
texture	52	C1
underestimate AW	52	B2

Unit 4	Page	CEFR level
anticipate AW	72	C1
application	72	C2
capability AW	72	C1
collaborate	72	C1
competency AW	64	C1
component AW	64	C1
enrich	72	C1
facilitate AW	64	C1
implication AW	72	C1
in demand	64	C1
inevitably AW	64	C1
insert AW	72	C1
integrate AW	64	C1
labor AW	64	C1
portable	72	C1
prominent AW	72	C1
retain AW	64	C2
sector AW	64	C1
state-of-the-art	72	OFF
widespread AW	64	C1

Unit 5	Page	CEFR level
alert	84	C1
clarify AW	92	C1
courageous	92	C1
detect AW	84	C1
exceptional	92	C2
exposure AW	84	C1
instinct AW	92	C2
irrational AW	84	C2
motivate AW	92	C1
obstacle	92	C1
portray AW	92	C2
predator AW	92	C1
scan	84	C1
scare	84	C1
struggle	92	B2
therapist	84	C1
trigger AW	84	C1
uncertainty	92	C1
verify	84	C1
weaken	84	C1

Unit 6	Page	CEFR level
accustomed to	104	C1
contradiction [AW]	104	C2
convert [AW]	104	B2
descendant	112	C2
habitat [AW]	112	C1
hardship	112	C1
harsh	112	C1
heritage	112	C2
interaction [AW]	104	C1
isolated	104	C1
livelihood	112	OFF
materialistic	104	C2
preservation	104	C1
principle [AW]	104	C1
profound [AW]	112	C2
pursue [AW]	104	C1
thrive	112	C1
transition [AW]	104	C2
ultimately [AW]	112	C1
undertake [AW]	112	C1

Unit 7	Page	CEFR level
accumulate [AW]	124	C2
allocate [AW]	132	C1
associate	124	C1
claim	124	C1
conduct [AW]	124	B2
criterion [AW]	132	C1
deposit	132	C1
impact [AW]	124	C1
interest [AW]	132	C1
loan	132	B1
overdo	132	C1
perspective [AW]	124	C1
promote [AW]	124	C1
prosperous	124	C1
reluctant	132	C1
reminder	132	C1
security [AW]	124	C1
transaction [AW]	132	C1
well-being	124	OFF
withdraw	132	C1

Unit 8	Page	CEFR level
abnormal [AW]	152	C1
address [AW]	144	C1
confidential	144	C1
consult [AW]	144	C1
consumption [AW]	152	C1
continually	152	C1
determine [AW]	152	C1
diagnose [AW]	144	C2
enhance [AW]	144	C1
frustrated	152	C1
hesitant	144	OFF
insight [AW]	152	C1
keep track of	144	C1
notify	152	C1
obtain [AW]	152	B2
overwhelming	144	C1
productivity [AW]	152	C1
surge [AW]	144	C2
tendency	144	C1
track	152	C2

Unit 9	Page	CEFR level
actual	164	B2
analytical [AW]	164	C1
awareness [AW]	164	C1
basis	164	C1
biased [AW]	164	C1
competent [AW]	164	C1
concept [AW]	164	B2
customary	172	C1
deepen	172	C1
ethical [AW]	172	C2
inferior [AW]	172	C1
innate [AW]	172	C2
intuition	164	C2
memorize [AW]	172	OFF
radical [AW]	172	C1
self-image	164	OFF
stem from	172	C1
superior [AW]	172	C1
unprecedented	172	C2
verbal [AW]	164	C2

Unit 10	Page	CEFR level
advocate [AW]	184	C1
alter [AW]	184	B2
call for	192	C2
coincide [AW]	192	C2
disastrous	192	C1
distribute [AW]	184	C1
evident [AW]	192	B2
exceed [AW]	192	C1
gene	184	C1
inadequate [AW]	192	C1
intense [AW]	184	C1
invaluable	184	C1
output [AW]	192	C2
proportion [AW]	184	C1
resistant [AW]	184	OFF
restriction [AW]	192	C1
scenario [AW]	192	C2
stick to	192	B2
surplus [AW]	184	C2
trait [AW]	184	C2

V. SPEAKING RUBRICS

Unit 1: HOSPITALITY AND TOURISM	Give a recruitment presentation for a job	4	3	2	1
Student name: **Date:** Use this rubric to assess each student's speaking. You can add other aspects of their speaking you'd like to assess at the bottom of the rubric, or use the space for more explanation. 4 = Excellent 3 = Good 2 = Satisfactory 1 = Needs improvement	**Content and Organization** • Describes the job. • Explains the qualifications, responsibilities, and benefits. • Gets the audience's attention at the start. • Includes questions or another technique to move smoothly between sections. • Organizes ideas in a clear and logical way.				
	Language Use and Fluency • Uses correct sentence structure, and language is easy to understand and follow. • Uses a variety of words, including phrases to handle questions, as well as words taught in the unit. • Speaks smoothly with few hesitations or breaks.				
	Body Language and Voice • Makes good eye contact and uses natural gestures. • Speaks loudly enough for everyone to hear. • Speaks at an appropriate pace.				

Unit 2: SOLVING URBAN CHALLENGES	Give a presentation about laws or rules	4	3	2	1
Student name: **Date:** Use this rubric to assess each student's speaking. You can add other aspects of their speaking you'd like to assess at the bottom of the rubric, or use the space for more explanation. 4 = Excellent 3 = Good 2 = Satisfactory 1 = Needs improvement	**Content and Organization** • Names the location and explains the laws or rules. • Explains the reasons for the laws and the different perspectives about them. • Has divided the pair presentation effectively. • Organizes ideas in a clear and logical way.				
	Language Use and Fluency • Uses correct sentence structure, and language is easy to understand and follow. • Uses a variety of words, including words taught in the unit. • Speaks smoothly with few hesitations or breaks.				
	Body Language and Voice • Makes good eye contact and uses natural gestures. • Speaks loudly enough for everyone to hear. • Speaks at an appropriate pace.				

Unit 3: BEAUTY AND APPEARANCE

Student name:

Date:

Use this rubric to assess each student's speaking. You can add other aspects of their speaking you'd like to assess at the bottom of the rubric, or use the space for more explanation.

4 = Excellent
3 = Good
2 = Satisfactory
1 = Needs improvement

Present fashion trends	4	3	2	1
Content and Organization • Explains the trends, giving a description of each and a time when each one started. • Has prepared appropriate visuals for display. • Organizes ideas in a clear and logical way.				
Language Use and Fluency • Uses correct sentence structure, and language is easy to understand and follow. • Uses a variety of words, including language for taking turns, as well as words taught in the unit. • Speaks smoothly with few hesitations or breaks.				
Body Language and Voice • Makes good eye contact and uses natural gestures. • Speaks loudly enough for everyone to hear. • Speaks at an appropriate pace.				

Unit 4: GOING GLOBAL

Student name:

Date:

Use this rubric to assess each student's speaking. You can add other aspects of their speaking you'd like to assess at the bottom of the rubric, or use the space for more explanation.

4 = Excellent
3 = Good
2 = Satisfactory
1 = Needs improvement

Give a presentation about a social media platform	4	3	2	1
Content and Organization • Names and describes the platform, giving a brief history. • Explains how the platform makes money and who the competitors are. • Explains how the platform facilitates globalization. • Describes the future of the platform. • Organizes ideas in a clear and logical way.				
Language Use and Fluency • Uses correct sentence structure, and language is easy to understand and follow. • Uses a variety of words, including words taught in the unit. • Speaks smoothly with few hesitations or breaks.				
Body Language and Voice • Manages nervousness while presenting. • Makes good eye contact and uses natural gestures. • Speaks loudly enough for everyone to hear. • Speaks at an appropriate pace.				

Unit 5: FACING YOUR FEARS	Give a presentation about a courageous person	4	3	2	1
Student name: **Date:** Use this rubric to assess each student's speaking. You can add other aspects of their speaking you'd like to assess at the bottom of the rubric, or use the space for more explanation. 4 = Excellent 3 = Good 2 = Satisfactory 1 = Needs improvement	**Content and Organization** • Describes the person and explains why they are courageous. • Organizes events in the person's life along a timeline. • Transitions smoothly from one part to the next. • Organizes ideas in a clear and logical way.				
	Language Use and Fluency • Uses correct sentence structure, and language is easy to understand and follow. • Uses a variety of words, including separable phrasal verbs, as well as words taught in the unit. • Speaks smoothly with few hesitations or breaks.				
	Body Language and Voice • Listens actively when their partner speaks. • Makes good eye contact and uses natural gestures. • Speaks loudly enough for everyone to hear. • Speaks at an appropriate pace.				

Unit 6: TRADITION AND PROGRESS	Interview and present about Gross National Happiness	4	3	2	1
Student name: **Date:** Use this rubric to assess each student's speaking. You can add other aspects of their speaking you'd like to assess at the bottom of the rubric, or use the space for more explanation. 4 = Excellent 3 = Good 2 = Satisfactory 1 = Needs improvement	**Content and Organization** • Explains who they interviewed and where they are from. • Explains how the location ranks on all four pillars. • Asks follow-up questions to get clarity. • Organizes ideas in a clear and logical way.				
	Language Use and Fluency • Uses correct sentence structure, and language is easy to understand and follow. • Uses a variety of words, including words taught in the unit. • Includes one or more rhetorical questions. • Speaks smoothly with few hesitations or breaks.				
	Body Language and Voice • Speaks with confidence. • Makes good eye contact and uses natural gestures. • Speaks loudly enough for everyone to hear. • Speaks at an appropriate pace.				

Unit 7: MONEY IN OUR LIVES

Student name:

Date:

Use this rubric to assess each student's speaking. You can add other aspects of their speaking you'd like to assess at the bottom of the rubric, or use the space for more explanation.

4 = Excellent
3 = Good
2 = Satisfactory
1 = Needs improvement

Give a presentation on how to save and manage money	4	3	2	1
Content and Organization • Describes three tips, explaining the benefits of each, and gives the source of their information. • Has collaborated fairly and responsibly with the group; work is divided evenly. • Organizes ideas in a clear and logical way.				
Language Use and Fluency • Uses correct sentence structure, and language is easy to understand and follow. • Uses a variety of words, including words taught in the unit. • Speaks smoothly with few hesitations or breaks.				
Body Language and Voice • Makes good eye contact and uses natural gestures. • Speaks loudly enough for everyone to hear. • Speaks at an appropriate pace.				

Unit 8: HEALTH AND TECHNOLOGY

Student name:

Date:

Use this rubric to assess each student's speaking. You can add other aspects of their speaking you'd like to assess at the bottom of the rubric, or use the space for more explanation.

4 = Excellent
3 = Good
2 = Satisfactory
1 = Needs improvement

Present on a wearable health care device	4	3	2	1
Content and Organization • Describes and explains the product. • Asks follow-up questions to get clarity. • Organizes ideas in a clear and logical way.				
Language Use and Fluency • Uses correct sentence structure, and language is easy to understand and follow. • Uses a variety of words, including language to transition between pros and cons, as well as words taught in the unit. • Speaks smoothly with few hesitations or breaks.				
Body Language and Voice • Engages with the audience. • Makes good eye contact and uses natural gestures. • Speaks loudly enough for everyone to hear. • Speaks at an appropriate pace.				

Unit 9: THE MYSTERIOUS MIND	Give a presentation on "study/learning hacks"	4	3	2	1
Student name: **Date:** Use this rubric to assess each student's speaking. You can add other aspects of their speaking you'd like to assess at the bottom of the rubric, or use the space for more explanation. 4 = Excellent 3 = Good 2 = Satisfactory 1 = Needs improvement	**Content and Organization** • Describes four study or learning hacks. • Explains the benefits of each hack. • Includes an introduction and closing. • Organizes ideas in a clear and logical way.				
	Language Use and Fluency • Uses correct sentence structure, and language is easy to understand and follow. • Uses a variety of words, including cause-and-effect expressions, as well as words taught in the unit. • Speaks smoothly with few hesitations or breaks.				
	Body Language and Voice • Uses gestures and facial expressions. • Makes good eye contact and uses natural gestures. • Speaks loudly enough for everyone to hear. • Speaks at an appropriate pace.				

Unit 10: THE FUTURE OF FOOD	Have a debate about a food-related issue	4	3	2	1
Student name: **Date:** Use this rubric to assess each student's speaking. You can add other aspects of their speaking you'd like to assess at the bottom of the rubric, or use the space for more explanation. 4 = Excellent 3 = Good 2 = Satisfactory 1 = Needs improvement	**Content and Organization** • Explains the question being debated. • Argues effectively for their position. • Concedes and then refutes by providing further evidence. • Follows debate rules. • Organizes ideas in a clear and logical way.				
	Language Use and Fluency • Uses correct sentence structure, and language is easy to understand and follow. • Uses a variety of words, including words to concede and refute, as well as words taught in the unit. • Speaks smoothly with few hesitations or breaks.				
	Body Language and Voice • Makes good eye contact and uses natural gestures. • Speaks loudly enough for everyone to hear. • Speaks at an appropriate pace.				

ACKNOWLEDGMENTS

The Authors and Publisher would like to acknowledge the educators around the world who participated in the development of the third edition of *Pathways Listening, Speaking, and Critical Thinking*.

A special thanks to our Advisory Board for their valuable input during development.

Advisory Board

Baher F. AlDabba, Amideast Gaza; **Hossein Askari**, Houston Community College; **Dilara Ataman Akalin**, TOBB University; **Andrew Boon**, Toyo Gakuen University; **Fatih Bozoğlu**, Antalya Bilim University; **Julie Cote**, Houston Community College; **Kristen Cox**, Global Launch at ASU; **Patricia Fiene**, Midwestern Career College; **Ronnie Hill**, Royal Melbourne Institute of Technology; **Greg Holloway**, University of Kitakyushu; **Ragette Jawad**, Lawrence Technological University; **Elizabeth Macdonald**, Sacred Heart University; **Daniel Paller**, Kinjo Gakuin University; **Kes Poupaert**, INTO Manchester; **Juan Quintana**, Instituto Cultural Peruano Norteamericano; **Anouchka Rachelson**, Miami Dade College; **David Ruzicka**, Shinsu University; **Gabrielle Smallbone**, Kingston University; **Debra Wainscott**, Baylor University

Global Reviewers

Asia

John Paul Abellera, San Beda College-Alabang; **Andrew Acosta**, Udonpittayanukoon School; **Jherwin Adora**, Department of Education Philippines; **Mubarak Ali**, Unilever; **Joan Arado**, TESDA PTS-Misamis Occidental; **Frederick Bacala**, Yokohama City University; **Katherine Bauer**, Clark Memorial International High School; **Richard Bent**, Kwassui Women's University; **Teresa Bolen**, Ryukoku University; **Johnny Burns**, Kansai Daigaku; **Darine Chehwan**, Rest-art Studio; **Simon Cornelius**, Kansai University; **Aurelio Da Costa**, UNICEF/Senai Language Centre; **Carlos Daley**, London Institute; **Maria del Vecchio**, Nihon University; **Ria De Ocera**, Udomsuksa School; **Michael Donzella**, Kaichi International University; **David Groff**, Meiji University; **Akiko Hagiwara**, Tokyo University of Pharmacy and Life Sciences; **Sisilia Halimi**, Humanities Universitas Indonesia; **Jane Harland**, Fukoka University; **Makoto Hayashi**, Nagoya University; **Patrizia Hayashi**, Meikai University; **Andrea Noemie Hilomen**, Private teacher; **Ha Hoang**, Au Chau Language School; **Ana Sofia Hofmeyr**, Kansai University; **Stephen Hofstee**, Kanto Gakuin University; **Stephen Howes**, Tokyo Seitoku University Fukaya Junior High School; **Yuko Igarashi**, Ritsumeikan University; **Mari Inoue**, Tokyo University of Science; **David Johnson**, Kyushu Sangyo University; **Sarita Joyaka**, Nongkipittayakhom; **Chong Jui Jong**, Universiti Sains Malaysia; **Yuko Kawae**, Kindai University; **Megumi Kobayashi**, Seikei University; **Mutsumi Kondo**, Kyoto University of Foreign Studies; **Gomer Jay Legaspi**, Caraga State University; **Indah Ludij**, Academic Writing Center, Universitas Indonesia; **Kelly MacDonald**, Fukuoka University; **Anh Mai**, Van Lang University; **Tiina Matikainen**, Tamagawa University; **Eiko Matsubara**, Rissho University; **Jason May**, Den-en Chofu Gakuen; **Sean Collin Mehmet**, Matsumoto University; **Mabell Mingoy**, Teach for the Philippines; **Mari Miyao**, Kyoto University of Foreign Studies; **Wah Mon**, Private teacher; **Masaki Mori**, Aoyama-Gakuinn University; **Gerald Muirhead**, Tohoku Gakuin University; **Charlotte Murakami**, Kurume University; **Duong Nguyen**, APU; **Ly Huyền Nguyễn**, FPT High School; **Vinh Nguyen**, Hanoi University; **Ngan Nguyễn**; **Thảo Nguyễn**, Gia Việt English Center; **MaiKhoi NguyenThi**, Danang Architecture University; **Takeshi Nozawa**, Ritsumeikan University; **Naomi Ogasawara**, Gunma Prefectural Women's University; **Mari Ogawa**, Meiji University; **Megumi Okano**, Keio University; **Hisako Osuga**, Meiji University; **Gellian Ostrea**, Manolo Fortich National High School; **Tina Ottman**, Doshisha University, Bukkyo University; **Ardy Paembonan**, SMA El-Shaddai Jayapura; **Anthony Paxton**, Ibaraki Prefectural Takezono High School; **Hong Pham**, Brendon Primary School; **Huong Pham**, Foreign Languages Specialised School, University of Languages and International Studies; **John Plagens** Lutheran College; **Javeria Rana**, The City School; **Rebecca Reyes**, Captain Albert Aguilar National High School; **Florencio Salmasan**, School of the Holy Spirit; **Sherri Scanlan**, Toyama Prefectural University; **Naoki Senrui**, Komazawa University; **Nanik Shobikah**, IAIN Pontianak; **Coleman South**, Saga National University; **Yukiko Sugiyama**, Keio University; **Pavloska Susanna**, Doshisha University; **Eri Tamura**, Ishikawa Prefectural University; **Yuko Tokisato**, Kansai University; **Saeko Toyoshima**, Tsuru University; **Janssen Undag**, Darunapolytechnic Technological College; **Carl Vollmer**, Ritsumeikan Uji Junior and Senior High School; **Isra Wongsarnpigoon**, Kanda University of International Studies

Europe

Ana Maria Andrei, Liceul Teoretic de Informatica; **Regina Bacanskiene**, Kaunas School; **Janice Bain**, Glasgow International College; **Oana Banu**, LPS; **Daniela Berntzen**; **Sarah Bishopp**, Kaplan International College London; **Anna Broumerioti**; **Cath Brown**, The University of Sheffield; **Laura Cannella**, Kaplan International College London; **Barbara Cavicchiolli**, INTO Manchester; **Ioana Mirela Cojocaru**, Liceul Tehnologic Anghel Saligny; **Viorica Condrat**, USARB; **Astrid D'Andrea**, I.I.S. Croce-Aleramo; **Liesl Daries**, English with Liesl; **Kurtis De Souza-Snares**, Kaplan International Pathways; **Elona Dhepa**, 7 Marsi; **Maral Dosmagambetova**, Lingua College; **Camelia-Adriana Dulau**, Simion Bărnuţiu; **Ruthanna Farragher**, Kaplan; **Olesia Fesenko**, Vyshhorod Lyceum "Suziria"; **Cristina Foltmann**, ITCS Abba Ballini; **Laura Gheorghita**, Scoala Gimnaziala Grigore Geamanu Turcinesti; **Marian Gonzalez**, Liceo de Idiomas Modernos; **Paulina Holesz**, Private teacher; **Lindsey Hollywood**, Universtiy of Liverpool International College; **Sarah Hopwood**, University of Nottingham International College; **Barbara Howarth**, Glasgow International College; **Barbara Howarth**, Glasgow International College; **Jana Jilkova**, ICV & Pedagogical Faculty; **Alina Loata**, Colegiul National Dimitrie Cantemir; **Ia Manjgaladze**, Access Program Teacher; **Christiana Mili**, Private teacher; **Laura**

Morrison, Glasgow International College; **Robert Pinkham-Smith**, University of Essex International College; **Yuliya Pokroyeva**, Private teacher; **Eva Rodaki**, Private teacher; **Alina Rotaru**, Twinkle Star; **Carme RR**, CEIP Joan Mas Pollença; **Tatiana Silvesan**, Centrul Scolar de Educatie Incluziva; **Bianca Somesan**, Palatul Copiilor Targu Mures; **Elena Strugaru**, Britanica Learning Centre; **Mina Vermot**, Miduca; **Matthew Wilson**, Brunel University London; **Emily Wright**, Arden University

Latin America and the Caribbean

Maria Aguilar, Universidad Nacional de La Rioja; **Karina Aldana**, Colegio la Asuncion; **Mariela Amarante**, Sunshine Academy; **Auricéa Bacelar**, Top Seven Idiomas; **Verónica Bonilla**, Universidad Anáhuac de Puebla; **Lucila Caballero**, MEDUCA; **Milagros Calderón Miró**, Colegio San Antonio IHM; **Maria Carrizo**, Nores; **Erika Ceballos**, Escuela Nacional Preparatoria; **Johana Coronel**, Private teacher; **Marcelo D'Elia**, Centro Britanico Idiomas; **Sophia De Carvalho**, Inglês Express; **Corina Diaz**, CCSA; **Isabela Dias**, Inglês Express; **Joseph Duque**, Unidad Educativa Leibnitz; **Esperanza Espejo**, Iteso; **Susana Espinosa**, ICPNA; **Carolina Ferreira**, Private teacher; **Matheus Figueiredo**, Private teacher; **Andrea Garcia Hernandez**, Bilingual School; **Alessandra Gotardo**, IYEnglish - Language & Culture; **Santo Guzmán**, JFK Institute of Languages, inc.; **Cecibel Juliao**, Meduca / Udelas; **Letícia Kayano**, Private teacher; **Sandra Landi**, Private teacher; **Patricia Lanners**, Universidad de las Americas Puebla; **Arenas Laura**, ITESO; **Diana Lopez**, ITSE; **Mario López Ayala**, Universidad Autónoma de Sinaloa; **Rosa Awilda Lopez Fernandez**, Universidad Acción Pro-Educación y Culturalic Dominicana; **Fabricio Romeo Mejia Lopez**, Academia Europea; **Silvia Luna**, Universidad Evangélica; **Manuel Malhaber Diaz**, Colegio Nacional San Juan De Chota; **Daniel Martins Aragão**, Private teacher; **Victor Hugo Medina Soares**, Cultura Inglesa Belo Horizonte; **Angélica Parada**, CBA; **Adela Perez del Viso**, Fundación E.S.Y.C.; **Byron Quinde**, Unidad Educativa Particular de la Asunción; **Maria Alejandra Quirch**, Instituto San Roman; **Joselyn Ramos Cuba**, UNMSM; **Jorge Reategui**, Universidad Continental; **Jazmin Reyes**, La Dolorosa; **Iliana Rivas**, ITESO; **Sheirys Hidalgo Ruiz**, Ministerio de Educacion Publica; **Adelina Ruiz Guerrero**, Instituto Tecnológico y de Estudios Superiores de Occidente; **Maribel Santiago**, Colegio de Bachilleres; **Margaret Simons**, English Center; **Margaret Simons**, English Center; **Sheily Sosa García**, ICPNA; **Jane Stories**, Private teacher; **María Trigos**, ITSX; **Henrique Ucci**, Liverpool English Institute; **Ana Carolina Vargas Arreola**, Colegio Vizcaya; **Laura Zurutuza**, ITESO

Middle East and Africa

Merve Akyiğit, Adana Doğa Schools; **Yousef Albozom**, America-Mideast Educational and Training Services; **Rehab Alzeiny**, IPS; **Rais Attamimi**, UTAS-Salalah; **Ezgi Avar**, Tuzla Doğa Lisesi; **Pınar Çakır**, Doğa Koleji; **Burçe Çimeli**, Doğa Koleji; **Christelle Gernique Djoukouo Talla**, Government Bilingual High School Ekangte; **Canan Dülger**, Doğa Koleji; **Manal ElMazbouh**, American University of the Middle East; **Fatma el-zahraa El-sayed zaki nassef**, Damietta Official Language schools; **Necmi Ersungur**, İtü Eta Vakfı Doğa Koleji; **Mary Goveas**, University of Bahrain; **Farhad Hama**, Sulaimani University; **Michael King**, Community College of Qatar; **Georgios Kormpas**, Al Yamamah University; **Volga Kurbanzade**, Okan University; **Eni Ermawati Lasito**, Lusail University; **Gonca Mavuk**, Atasehir ITU Doga College; **Amina Moubtassim**, ALC; **Doaa Najjar**, PISOD; **Mohammad Esmaeel Nasrabadi**, Private teacher; **Naki Erhan Ozer**, Doga Schools; **Rehab Raouf**, Al Safwa School; **Nurhayat Şenman**, Özlüce Doğa Koleji Lise; **Choukri Serhane**, CHSS; **Hussam Tannera**, America-Mideast Educational and Training Services; **Pedro Vemba**, Liceu do Soyo; **Cüneyt Yüce**, Istanbul Okan University

USA and Canada

Galyna, Arabadzhy, St. Cloud State University; **Elizabeth Armstrong**, Midwestern Career College; **Judy Bagg**, Pierce; **Karin Bates**, Intercambio Uniting Communities; **Mandie Bauer**, ASC English; **Elisabeth Bowman**, Schoolcraft College; **Teresa Cheung**, North Shore Community College; **Colleen Comidy**, Seattle Central College; **Jacquelin Cunningham**, Harold Washington College; **Jean Danic**, Hillsborough Community College; **Rosalia dela Cruz**, NorQuest College; **Christine Dick**, Arizona State University; **Yvonne Dunham Slobodenko**, University of Tennessee at Chattanooga; **Karen Eichhorn**, International English Center; **Thomas Fox**, Dallas College; **Diana Garcia**, Union County College; **Bertha George**, Union County College; **Thomas Germain**, University of Colorado Boulder; **Debra Gibes**, Mott Community College; **John Glover**, Old Saybrook High School; **Christine Guro**, University of Hawaii at Manoa; **Carrie Hein-Paredes**, MATC; **Deanna Henderson**, Language Consultants International; **Tom Justice**, North Shore Community College; **Evan Kendall**, Los Angeles City College; **Michael Kelley**, Hillsborough Community College; **Karen E. Kyle**, Aims Community College; **Laura Lamour**, Florida International University; **Maureen Lanseur**, Henry Ford College; **Heidi Lieb**, Bergen Community College; **Layla Malander**, PLACE/Colorado State University; **Tim Mathews**, Nashville State Community College; **Richard McDorman**, Language On; **Susan McElwain**, Mohawk College of Applied Arts and Technology; **Jason McKenzie**, Apex Language and Career College; **William Miller Jr.**, H.EN; **Lilia Myers Van Pelt**, Colorado State University Pueblo; **Sandra Navarro**, Glendale Community College; **Linda Neuman**, Anne Arundel Community College; **Susan Niemeyer**, Los Angeles City College; **Mariah Nix**, Lumos Language School; **Cheryl Pakos**, Union County College; **Jim Papple**, York University; **Cora Perrone**, Southern CT State University; **Deborah Pfeifer**, Fort Hays State University; **Loretta Quan**, Schoolcraft College; **Thomas Riedmiller**, University of Northern; **Lisa Rivoallon**, Gavilan College; **Noele Simmons**, George Mason University; **Pamela Smart-Smith**, Virginia Tech; **Kelly Smith**, English Language Institute, UCSD Extension; **Brandt Snook**, University of Louisiana – Lafayette; **Shoshanna Starzynski**, Global Launch, Arizona State University; **Kirsten Stauffer**, Immigrant and Refugee Center of Northern Colorado; **JoAnn Stehly**, North Orange County Community College District; **Karen Vallejo**, University of California, Irvine; **Sharifeh Van Court**, Dallas College; **Melissa Vervinck**, ESL Institute at Oakland University; **Christy Williams**, INTO USF; **Paula Yerman**, Los Angeles City College

CREDITS

Illustrations: All illustrations are owned by © Cengage.